Pathways to Teaching Series

Assessment Throughout the Year

MARK R. O'SHEA
California State University, Monterey Bay

NATIONAL CENTER FOR EDUCATION INFORMATION

NATIONAL CENTER FOR
EDUCATION INFORMATION

Merrill
is an imprint of

Upper Saddle River, New Jersey
Columbus, Ohio

Library of Congress Cataloging-in-Publication Data

O'Shea, Mark R.

Pathways to teaching series: assessment throughout the year/Mark R. O'Shea. — 1st ed.

p. cm.

ISBN-13: 978-0-13-513057-5

ISBN-10: 0-13-513057-3

1. Educational tests and measurements—United States.   2. First year teachers—United States.   I. Title.

LB3051.O69 2009

371.26—dc22

2008011270

Vice President and Executive Publisher: Jeffery W. Johnston
Executive Editor: Darcy Betts Prybella
Editorial Assistant: Nancy J. Holstein
Project Manager: Sarah N. Kenoyer
Production Coordinator: Sarvesh Mehrotra/Aptara, Inc.
Design Coordinator: Diane C. Lorenzo
Cover Design: Jeff Vanik
Cover Image: Jupiter Images
Operations Specialist: Susan W. Hannahs
Director of Marketing: Quinn Perkson
Marketing Manager: Erica DeLuca
Marketing Coordinator: Brian Mounts

This book was set in Garamond by Aptara, Inc. The book and cover were printed and bound by Courier Stoughton.

Photo Credits: Chapters 1 and 2: Patrick White/Merrill; Chapters 3 and 4: Anthony Magnacca/Merrill; Chapter 5: Maria B. Vonada/Merrill; Chapter 6: Anthony Magnaca/Merrill; Chapter 7: Getty Images–Photodisc; Chapter 8: David Mager/Pearson Learning Photo Studio

Pearson Education Ltd., London
Pearson Education Singapore, Pte. Ltd.
Pearson Education Canada, Inc.
Pearson Education–Japan
Pearson Education Australia PTY, Limited

Pearson Education North Asia, Ltd., Hong Kong
Pearson Educación de Mexico, S.A. de C.V.
Pearson Education Malaysia, Pte. Ltd.
Pearson Education Upper Saddle River, New Jersey

Merrill
is an imprint of

10 9 8 7 6 5 4 3 2 1
ISBN-13: 978-0-13-513057-5
ISBN-10:   0-13-513057-3

DEDICATION

Assessment Throughout the Year *is dedicated to beginning teachers. New teachers may be early deciders who have wanted to teach since they entered elementary school, or they may be late deciders who come to teaching after preparation for, or experience in, other lines of work. The author of this book sought his teaching credentials following military service during the Vietnam War. Whatever your past history or prior accomplishments, you, the beginning teacher, have in your hands the opportunity to make a difference in the lives of young people, one person at a time. Go forth and teach. And be proud that every day you do not have to explain to others the purpose of your labors or the value in the work that you do.*

AUTHOR BIOGRAPHY

Dr. Mark O'Shea is a professor of education at California State University–Monterey Bay. Following 11 years of secondary school teaching and curriculum leadership, Dr. O'Shea embarked on his career as a teacher educator. His research interests focus on the identification of the skills and knowledge teachers need to succeed in standards-based classrooms. He is also involved in school reform efforts across the nation, from California to Alabama. He is the author of *From Standards to Success: A Guide for School Leaders* published in 2005 by the Association for Supervision and Curriculum Development. Dr. O'Shea invites correspondence from readers at Mark_OShea@CSUMB.edu.

PREFACE

This book on classroom-based assessment is intended for aspiring or new teachers who will be entering classrooms in the midst of our current school reform movement. As part of the *Pathways to Teaching Series,* it is meant to be accessible to teacher candidates in traditional and alternative certification programs who will be applying assessment skills in daily practice immediately or within a few months of entering their teacher preparation program. These new teachers are not likely to encounter a world of teaching that they observed as students in their elementary or high school days. Rather, they will experience state curriculum standards and new forms of assessment that derive in part from No Child Left Behind legislation. *Assessment Throughout the Year* is intended to augment conventional instruction in the principles of testing and measurement through these new approaches to learning assessment practices, including:

▶ Helping new teachers prepare for assessment experiences as they are likely to encounter them through the school year

▶ Bringing new practices in assessment to life through a series of classroom vignettes and scenarios

▶ Presenting learner objectives, graphic organizers, and essential assessment vocabulary at the beginning of each chapter to prepare the reader for the content that follows

▶ Providing authentic exercises focused on applications in school settings that often result in products to use in the classroom

▶ Placing special emphasis on new perspectives to guide learners to the achievement of state curriculum standards

Schools have undergone enormous change in the last 10 years in response to the standards movement. Teachers are using standards-aligned curriculum materials and benchmark testing programs to monitor student progress toward success on spring standards-based exams. More than ever before, teachers are collaborating in the planning of common assessments and the examination of student work in relation to expectations of the standards. This text vividly depicts these practices through school-based vignettes.

For new teachers working in schools where curriculum pacing, benchmark tests, and state-standards exams are emphasized, *Assessment Throughout the Year* illustrates how to use:

▶ State standards in the formulation of educational objectives and describing instructional targets

▶ State standards assessment data to plan for instruction at the beginning of the school year

▶ Teaching practices where curriculum pacing and benchmark assessments frame the curriculum

▶ Formative assessment to evaluate the effectiveness of standards-based instructional plans

▶ Alternative forms of summative assessment to evaluate student achievement of knowledge and skills described in state curriculum standards

▶ Guidelines for evaluating student work, determining grades, and assigning course marks in standards-based instructional settings

New teachers arriving to work in progressive settings will experience success if they have mastered the skills of standards-based assessment and collaborative planning for the improvement of instruction. *Assessment Throughout the Year* has been written to help guide their way.

ACKNOWLEDGMENTS

I wish to thank Emily Feistritzer, President of the National Center for Education Information, and Debbie Stollenwerk, formerly the executive editor at Merrill, for offering me the opportunity to prepare this message to future educators. Darcy Betts Prybella and Nancy J. Holstein of Merrill provided me with patient encouragement and feedback during the early formative development of the manuscript.

I want to thank my staff who work diligently in the background assisting me with my day-to-day responsibilities as I work on my scholarship in teaching and learning in our standards-based world. I want to thank Christina del Porto of the teacher internship program that I coordinate for California State University—Monterey Bay (everyone knows it's Christina who runs the program). I want to thank Sophia Vicuna who manages so many of my projects for me. She is the sunshine of all my days in the office. And thank you, Sundy Sosavanh, for helping with the preparation of the manuscript. I need to acknowledge my wife, Lorraine O'Shea, a natural teacher if there ever was one. The preparation of this manuscript depended on the kind assistance of reviewers. Their invaluable assistance over many months of writing and revision made this writing project a truly collaborative effort, and it is my pleasure to recognize them here. They are C. Jay Hertzog, Slippery Rock University of Pennsylvania; Pamela D. Parkinson, Western Governors University; Robert S. Ristow, St. Ambrose University; Michele Spires, Western States Certification Consortium; and Eileen Wetmiller, Eckerd College.

BRIEF CONTENTS

CONTENTS

Chapter 1

Classroom Teaching and Assessment: Then and Now

LEARNER OBJECTIVES

At the conclusion of this chapter, the reader will be able to

▶ Differentiate between conventional classroom assessment in the 1980s and current practice brought about by No Child Left Behind legislation and related reform initiatives.

▶ Describe changes in assessment practice resulting from the current reform environment.

▶ Describe six policy initiatives that drive changes in educational assessment.

▶ Identify five categories of classroom-based assessment.

GRAPHIC ORGANIZER

Teaching and Assessment, 1983	Teaching and Assessment, 2007
Teachers plan and assess in isolation from others. They alone decide what will be taught with low accountability for student achievement.	Teachers collaborate in their work as they plan lessons and evaluate student progress. Teachers work with state curriculum standards with high accountability for student achievement.

Six policies leading to these changes:

1. Shift of power over curriculum
2. Resolution of curriculum questions
3. High-stakes testing by state authorities
4. Blending between classroom and large-scale assessment
5. Blurring of distinctions between instruction and assessment
6. Teacher skills and abilities open to review by others

Types of assessment and how they have changed:

1. Preinstructional assessment focused on student achievement of state standards
2. Diagnostic assessment supports learning for students with special needs
3. Formative assessment increased in significance
4. Summative assessment measures standards achievement
5. Large-scale assessments are higher-stakes and standards focused

ASSESSMENT VOCABULARY

Preinstructional assessment: Methods by which the teacher learns the aptitudes, dispositions, and prior achievement of students before the start of the school year.

Diagnostic assessment: Tests and other instruments for the purpose of evaluating an individual's capabilities, perhaps as part of a referral process.

Formative assessment: Assessment focused on guiding instruction and helping students learn.

Summative assessment: Assessment used to evaluate learning, often for the purpose of assigning grades.

Large-scale assessments: Examinations administered to large populations of subjects.

Standardized tests: Large-scale assessments administered under uniform procedures for the purpose of comparing the performances of one or more subjects to a comparison group.

State standards test: A test that measures the extent to which subjects have achieved the skills and content of a state's curriculum standards.

INTRODUCTION

In the fall of each year, new teachers are hired and begin their teaching careers. Most of these neophytes graduated from public schools, perhaps as recently as 5 or 6 years earlier. For the most part, they anticipate returning to classrooms similar to those they attended as students, with the same daily routines of teaching and learning. And why not? For decades schools have proceeded through one academic year after another with little change in the general routine. Teachers have been planning lessons, teaching classes, and administering tests in much the same way for decades, or so it would seem. In truth, a revolution in daily school routines and practices has been underway for at least two decades, and these changes have begun to accelerate in the last 5 or 6 years (Tyack & Cuban, 1995). Teaching and assessment practices are changing as the result of a great reform movement in public education that began in 1983 with the publication of the seminal report, *A Nation at Risk*, by the National Commission on Excellence in Education (1983). Prior to that watershed event, declines in student test scores and a general sense of dissatisfaction in student achievement had led to decreasing confidence in our public schools. In exceptionally strong language, *A Nation at Risk* called for substantial reforms in public education. Fifteen years after that clarion call for school improvement, coherent changes in educational policy began to emerge (Tyack & Cuban, 1995).

Under the direct influence of Presidents George Bush and Bill Clinton, each state developed kindergarten through high school (K–12) curriculum standards that specify what students are to know or be able to do in important core curriculum subjects. Throughout the late 1990s, states continued to make progress in developing state curriculum standards. They also developed new curriculum frameworks based on the standards to guide teachers in meeting these new instructional targets. The pace of these changes accelerated with reauthorization of the Elementary and Secondary Education Act, which President George W. Bush signed into law in 2002 as No Child Left Behind (NCLB) (NCLB, 2001).

When NCLB became law, strict accountability measures were enacted to ensure full implementation of state curriculum standards. Under NCLB, the federal government used the standards movement to require higher levels of student achievement in all states. The new law required each state to develop assessments for Grades 3 through 8 to measure student achievement gains in language arts and mathematics. Further, each state was required to publicly identify schools that failed to demonstrate adequate yearly progress (AYP) in student achievement growth, as measured by the new **state standards exams**. By 2005, every state required annual testing of children in the elementary grades covered by the law; science was added as an additional subject to be tested for in 2008 (Porter, Linn, & Trimble, 2005).

The impact of these changes has been felt across the country. Underperforming schools with poor student test outcomes are facing consequences that would have been unheard of in the 1980s. For instance, school districts must inform parents of their right to move their child to another school when the school fails to make adequate yearly progress.

Principals have lost their jobs when student test scores have not improved. Annual school report cards that are issued by each state government often embarrass teachers and school leaders when students do not achieve state standards.[1]

Faced with these consequences, many school districts have experienced dramatic changes in expectations for teaching, learning, and assessment that are visible in teachers' daily practice. If teachers who left the profession more than 3 years ago were to return to their prior assignment, their biggest surprise would likely be the extent to which accountability for student academic achievement has found its way from federal legislation to the teacher's desk of every classroom. In the vignettes that follow, we will visit two classrooms, one of the late 1980s and one in today's reform environment, to understand the significance of education policy change in the daily lives of teachers.

A vignette of middle school teaching in 1983:

Janet Morehouse is sitting at her desk in Room 347, where she has been teaching Introduction to Life Science to seventh graders for the last 6 years. She is grading student homework at the end of the day during the hour or so following student dismissal, when a teacher may be alone with thoughts and concerns for students' progress. She is looking over student homework and student marks in her grade book when she is interrupted by a knock at the door.

"Hi, Janet, it was so quiet down at this end of the hall I thought everyone in the science wing had gone home," declared Susan Toliver, Janet's close friend and colleague, who had come to West Valley Middle School with Janet when it opened in 1977.

"Oh, hi, Susan. I'm just grading some of today's class work and some homework I previously collected but haven't managed to review until now, and I dare say, I'm more than a little worried," Janet responded with a tone of concern in her voice.

"Aren't they doing well? You have always succeeded with your seventh graders since I've known you," replied Susan.

Janet continued to express her concern, "Well, maybe not this time. I've struggled to help these students understand DNA and protein synthesis, but the class work and homework results are terrible this year, and I'm sure my students aren't going to do well on the unit test I'm giving tomorrow. I know this material is hard for them. Maybe I'm not spending enough time going over the details of the process. The text seems to cover this material well enough, and the publisher's unit test seems to match up with the content conveyed by the book. Maybe the department selected a textbook that's just too hard for our students."

"Uh oh," responded Susan. "Have Juanita and Jack experienced the same kind of difficulties?"

"I'm not sure," Janet said. "I haven't really checked with them about their students' progress since the start of the year, and they have new teaching assignments this year as well. We sometimes talk at lunch or during department meetings with respect to student progress, but I don't want to pry, if you know what I mean."

This vignette of teaching in the year that *A Nation at Risk* was released displays the nature of teaching that was common at that time and may still be found in settings where reform has been slow. It portrays a vision of teaching as a relatively lonely and isolated profession. In 1983, teachers rarely interacted with each other on matters of teaching, curriculum, and student evaluation. Typically, teacher interaction was social in nature, often restricted to inconsequential issues and personal life matters (Flinders, 1988). Neophytes coming into the faculty dining area who chose to talk about their teaching experiences during lunch would be told, "We don't talk shop here." Even today, too many teachers have no idea how the teacher in an adjacent classroom plans instruction, grades student work, or assigns grades.

The world of work for teachers in 1983 can be attributed in part to pervasive autonomy in the selection of curriculum resources, topics to be taught, methods for evaluating student work, and assignment of student grades. In 1983, a student taking General Biology from one teacher might experience quite a different curriculum than students of another teacher in the same building teaching the same subject, even with the same textbook. The current reform movement and the imposition of state control over curriculum in the form of content standards are changing this view of teaching. In more progressive settings, the days of teacher isolation and professional discretion are long past (Darling-Hammond, 1996). Note the circumstances in our second vignette that introduce two teachers, Sandra Ruiz and Carl Johnson, as they prepare to attend a weekly collaborative planning session of U.S. history teachers in Lost Valley High School.

A vignette of high school teaching in 2007:

As Mrs. Ruiz looked at the classroom clock, she noted that her two o'clock meeting time was rapidly approaching. All students in the school were given early dismissal at 1:00 p.m. to attend special Wednesday afternoon activities scheduled each week by the school district. For the last 45 minutes, Mrs. Ruiz has been looking over several documents spread out on her desk. These include her teacher's edition of the locally adopted U.S. history textbook, the state's social studies/history framework (including the state social studies and history standards), several items she obtained from the Internet about pioneers who settled into her county in California, and her district's curriculum pacing guide. Mrs. Ruiz has been concentrating on the history standards that she and her colleagues are expected to achieve within the next 2 weeks. She is anxiously trying to complete two tasks before the meeting: (a) to decide on the specific content within the standards to teach before next Wednesday, and (b) to write two or three descriptions of student products that would demonstrate achievement of the selected content. As she is deep in thought attempting to make sense of all her resources, Mr. Carl Johnson knocks at the door to announce his presence.

"Are you ready, Sandra? Do you have your student work samples we will review at our meeting today?" he asks.

"Yes, I'm all set," responded Sandra. "I don't think we both need to bring pacing guides. If you bring yours, I'll bring along a copy of the language arts frameworks so we can include one or more standards to integrate into our next lesson."

As the two teachers went down the hall to meet with two other U.S. history teachers, they conversed along the way about upcoming activities.

"I hope we can catch up with the pacing guide within the next few weeks," said Carl. "We have our common benchmark exam scheduled for November 5, and from my estimation, we have 12 more standards to achieve that are assessed on that exam."

Sandra was confident that students were doing well. She put Carl at ease by saying, "I wouldn't be worried. Do you remember when we met last summer that we decided to move three standards from the current assessment period into the next one? That decision took some pressure off us. Don't you recall that our state test report identified several standards in need of additional development at this time of the year? We gave ourselves some more time with the next three standards, so we aren't nearly as rushed as we were last year."

In this vignette, we see differences in the daily lives of teachers when compared to conventional teaching as practiced in 1983. Today's teachers are working closely together, bound by common instructional targets that arise from state content standards. The targets are specific student behaviors or products that will demonstrate understanding of state content standards. In 1983, teachers typically talked in terms of content they would cover, or teach, rather than target behaviors they expected to see in their students (Putnam & Borko, 2000). Both Carl and Janet think about student outcome behaviors that result from their teaching, and they evaluate the outcome behaviors by relating them back to the standards to be achieved.

In 2007, Sandra and Carl met at least every Wednesday afternoon to plan standards-achieving lessons with their colleagues. These meetings stand in sharp contrast to the relative teacher isolation experienced by Janet Morehouse in the first vignette. It is evident that Sandra and Carl have prepared for a joint planning meeting, and that they are anticipating a collaboratively developed assessment experience that will prepare their students for the new high-stakes tests that have arisen since President Bush signed No Child Left Behind into law (Little, Gearhart, Curry, & Kafka, 2003)

They also seem to be using a variety of resources associated with the standards movement that were not a concern to teachers back in 1983. In the vignette, we heard about pacing guides and curriculum frameworks in addition to textbooks. These teachers recognize that they need to work together to ensure the success of all the children enrolled in U.S. History in their school. Although not all their lessons are planned collaboratively, major lessons and projects are developed during common planning time, and all major tests are developed collaboratively and administered to all students taking U.S. History on the same day. These teachers will work independently from their peers while teaching classes, but teacher isolation with respect to instructional planning, assessment planning, and student work evaluation has been replaced with collaboration and sharing of expertise.

The teaching lives of Sandra and Carl are quite different from those of Janet and Susan back in 1983. By contrast, Sandra and Carl have learned about collaboration, curriculum pacing, benchmark assessment practices, and the analysis of student test results for the improvement of teaching and learning. They have also learned to accept responsibility for the quality of teaching and student learning in all U.S. history classes taught by teachers in their planning group. They are clearly not teaching in isolation from each other.

We have seen through the two contrasting vignettes that the professional lives of teachers have changed in recent years and that these changes seem to be most evident in the collaborative nature of planning and assessment activities conducted by teachers, the resources that teachers use, and the expectations for student achievement that are emphasized through strong accountability measures. Our vignettes illustrate major changes underway in public education that point the way to new futures in teaching and learning not thought possible by teachers some 20 years ago.

SIX NEW DIRECTIONS IN TEACHING, LEARNING, AND ASSESSMENT

How did this new world of public school teaching come to pass? Prospective teachers may have anticipated some changes in the teaching profession since they attended public school, and they may have heard about heightened accountability for student achievement under NCLB regulations, but they may not have anticipated the implications of this legislation for their own teaching careers. We will examine a number of sweeping policy changes that have taken place in the last 15 years that have given rise to a new world of teaching in public education.

1. **Local control of the curriculum has declined as states determine what is to be taught in classrooms.** Historically, the curriculum taught in America's public schools was under the control of local public school districts (Cohen & Spillane, 1992). Across the country, boards of education composed of elected or appointed community members determined the curriculum to be conveyed at elementary school grades and in secondary school subjects. Typically, these boards of education gave teachers and administrators substantial discretion in the selection of textbooks and other curriculum resources. For the most part, teachers prepared their own exams and assigned students grades with only limited involvement of the principal.

In the current educational climate, local boards of education may add to the curriculum imposed by state curriculum content standards, but they may not disregard them. States that fail to impose content standards on local school districts can ultimately lose their eligibility for federal funding of public education. Accountability for the achievement of the skills and content described in the standards is ensured through high-stakes testing programs that are administered every spring to all students in Grades 3 through 8 in mathematics and language arts. Recently, states have also begun to assess science in three different grades, and many states have implemented high school graduation tests based on their state's standards.[2]

States that fail to monitor the progress of all public school districts as they demonstrate achievement of adequate yearly progress will be in jeopardy for sanctions from the federal government in the form of reduced federal funding and eligibility of school districts for federal grants and loans. No Child Left Behind accountability passes directly through state departments of education to local school districts. This accountability movement has dramatically reduced control over the curriculum by local boards of education and placed it in the hands of state and federal authorities, who determine the curriculum standards to be met and the assessments that measure student progress in learning.

2. Essential curriculum questions have been resolved. Prior to the emergence of state content standards, educators in towns across America wrestled with essential questions related to the purposes of public education, including, "What should be taught in the schools?" "What essential knowledge should be conveyed in each subject?" and "At what grade level and in what subjects should certain concepts, ideas, and skills be conveyed?" (Popkewitz, 1997). These time-honored questions, and their consequent question, "What is to be tested?" have been largely resolved through the imposition of state curriculum standards.

This is not the case in other subject areas outside the core curriculum identified in NCLB. There is opportunity for teachers, particularly in secondary schools, to supplement the content of the standards with additional material suited to student interests and social needs in elective courses. Nevertheless, the adequate yearly progress stipulation of NCLB has nearly eliminated teacher discretion over the curriculum.

This loss of control is particularly evident in school settings in which curriculum pacing guides or pacing calendars have been installed. These mechanisms are used by school districts to determine the sequence and pace with which standards are conveyed through the school year. Additional factors, including benchmark testing programs, which will be discussed in Chapter 6, go further in limiting teacher discretion with regard to the content and skills that are conveyed in the classroom.

New teachers using this book as a guide to beginning professional practice will notice that choices over areas of the curriculum to be emphasized or developed at length will be limited in comparison to the discretion exercised by teachers they encountered during their own secondary school days. More than ever, teachers with common instructional assignments (e.g., U.S. History) can actually be found teaching similar content in every classroom. In the past, one teacher might stress the Civil War and Reconstruction at the expense of Manifest Destiny, whereas a teacher across the hall focused on the Industrial Revolution. Students encountered different curricula in sections of the same course due only to the luck of the draw in terms of the teacher to whom they were assigned. State curriculum standards and their assessment have put a halt to this flexibility in teaching practices in all but a few school districts.

3. State-level control over the curriculum has changed assessment. In 1983, secondary school teachers typically taught courses of 20 units that included a unit test every 2 or 3 weeks. Quizzes and written assignments constituted other forms of assessment that kept students focused on instruction. At the end of the year, some students took **standardized tests** so the school could compare its students' performances with similar students across the country, but the standardized tests had no bearing on courses of study (Linn, 2000). Teachers typically made up their own tests, which may have differed substantially from tests constructed by other teachers of the same course.

One exception to school-level decision making with respect to testing and other forms of assessment evident in 1983 is the Advanced Placement program sponsored by the College Board (Rothschild, 1999). The exams administered by this program, prepared with the assistance of scholars of various disciplines in universities across the country, measure student knowledge in relation to course completion expectations set for college and university students.[3] However, these are elective exams, and only a few students in most high schools enroll in the preparatory courses, pay fees, and take these exams on a voluntary basis.

The high-stakes state standards tests, by contrast, are required of all students who complete designated core curriculum courses in math, English, social studies, and science in the general academic curriculum. They are not elective tests, and the consequences for poor performance affect all students in the school because the school as a unit of performance is evaluated. The schoolwide affects of state standards testing are diminishing teachers' reliance on independently developed assessment procedures to evaluate student progress and course completion.

Teachers in the first decade of the 21st century are centering assessment activities on standards achievement in general and on student success with state standards exams in particular. Unit tests, benchmark tests, quizzes, reports, and portfolios are enriching the assessment landscape as they hopefully will lead to high test scores on the state standards tests administered at the end of each academic year. This preoccupation with assessment is largely driven by the need for each school to demonstrate adequate yearly progress and thus avoid possible sanctions for underperformance.

4. Classroom assessment is affected by large-scale assessment. In years past, the relationship between the curriculum of the classroom and items on standardized tests was limited, and the exams were low stakes for schools and districts. The few exams that related to students' futures, typically related to the college admission process, did not measure school quality directly. Teachers taught content toward assessment targets of their own making. Typically, these targets were measured by quizzes and tests written by the teachers who administered them.

In secondary school grades, midterm exams and final course exams were sometimes included as part of the course curriculum. If midterm and final exams had a great impact on final grades, teachers probably spent one or two class sessions reviewing for these relatively important exams. With the advent of state standards exams, "teaching to the test" has become common, largely because these new exams are used to evaluate school effectiveness (Popham, 2001). In some communities, students with poor prior testing records have been scheduled into classes with the express purpose of preparing them for the exam through focused use of test prep curriculum materials. Many school districts are installing benchmark testing programs that call for periodic exams to evaluate achievement of selected state standards taught over several weeks' time. These exams emulate the state standards exams in both format and content.

Many progressive school districts appoint assessment committees to review the items and content of the state standards exams as they receive test reports in the summer following spring test administration. These committees look for test items that challenged students in the district and included these items, or questions like them, on the benchmark exams to be administered for the next year. As a result of these practices, assessments through the academic year have grown to serve two purposes: evaluation of student performance for content recently conveyed and assessment of student progress toward successful performance on state standards exams to be administered in the spring.

5. Distinctions between instruction and assessment have begun to blur.   An additional distinction between assessment practices of the past and those that are emerging in classrooms today is the variety and purpose of the assessment that takes place in classrooms (Rothman, 1997). Formerly, teachers focused their attention on weekly quizzes and end-of-unit exams for the purpose of recording the grades that made up quarterly and semester marks on report cards. In today's reform environment, assessment takes on many forms because of the increased diversity of students in today's general education classroom. As more English language learners (students whose primary language is not English) and students with special needs enroll in general education studies, the need to provide alternative means by which these students can express understanding of subject matter has led to increased variety in assessment, including the use of performance assessment methods that differ from traditional literacy-dependent methods of evaluation such as essay questions and multiple-choice items.

The current emphasis on differentiated instruction has also contributed to increased use and variety of assessment practices (Tomlinson, 1999). In today's classroom, student differences in learning styles and learning abilities are acknowledged and built on. In the differentiated classroom, assessment is viewed as a daily, ongoing activity that the teacher uses to gain deeper insights into individual student acquisition of knowledge and skill. As a result of these continuing **formative assessments**, the teacher modifies individual and group instruction to achieve learning goals identified for all students through state curriculum standards. The new instructional practices of the inclusive and differentiated classroom depend on high-quality assessment methods that weave through the instructional events of the day.

6. Teachers are sharing their teaching skills as they plan collaboratively.
Sandra and Carl's working environment, which was described in our second vignette, illustrates a collaborative, open environment where teachers work as interdependent colleagues in many aspects of teaching. In particular, these teachers work closely as they plan instruction, assess student learning progress, and evaluate student work. If Janet and Susan, our two teachers in the first vignette, were transported forward in time to the school where Sandra and Carl teach, they would experience a period of adjustment and perhaps some anxiety as they found themselves working in settings where their ideas, educational process understandings, and subject matter knowledge would be open to scrutiny by their new colleagues.

Several challenges are associated with collaborative planning, collaborative student work evaluation, and the use of common assessments. Teachers who work in these settings are constantly disclosing their subject matter knowledge strengths and weaknesses to their colleagues as they describe the quality of work they expect to see in a good student performance. When two teachers work together to interpret curriculum standards and translate the knowledge and skill statements of the standards into descriptions of student knowledge production, they reveal their understanding of content and curriculum planning to each other.

Additional concerns may surface as teachers collaboratively examine student work. At some point in time, one teacher's set of student products may fall short of the performances seen in the work of a colleague's students. Differences in student performance are also likely to surface when students in two different classrooms take common examinations. Teachers who find their students performing below the average of students taught by other teachers may feel some unease regarding perceptions of their teaching skills.

These changes in the profession may come as a surprise to new teachers who attended school during times of more conventional teaching. It is important for new teachers to understand that the activities of teachers they witnessed in classrooms 10 or more years ago are disappearing from schools across America. Teacher candidates should be mindful of reform conditions present in schools they visit during student teaching, internship teaching, or other forms of professional practice. Adjustments to collaborative ways of performing traditional teaching functions, including planning, instruction, and student work evaluation, are usually easier to make during the first years of teaching than they are after routines and operational procedures have become habits of professional practice (Darling-Hammond & McLaughlin, 1995).

AN OVERVIEW OF ASSESSMENT PURPOSES AND METHODS: THEN AND NOW

We have seen that the world of teaching is changing as a result of curriculum and assessment reforms largely driven by NCLB legislation and widespread focus on K–12 curriculum standards. No aspect of teaching has been affected more by these reforms than the assessment practices of teachers in progressive schools. What are the different kinds of assessment that involve classroom teachers, and how have each of these been modified in recent years? We will answer this question with a brief survey of the field of classroom assessment prior to exploring assessment purposes and methods in detail in later chapters. We will conduct this introductory survey of the field of classroom assessment in a chronological manner. We will examine testing as it might unfold through the academic year, beginning, as it should, before students arrive for their first day of school.

Preinstructional Assessment: Understanding Learners and Their Needs

In late summer, prior to the arrival of students for the start of the academic year, teachers anticipate the skills and abilities they will encounter in students who will soon be seated in their classrooms. Although some teachers may choose only to speculate about the relative abilities of their students or how well prepared their students will be for the start of the school year, others take action to learn about their students prior to the onset of instruction. Some of this activity may take place before the first day of school, and a few activities may be planned for students during the first week of classes before full engagement with the curriculum. All activity relating to learning about students that falls before teaching begins can be placed into the category of **preinstructional assessment.**

In elementary schools across the country, teachers spend several days before the start of the school year preparing their rooms and bulletin boards in an effort to provide students with an attractive and motivating learning environment. Many of these teachers take time to visit the main office, where they will learn about students enrolled in their grade-level teaching assignment. Secondary school teachers, typically less inclined to make substantial preparations to their classroom environment, are nevertheless interested in learning about students with special needs for whom they will need to make accommodations (Taylor-Greene et al., 1997). Although new teachers may not give much thought to these kinds of preparations as they consider the first day of regular classes and their new role as a classroom leader, they can probably recall with little prompting the preinstructional assessment activities they experienced long ago when they were elementary school students.

The stereotype of assessment conducted during the first day of school has either been directly experienced, or talked about, by everyone who has reminisced with others about their school days. Following introductions and perhaps a review of classroom rules, the teacher asked students to write an essay about their experiences during summer vacation. It is doubtful that many people who have considered the pervasive nature of this assignment for the first day of school have ever wondered why teachers conducted this activity. Perhaps the purpose of the assignment was to judge the relative writing abilities of students who were new to the classroom. For decades teachers have sought information about the abilities and special needs of their students prior to the first day of class (Feiman-Nemser, 2003). In some instances, the teacher might look at school records of students soon to be taught to find information about their performance at the preceding grade level.

Teachers have been using a wide variety of information sources to ascertain student attitudes, dispositions toward school and learning, and readiness to learn the subject matter they will soon be teaching. Airasian (2000) referred to teacher efforts to understand students, their interests, and their motivations before teaching begins as "sizing up assessment." When teachers focus on student capacity to learn in their classroom, they are likely to turn their attention to scores from a standardized test battery consisting of student achievement scores in core subject areas and subskills in two critical areas: math and reading. Subskills in reading might include vocabulary, word analysis, or punctuation. These exams would compare the performance of each new student with other students of the same grade level in the school district and with a national sample of similar students.

Typically, students would be assigned a percentile rank that would identify the percentage of students in their school district, or in a national sample of students, that obtained a lower or equal raw score of correct items in each category of performance reported (Linn & Gronlund, 2000). Armed with this information, a teacher could infer the relative abilities of students and how likely they were to perform in various subjects during the academic year. As we shall explore later, it is possible to make incorrect inferences using this kind of information, especially if it is used in isolation from other assessment information concerning similar skills.

In recent years, the influence of standardized achievement tests has waned substantially as student performance on state standards exams has begun to displace exams that compare one student's performance with other students. State standards exams, in contrast to conventional standardized tests, compare a student's performance with a target performance usually labeled "proficient." If state test writers determine that students must identify the correct answer, or provide a correct answer, to 35 of 50 similar items on a state standards test, then students who answer fewer than 35 items will be deemed "basic," "below proficient," or a similar determination that denotes less-than-satisfactory performance in acquiring the skills and knowledge of state standards (Meier, Cohen, & Rogers, 2000).

If today's teachers examine student records to see statewide test results, they are likely to find student performance scores qualified with terms that include "basic," "proficient," or "advanced," rather than a percentile rank score typically reported for the standardized tests that were used in the past. These new exams measure student achievement of content and skills of the curriculum in relation to expectations held for all students, not in terms of relative performance in general fields of knowledge that may or may not have been taught in the prior grade (Hamilton, Stecher, & Klein, 2002). State standards tests are more effective in assessing student achievement in relation to the curriculum the student has actually encountered.

Teachers can turn to other information besides standardized tests and state standards tests to learn about student knowledge before the school year begins. Grade reports and commentary provided by the teacher from the prior academic year are often viewed by teachers as the most reliable predictors of future student performance in subject areas that are taught in each grade in a developmental manner (Wilson & Berne, 1999). Although this information may be useful in corroborating inferences formed when standards test achievement records are also known, they may not be useful if they lead the teacher to form unwarranted negative perceptions about a student's ability to perform well in the subsequent year. Year-to-year disparities in student performance often occur due to a variety of factors, including student maturation, changes in personal circumstances in the home, or the relationship between the student and the former teacher.

In addition to test scores and grade reports for all students in a class, teachers will also want information concerning particular students for whom they may need to provide special attention. Teachers want to know if they are enrolling students with special needs, which could include students with disabilities or those who are English language learners (ELLs). Schools are obliged to provide information to teachers on a need-to-know basis regarding special-needs students. In the event of a learning or other form of disability, teachers should have access to information in the Individual Educational Plan (IEP) for guiding students to achieve learning goals included in these plans (Doolittle, 2002). Recently enacted legislation, including Section 504 of the Adults with Disabilities Act, which mandates the inclusion of students with disabilities into the general education curriculum, also specifies the information and support services that general education teachers are entitled to receive to meet the educational goals for these students. This important legislation, which affects teachers as they perform their duties in classrooms with special-needs students, is the Individuals with Disabilities Education Act (IDEA) with additional specifications added in its subsequent reauthorization in 2004 as the Individuals with Disabilities Education Improvement Act (IDEIA).[4] Other students may need specialized educational services because of their language and cultural history. When students are raised in families where languages other than English are spoken, they often struggle to understand instruction provided by teachers instructing only in English. These students are referred to as English language learners (ELLs).

English language learners may be in need of specialized services or instructional approaches that help them acquire English skills while learning subject matter. Depending on the state in which the teacher is employed, assessment information may be provided that informs the teacher of grade equivalent information about the English language skills of these students. Additionally, specific professional development may be available to teachers of ELL students in the use of instructional strategies for these learners. Often referred to as specially designed academic instruction in English (SDAIE), or sheltered English instruction,[5] these methods help ELL students comprehend teachers who use English in the classroom, and they can be customized to meet the particular challenges of individual students as they are assessed using diagnostic tests of English language acquisition (Goldenberg, 1996).

English language learners are now appearing across America in school districts that previously had minimal or no enrollment of these special-needs students. For years, only California, Arizona, New Mexico, and Texas focused attention on ELL students and their needs. Recently, states in the central and eastern portions of the United States have reported substantial increases in their ELL populations (Carrasquillo & Rodriguez, 2002). Increasing numbers of teachers who work and live in states other than border states are encountering these learners, and they are making adjustments in the curriculum for them.

Finally, the teacher can perform an assessment of student readiness to learn through the administration of a preinstructional test based on the curriculum to be taught through the year. Teachers want to know what students may already know about subject matter to be taught in their classroom. Also, teachers want to know how well students have mastered knowledge and skills in the lower grades that are essential building blocks to learning in the grade or course they will be teaching. Fortunately, in this modern era involving a mandated curriculum aligned with state content standards, it is possible to construct a test that serves both of these purposes. Many states release previously administered state standards exams or selected test items that appeared on their state standards tests. By using selected released items of the standards test that students took at the close of the prior year and released items that measure student achievement for the upcoming year, the teacher can learn how much information from last year's standards students have retained and how well prepared students are to acquire knowledge that will be assessed in the current grade. It is important that this kind of preassessment not be used to grade student performance, and information gleaned from this assessment should be corroborated with other information about student achievement previously discussed prior to making inferences about student learning needs (Stiggins, 1997).

Diagnostic Assessment

Diagnostic assessment exams are used in schools to identify underlying causes of learning difficulties experienced by individual students (Nitko, 2001). These specialized exams are usually called for when a teacher notices that the academic performance or behavior of a student deviates sufficiently from class group norms to be a cause for concern. Alternatively, the teacher may notice some aspect of the student's general behavior, deportment, or attitude that suggests the need for an intervention.

These specialized exams are administered by properly credentialed professionals who are able to interpret the test results. A school psychologist or counselor will typically administer a diagnostic exam to a student who has been referred by a teacher, a parent, or another professional who has expressed a concern about a student's progress in school. In contrast to standardized tests or classroom-based assessments, diagnostic exams are administered to one student at a time.

The use of diagnostic assessments typically lies beyond the range of responsibilities of the classroom teacher. Nevertheless, teachers need to know the purposes of these exams and their value to student learning to make a proper referral when such exams are indicated. In the event a teacher senses a difficulty in student learning, poor disposition toward school, inappropriate social development, or low self-regard, it may be appropriate to inform parents and medical service providers of the need to delve more deeply into underlying causes of the student's stress or underperformance.

Diagnostic exams may be used to assess general abilities or special learning problems associated with certain aspects of the curriculum.[6] For instance, certain reading diagnostic exams can be used to identify disabilities, such as dyslexia, that interfere with reading ability. If a teacher were to notice that one student in a class is not responding to reading instruction, then the administration of a specialized diagnostic exam would help clinical experts in the school system identify the cause of the student's slow progress in reading skills development. When the test score on the reading diagnostic exam becomes available, the professional who is able to make a diagnosis will corroborate the test results with other evidence related to the student's performance in reading. It is important that conclusions about student learning difficulties be reached through the analysis of several types of data, not simply one test score from a single administration of a diagnostic exam.

Teachers who are new to the profession or new employees of a school district should learn the procedures for referring students of concern to school professionals who will conduct diagnostic assessments if an assessment is needed. Appropriate officials include the principal, the district's school psychologist, a school social worker, or a guidance counselor. Typically, the point for first referral is likely to be a grade-level team leader in an elementary school setting, a department chair in a secondary school, or the school principal.

A school referral form will probably need to be completed, along with a description of the circumstances that led the new teacher to be concerned about the progress or well-being of the learner in question. If school policies regarding student referrals and diagnosis of student difficulties are available, a review of these policies should be sufficient to guide the teacher to appropriate action when concern for a student arises. If the new teacher is not provided with policy guidelines or procedures for student referrals, it is best to make a request for this information and to review it when it is made available.

Formative Assessment

All former students recall the use of tests and quizzes to assign grades and report on student achievement, but few of us who attended school several years ago recall a teacher's use of assessment tools to guide their instructional planning. In recent years, assessment practices have increased in variety and frequency, and they have taken on many purposes that were not prevalent in schools in prior decades. Formative assessment, or the use of assessment practices to guide instructional planning and teaching practices, is a relatively new practice that today's teachers are expected to have in their professional repertoire.

Assessment has always served multiple purposes, and the improvement of instruction is among these. Teachers need to ascertain whether or not their students are acquiring information and skills before it is too late to take corrective action. The importance of formative assessment to effective learning is supported by research into student knowledge and skill acquisition (Black & William, 1998). On occasion, teachers wonder why students are not progressing as content is presented in the classroom. There may be many reasons why students find one area of learning to be particularly difficult or hard to retain, whereas another area is easily acquired and understood by most students (Gardner, 1983). Formative assessment techniques can help teachers recognize when students are facing challenges, and they can also lead to solutions for resolving student learning problems. They can help teachers identify specific areas of the curriculum that pose challenges to students, including misconceptions.

Cognitive psychologists have described the challenges to learning that result when students bring misconceptions or other forms of mistaken understanding to the learning experience. Misconceptions have been demonstrated to limit student retention of accurate information conveyed in class. When students learn mistaken information, particularly in relation to a new concept to be understood or a multistep procedure to be acquired, research has demonstrated that the incorrect information is difficult to dislodge if not corrected soon after the flawed learning experience (Griffiths & Preseton, 1992). When formative assessment is performed frequently, errors in student understanding are readily identified before they become entrenched. Additionally, formative assessment can be used to identify gaps in student learning or minimal understanding that needs to be supplemented with more information.

WHAT RESEARCH CAN TELL US ...

• About Incorrect Learning

Psychologists have identified the tendency for learners to readily acquire and persist in the use of incorrect procedures, knowledge, or routines. They have even noted that learners have a tendency to persist with the use of incorrect knowledge or routines even after the teacher has provided correct information. This retention of incorrect knowledge and its ease of acquisition is sometimes referred to as negative transfer. This problem surfaces most often when new, but incorrect, learning is similar to prior, but correct, learning. Woltz, Gardner, and Bell (2000) reported on this phenomenon in their report, "Negative Transfer Errors in Sequential Cognitive Skills: Strong-but-Wrong Sequence Application," published in the *Journal of Experimental Psychology, Learning, Memory, and Cognition.*[7]

One purpose of formative assessment is to guide students toward success on major exams and to the achievement of higher grades at the end of marking periods. With the advent of the current reform environment, new purposes and methods of formative assessment have emerged to guide students toward success on a more focused outcome. This outcome is the successful performance of all students on state standards exams administered in the late spring of each academic year.

In a standards-based classroom or school, formative assessment is focused on student achievement of curriculum standards as well as on traditional learning goals. The curriculum standards are translated by the teacher into descriptions of student products or performances, and these student outcomes become the target of instruction. When students meet instructional targets in today's reform environment, they have achieved one or more standards that may be tested on the state exam. The student product or performance may take the form of a written statement, an oral answer to a spoken question, a written solution to a problem, or the construction of a graph or diagram (O'Shea, 2005).

When teachers plan lessons to achieve instructional targets, they use language that specifies the nature of a proficient student performance they expect to see. During the course of daily instruction, they observe student efforts to achieve the targets. After students complete their daily work, the teacher collects the work and evaluates it in relation to the expectations set out in the performance descriptions in the instructional objectives of the daily lesson plan. Through this analysis, the teacher assesses student daily progress toward the achievement of state content standards. The following vignette of standards-based teaching that incorporates formative assessment for the achievement of state content standards may clarify some of these reform activities. This vignette describes two history teachers in a contemporary high school.

> Sandra and Carl, two U.S. history teachers at Lost Valley High School, are trying to translate a learning expectation from a California history/social science standard into a standards-achieving instructional target. Carl has just joined Sandra in a collaborative planning meeting to work on a standards-based lesson for next week. He brings her attention to History-Social Science Standard 11.3, Students analyze the role of religion played in the founding of America, its lasting moral, social, and political impacts, and issues regarding religious liberty (California Department of Education, 2005).
>
> "Sandra, I think this standard is a little vague. What do you think we are supposed to be getting at?" asked Carl.
>
> "Well, it's pretty clear that they are asking us to have students understand religious intolerance, particularly as experienced by Mormons, Catholics, and Jews. Perhaps we can bring in some events involving the experience of the Mormons as they moved west toward Utah," answered Sandra.
>
> Carl responded to this new focus by suggesting, "We could have them study the events in Nauvoo, Illinois, where Mormons were massacred before heading west to Utah."
>
> Sandra added, "We could ask them to research that event and write a report, identifying the reported causes of the persecution, historical explanations for their expulsion, and the response of the Mormon community to this action."
>
> "Okay," said Carl, adding, "but what specific things should they include in the report that would be good enough to be a proficient response?"

In this brief vignette, we see Carl and Sandra talking about topics included in a California history-social science standard. They are attempting to transform the content statements of the standard into a description of a student product, a collaboratively developed report that would demonstrate student mastery of the content. They are also considering the characteristics of a proficient report. After the lesson is taught, they will use their description of a successful report as an assessment tool by comparing it to samples of student reports that result from their instruction. Here, the report serves as a formative assessment of student acquisition of a history–social science standard.

Clearly, teachers are interested in achieving instructional goals that extend beyond the limited domain of state content standards (Abrams, Pedulla, & Madaus, 2003). These may include the larger societal goals involved in preparing young people to contribute to a diverse, multicultural society.

Teacher instructional priorities also include instructional goals in curriculum areas for which state content standards are not written. These goals can also be written as instructional outcomes to be assessed in daily classroom interaction with students. As we shall see in Chapter 5, conventional classroom observation and measurement techniques can be combined with newer techniques involving rubrics, observation checklists, and student self-assessment methods to ensure student achievement of standards-based instructional goals and other important goals.

Summative Assessment

As teachers and former students, we are all familiar with **summative assessment**. This measurement function evaluates student work and performances to assess achievement of learning targets. It is primarily used to provide students with a grade for work completed and, ultimately, final marks in courses. As former students, all teachers are familiar with final exams, unit tests, blue book exams, and final projects that raised their anxiety during the school year. For many of us who have had recent experience as students in higher education, perhaps in courses that prepare us to teach a particular subject matter, the experience of summative assessment is not a fond recollection. In some instances, final marks are determined based on only one or two exams. Although summative assessments have typically taken the form of final exams or papers, they can also include all manner of student performances used to assess the acquisition of knowledge or skills described in course descriptions or syllabi. Reports, papers, projects, speeches, dramatic performances, and other works of art are types of summative assessments.

In recent years, the purposes of summative assessment have expanded in the context of the current educational reform movement. Over time, instructors have come to understand that all forms of assessment should serve multiple purposes and that some of these purposes should serve the goal of improving teaching and learning. Teachers have learned to analyze the results of tests to identify areas of student underperformance. Armed with this information, teachers can use results of test performance analysis to improve instruction.

In addition, teachers are now involving students in several decision-making elements of the assessment process. When students are informed of subject matter to be covered on a test, the nature of the exercises they will encounter, and a role in the development of assessment instruments, they learn to succeed in their role as students (Stiggins, 1997). Across the United States, teachers are working harder to help their students succeed with high-stakes assessments.

With the advent of state standards exams as part of NCLB compliance, traditional summative assessments are taking on a role attributed to formative assessments, that of preparing students for success on these important exams. Also, new exams have appeared in many progressive school districts that are expressly intended to lead students to success on the state standards exams (Herman & Baker, 2005). Most teachers have become mindful of the learning expectations in their state's standards. Using information from their state department of education, they analyze test questions used on prior state exams, and they review information about state standards that are likely to be tested. Using this information, they augment their summative tests with test items resembling those that are likely to appear on the standards tests. Secondary school teachers can inform their students about this process and let them know that selected test items will closely resemble items they may encounter on the state exam. When they review test results with their students, they can inform them about the progress they are making toward course grades and simultaneously advise them about the likelihood of a proficient performance on the state test (O'Shea, 2005).

School districts are now installing a new form of exam called a benchmark test. These tests may be either formative or summative in nature. In the former case, school districts administer the exam to all students taking the same course or enrolled at the same grade level. The information that results from this test is used to advise students and teachers about the progress they are making in understanding state standards.

In some instances, these exams are used as unit exams or exams of similar stakes in relation to student grades. Regardless of the evaluative purposes to which these exams are used, they vary with conventional practice because they are commonly administered to all students experiencing the same component of the school curriculum. Traditionally, teachers have administered their own tests to their students. Benchmark testing is one part of an initiative that is bringing the reform culture of teaching to schools. Common planning and common assessment is a natural outcome of benchmark testing.

All teachers are concerned about the quality of their tests. They want them to be fair, equitable, and useful for evaluating student knowledge. Due to the high stakes associated with summative assessments, teachers are concerned that tests truly measure the skills and knowledge expected of students and that they measure these students' attributes fairly.

Standardized Tests and Related Large-Scale Assessments

Another common recollection that former students retain is the standardized tests and other **large-scale assessments** taken in classrooms, cafeterias, or gymnasiums where students sat in row after row of exam stations. Perhaps we only vaguely understood the purposes of the exams we were taking. Typically, these tests had no bearing on course grades, but sometimes they were influential in determining the curriculum to which we would be exposed. For the most part, these exams resulted in a test score that would be compared with the scores of all other students taking the exam. These exams were administered under tightly controlled conditions to ensure that each student had the same opportunity to perform well on the exam, whether they were taking it in the room next door or in another state (Ediger, 2000).

Standardized examinations are prepared by companies that understand principles of large-scale assessment. Because of the way they are constructed and administered, they can be used to compare the performance of one student with the performance of another student, with all the students in a class or school, or with all the students taking the same exam across the country. Although scores may be reported in many different ways, percentile ranks are typical. These rankings show the performance of a student in relation to various populations of students. For instance, a student in the 76th percentile may have performed as well or better than 76% of the students in the school district or in the nation, depending on the specific comparative information provided.

Standardized tests are constructed for several purposes, and three of these include measurement of aptitude, achievement, or some characteristic of the test taker, such as intelligence (Thorndike, 2005). Many teachers are familiar with the Scholastic Aptitude Test (SAT)[8] or the ACT (originally known as the American College Testing Program), which are intended to evaluate a public school student's comparative ability to perform well in college. Higher education institutions use information from these tests to assess the likelihood that an applicant will succeed as a student and the relative standing of the applicant in comparison with others who have applied for admission.

Standardized tests that compare the knowledge and skills of one student with the knowledge and skills of other students are referred to as achievement tests. These tests tend to evaluate a student's growth in knowledge and skills for comparison with students of the same age or grade level. Students who score high may be guided into a more challenging college preparatory curriculum. Students who score relatively low may be diverted from challenging courses. In the past, these achievement exams were quite influential in determining the guidance students would receive regarding their academic experiences. Recently, educators have come to understand that standardized tests of this nature may be measuring attributes of the environment in which the student matured, including the richness of the curriculum in schools attended by students. There is concern that reliance on standardized tests to guide student learning experiences places privileged students at an unfair advantage over others who attend schools in poor communities (Popham, 2004).

Large-scale assessments may also be administered to particular groups of students to assess attributes of concern for special learners. For instance, English language learners may take an exam to determine the nature of the English language development curriculum to which they will be assigned.

In recent years, public attention has been focused on a new large-scale assessment. These are the exams used to assess student achievement of state content standards in core subjects at various grade levels. State standards tests are rapidly replacing standardized achievement tests for the purpose of measuring the effectiveness of a school or school district (Barksdale-Ladd & Thomas, 2000). State standards exams are not intended to compare the performance of one student, or a group of students, with other students of a larger population. Rather, they assess the extent to which students have mastered the content and skills of their state's curriculum standards. Although these tests can be used to assess student achievement for guidance purposes, they are more often used to compare a school or district with other schools and districts across the state after the exam is administered.[9]

Testing in its various forms dominates much of the current reform environment in public education. Test literacy is now more important then ever, particularly for those new to teaching (Stiggins, 2001). The brief overview of assessment purposes and assessment tools we have provided here alludes to the confusion about tests and testing that persists today. For instance, standardized testing programs, such as the Scholastic Aptitude Test, and state standards testing programs, which are used to determine adequate yearly progress under NCLB, are very different examinations that are used for quite different purposes, even through they share the common term *standard* within them.

In the chapters that follow, we will review the purposes and methods of assessment provided in our overview in greater depth with the intent to guide teachers in the preparation, selection, and use of classroom assessments during their early years of teaching. It is not intended to be a detailed study of assessment methods. Special emphasis will be placed on the use of assessments as they are experienced and are emphasized during the academic year.

Summary

Since the publication of *A Nation at Risk* in 1983, educational reform in the United States has continued unabated. In the last 15 years, state curriculum standards have emerged, and federal legislation titled No Child Left Behind has mandated state tests that hold educators accountable for student achievement of the standards. These developments are largely responsible for changes in classroom assessment in public schools. New policies have emerged that link classroom assessment with state standards achievement. These policies are leading teachers to work together collaboratively in the development of instructional plans, assessments, and the evaluation of student work.

Several forms of assessment have been affected by changes in policy resulting from educational reform, whereas other forms of assessment have gained in significance due to the increasing diversity of America's classrooms. Preinstructional assessments, formative assessments, summative assessments, and large-scale assessments have all become more prominent and more frequently used due to increased accountability for learning outcomes resulting in part from NCLB (Tyack & Cuban, 1995). The increase in the number of students with special needs in general education classrooms has increased the need for diagnostic assessments and special exams intended to measure English language acquisition. Knowledge in the construction, selection, and use of various kinds of assessment has become increasingly important for new educators.

Exercises

1. Read the Findings and Recommendations sections of the 1983 report of the National Commission on Educational Excellence. Evaluate the extent to which the recommendations have been responded to in the more than 20 years since this report was published. Provide some details about the achievement of recommendations in the categories of Content, Standards and Expectations, Time, Teaching, and Leadership and Fiscal Support.

2. Review the No Child Left Behind implementation plan for your state as found on the website of your state's department of education. Take particular note of expectations for student assessment, how adequate yearly progress is measured, and requirements for highly qualified teacher status. Comment about two or three policy positions that your state authority describes on its website with regard to fairness and feasibility of implementation.

3. Contrast the vignette of the teaching episode of 1983 (Janet and Susan) with the one from 2007 (Sandra and Carl). Describe differences in teacher professional practice in the following areas:

   • Selection and use of instructional materials
   • Planning lessons
   • Deciding what to teach
   • Examining and evaluating student work
   • Planning quizzes, tests, and other forms of assessment

4. Consider the changes in teaching practices that have taken place during the last few years. Describe your comfort level in working in a school where the following teaching behaviors are expected.

   • Using state standards and other state documents to identify instructional goals
   • Writing instructional outcomes as descriptions of student products or behaviors and presenting them to two colleagues for their review and suggestions
   • Teaching lessons and units that were coplanned with colleagues toward goals determined through collaborative planning

- Evaluating student work from your class with two other colleagues who will also present their students' work
- Planning and administering common assessments with colleagues and grading the work of your students and your colleague's students in a collaborative assessment session

5. In the current reform environment, teachers must lead their students to the achievement of state standards that are assessed by high-stakes tests. Schools must make adequate yearly progress in test achievement growth through 2014 or face sanctions. Following a reading of these stipulations and others required by No Child Left Behind, provide a statement of support or rejection of this important federal law from your perspective as a teacher.

6. In this chapter, six new policies have been identified that guide changes in teaching and learning. With which of these do you agree? Why? Identify those policies that you believe are unfortunate developments and state why you are dissatisfied with them.

7. Several forms of preinstructional assessment were described in Chapter 1, including state test results for students administered at the close of the prior year; reviews of teacher reports, grades, and teacher commentary from the prior year; reviews of test reports and individual educational plans of special-needs students; and administration of a pretest focused on student understanding of last year's and this year's standards. Consider the grade level, subject area(s), and setting in which you are, or anticipate to be, teaching. Which of the described methods of obtaining information about your students would be most valuable to you as a teacher? Why is this method important? Which procedures would you not use and why?

8. Provide a brief explanation for this observation: "Across America, the diversity of students in general education classrooms is increasing. This diversity includes English language learners and students with disabilities. Therefore, the need for effective diagnostic assessments has also increased."

9. Although there has always been value in providing students with formative assessments to guide their learning, mandates associated with NCLB have placed increased need for formative assessment in general education classrooms. Describe how formative assessment has changed its purposes with this legislation.

10. Large-scale assessments include aptitude tests and achievement tests. Among achievement tests, standardized tests and state standards test are now predominant. Distinguish between the nature and the purpose of state standards tests and conventional standardized tests.

Resources and Suggested Readings

A Nation at Risk remains preeminent among national reports on public education as the impetus for the educational reform movement launched with its publication in 1983. The following quotation, from the introduction to the report, illustrates the strident tone of the report:

> If an unfriendly foreign power had attempted to impose on America the mediocre educational performance that exists today, we might well have viewed it as an act

of war. As it stands, we have allowed this to happen to ourselves. We have even squandered the gains in student achievement made in the wake of the Sputnik challenge. Moreover, we have dismantled essential support systems which helped make those gains possible. We have, in effect, been committing an act of unthinking, unilateral educational disarmament. (*A Nation at Risk*, a report of the National Commission on Educational Excellence)
A complete copy of the report is available at:

www.ed.gov/pubs/NatAtRisk/index.html.

Other prominent reports that have influenced the current reform movement include: *A Nation Prepared: Teachers for the 21st Century*. Sponsored by the Carnegie Corporation of New York, Vol. 1/No. 3, Fall 2003, available at:

www.carnegie.org/results/03/pagetwo.html.

What Matters Most: Teaching and America's Future, a report of the National Commission on Teaching and America's Future, available at:

http://documents.nctaf.achieve3000.com/WhatMattersMost.pdf.

Collectively, the national reports led us ultimately to the sweeping reauthorization of the Elementary and Secondary Education Act, now known as No Child Left Behind, which was signed into law by President George W. Bush in 2002. The report is available at:

www.ed.gov/nclb/landing.jhtml.

Other resources on changes and trends in assessment described in Chapter 1 include Linn, R.L. (1993). Educational assessment: Expanded expectations and challenges. *Educational Evaluation & Policy Analysis, 15*(1), 1–16. Black, P., & William, D. (1998).
Inside the black box: Raising standards through classroom assessment. *Phi Delta Kappan, 80*(2), 139. This article is available at:

www.pdkintl.org/kappan/kbla9810.htm.

References

Abrams, L. M., Pedulla, J.J., & Madaus, G. F. (2003). View from the classroom: Teachers' opinions of statewide testing programs. *Theory into Practice, 24*(1), 18–29.

Airasian, P. W. (2000). *Assessment in the classroom: A concise approach* (2nd ed.). New York: McGraw-Hill, p. 32.

Barksdale-Ladd, M. A., & Thomas, K. F. (2000). What's at stake in high-stakes testing: Teachers and parents speak out. *Journal of Teacher Education, 51*(5), 384–397.

Black, P., & William, D. (1998). Inside the black box: Raising standards through classroom assessment. *Phi Delta Kappan, 80*(2), 139–149.

California Department of Education. (2005). *History-social science framework for California public schools*. Sacramento, CA: Author.

Carrasquillo, A. L., & Rodriguez, V.(2002). *Language minority students in the mainstream classroom* (2nd ed., *Bilingual Education and Bilingualism*, 33). Clevedon, UK: Multilingual Matters.

Cohen, D. K., & Spillane, J. P., (1992). Policy and practice: The relations between governance and instruction. *Review of Research in Education, 18*(1), 33–49.

Darling-Hammond, L. (1996). The quiet revolution: Rethinking teacher development. *Educational Leadership, 53*(6), 4–10.

Darling-Hammond, L., & McLaughlin, M. W. (1995). Policies that support professional development in an era of reform. *Phi Delta Kappan, 76*(8), 597.

Doolittle, A. E. (2002). Classroom assessment: What teachers need to know. *Journal of Educational Measurement, 39*(1), 85–90.

Ediger, M. (2000). Purposes in learner assessment. *Journal of Instructional Psychology, 27*(4), 244.

Feiman-Nemser, S. (2003). What new teachers need to learn. *Educational Leadership, 60*(8), 25–29.

Flinders, D. J. (1988). Teacher isolation and the new reform. *Journal of Curriculum and Supervision, 4*(1), 17–29.

Gardner, H. (1983). *Frames of mind: The theory of multiple intelligences.* New York: Basic Books.

Goldenberg, C. (1996). Commentary: The education of language-minority students: Where are we, and where do we need to go?, *The Elementary School Journal, 96*(3), 353–361.

Griffiths, A. K., & Preston, K. R. (1992). Grade 12 students' misconceptions relating to fundamental characteristics of atoms and molecules. *Journal of Research in Science Teaching, 29*(6), 611–628.

Hamilton, L. S., Stecher, B. M., & Klein, S. P. (2002). Making sense of test-based accountability in education. Santa Monica, CA: Rand.

Herman, J. L., & Baker, E. L. (2005). Making benchmark testing work. *Educational Leadership, 63*(3), 48–54.

Linn, R. L. (2000) Assessments and accountability. *Educational Researcher, 29*(2), 4–16.

Linn, R. L., & Gronlund, N. E. (2000). *Measurement and assessment in teaching.* Upper Saddle River, NJ: Prentice Hall.

Little, J. W., Gearhart, M., Curry, M., & Kafka, J. (2003). Looking at student work for teacher learning, teacher community, and school reform. *Phi Delta Kappan, 85*(3), 184–192.

Meier, D., Cohen, J., & Rogers, J. (2000). *Will standards save public education?* Boston: Beacon Press.

National Commission on Excellence in Education. (1983). *A nation at risk: The imperative for educational reform.* Washington, DC: U.S. Government Printing Office. Available at: www.ed.gov/pubs/NatAtRisk/index.html.

Nitko, A. J. (2001). *Educational assessment of students.* Upper Saddle River, NJ: Prentice Hall.

No Child Left Behind (NCLB) Act of 2001, Pub. L. No. 107–110, 115Stat. 1425. (2001). Washington, DC: U.S. Department of Education. Available at: www.ed.gov/nclb/landing.jhtml.

O'Shea, M. R. (2005). *From standards to success: A guide for school leaders.* Alexandria, VA: Association for Supervision and Curriculum Development.

Popham, W. J. (2001). Teaching to the test? *Educational Leadership, 58*(6), 16–20.

Popham, W. J. (2004). A game without winners. *Educational Leadership, 62*(3), 46–50.

Popkewitz, T. S. (1997). The production of reason and power: Curriculum history and intellectual traditions. *Journal of Curriculum Studies, 29*(2), 131–164.

Porter, A. C., Linn, R. L. & Trimble, C. S. (2005). The effects of state decisions about NCLB adequate yearly progress targets. *Educational Measurement, 24*(4), 32–39.

Putnam, R. T., & Borko, H. (2000). What do new views of knowledge and thinking have to say about research on teacher learning? *Educational Researcher, 29*(1), 4–15.

Rothman, R. (1997). *Measuring up: Standards, assessment and school reform.* San Francisco: Jossey-Bass.

Rothschild, E. (1999). Four decades of the advanced placement program. *The History Teacher, 32*(2), 175–206.

Stiggins, R. J. (1997). *Student-centered classroom assessment.* Upper Saddle River, NJ: Merrill/Prentice Hall.

Stiggins, R. J. (2001). *Student-involved classroom assessment* (3rd ed.). Upper Saddle River, NJ: Merrill/Prentice Hall.

Taylor-Greene, S., Brown, D., Nelson, L., Longton, J., Gassman, T., Cohen, J., et al. (1997). School-wide behavioral support: Starting the year off right. *Journal of Behavioral Education, 7*(1), 99–112.

Thorndike, R. M. (2005). *Measurement and evaluation in psychology and education* (7th ed.). Upper Saddle River, NJ: Merrill/Prentice Hall.

Tomlinson, C. A. (1999). *The differentiated classroom: Responding to the needs of all learners.* Alexandria, VA: Association for Supervision and Curriculum Development.

Tyack, D. B., & Cuban, L. (1995). *Tinkering toward utopia: A century of public school reform.* Cambridge, MA: Harvard University Press.

Wilson, S. M., & Berne, J. (1999). Teacher learning and the acquisition of professional knowledge: An examination of research on contemporary professional development. *Review of Research in Education, 24,* 173–210.

Woltz, D. J., Gardner, M. K., & Bell, B. G. (2000). Negative transfer errors in sequential cognitive skill: Strong-but-wrong sequence application. *Journal of Experimental Psychology, Learning, Memory, and Cognition, 26*(3), 601–625.

Endnotes

1 School report cards are described on the No Child Left Behind website of the U.S. Department of Education: www.ed.gov/nclb/accountability/schools/accountability.html.

2 Policies from NCLB that may result in sanctions are identified at: www.ed.gov/policy/elsec/guid/states/index.html.

3 Advanced Placement programs sponsored by the College Board are described at: www.collegeboard.com/student/testing/ap/about.html.

4 Individuals with Disabilities Education Act, or IDEA, as described at: http://idea.ed.gov/, subsequently reauthorized as the Individuals with Disabilities Education Improvement Act.

5 Specially designed academic instruction in English is defined at: http://en.wikipedia.org/?title=SDAIE. Wikipedia's definition is followed by a listing of representative SDAIE strategies. In other settings outside western states, SDAIE is referred to as sheltered English instruction.

6 Comprehensive resource for learning more about diagnostic assessments as they apply to students with special needs can be found at: Lerner, J. W. (2000). *Learning disabilities: Theories, diagnosis, and teaching strategies* (8th ed.). Boston: Houghton Mifflin.

7 Department of Educational Psychology, University of Utah, Salt Lake City, UT 84112–9255, woltz@gse.utah.edu. Three experiments investigated the role of processing sequence knowledge in negative transfer within multistep cognitive skills. In Experiments 1 and 2, more training resulted in higher error rates when new processing sequences that resembled familiar ones were introduced in transfer. Transfer error responses were executed with the same speed as correct responses to familiar sequence trials, and the errors appeared to be undetected by the performers. Experiment 3 tested whether the effects of sequence learning were attributable to explicit or implicit knowledge of processing sequences. Evidence favored the implicit learning interpretation. Findings are discussed in relation to earlier demonstrations of the Einstellung effect and to current taxonomic theories of human error.

8 Note: Information about the SAT is available from: www.collegeboard.com/splash/, *Sex differences in the academic performance of scholastic aptitude test takers,* College Board Report No. 84–8

9 Sanctions for failing to demonstrate adequate yearly progress stipulated in No Child Left Behind may be found at the U.S. Department of Education webpage: www.cde.ca.gove/re/pn/fb/yr04nclb.asp.

Chapter 2

Essential Principles of Assessment and Evaluation

LEARNER OBJECTIVES

At the conclusion of this chapter the reader will be able to

▶ Distinguish between fair and unbiased assessments and biased assessments.

▶ Distinguish between reliability and validity.

▶ Describe different kinds of assessment validity.

▶ Characterize valid and reliable classroom assessments.

GRAPHIC ORGANIZER

ASSESSMENT VOCABULARY

Accuracy: The extent to which a measure is free from error. A measurement instrument is accurate if the same value is obtained in repeated trials and the value conforms to an accepted standard.

Binomial distribution: A probability function that expresses the likelihood of obtaining a possible total of two alternative outcomes when an independent event with only two possible outcomes is repeated for a given number of trials (e.g., flipping a coin 17 times).

Content validity: The extent to which a test or other form of assessment is representative of a body of knowledge typically conveyed in a curriculum.

Construct validity: The ability of an assessment to measure some underlying trait of an examinee (e.g., intelligence or motivation).

Miller Analogies Test: An admission examination often used for graduate programs in the social sciences.

Precision: The property of a measurement tool to generate the same quantitative or qualitative data in repeated measures of an unchanging attribute.

Predictive validity: The extent to which an assessment process leads to a score or outcome that correlates with the likelihood of some future event.

Reliability: Related to precision, it is the ability of an assessment tool and its administration to obtain the same results for repeated measures of the same attribute.

Speeded test: An assessment administered with intentional time constraints to measure rapid performance of a skill or a series of tasks.

Test-wiseness: The ability of some examinees to score high on an assessment through understanding of the nature and purposes of test items.

Title I: A section of the Elementary and Secondary Education Act that provides supplemental funding for low-income children.

Validity: The measures of the goodness of fit between an assessment tool and a property it is intended to measure.

INTRODUCTION

Classroom-based assessment has taken on new proportions and influence within our current reform movement in education. Expectations for increased accountability have linked classroom assessment to the high-stakes tests that are administered toward the close of each academic year (Rothman, 2002). As educators, we need to be sure that our assessment practices are fair. We want our tests, quizzes, assignments, and projects to provide each and every student with an equal chance to perform well and receive a good grade. Further, we do not want any individual, or group of students, to have an advantage over other test takers because of factors in the assessment process that are unrelated to the skills or content to be measured. In this chapter, we introduce principles and concepts of assessment intended to maximize fairness in the classroom assessment process.

We will explore important assessment concepts that form the foundation of fairness in educational measurement, including reliability, validity, and freedom from bias. Some of these concepts are grounded in commonsense understandings that are easily applied by any professional concerned with fairness for all students. Other concepts, including varied forms of validity and measures of reliability, are more difficult to grasp and can require expertise to apply when constructing an assessment instrument. Nevertheless, essential elements of these more sophisticated concepts can be applied by teachers as they develop tests and quizzes. This chapter will show how these concepts can be used in the classroom by professionals new to teaching.

AN EXPERIENCE IN CONTEMPORARY ASSESSMENT

In American life, participation in compulsory education is a commonly shared experience. For most of us, this means public school attendance from kindergarten through 12th grade. By the time we reach middle or high school, the experience of testing and other forms of assessment are part of the landscape of school life, with attendant anxiety, concern for a good outcome, and ultimately, good marks on report cards. As adults, we have no more than vague recollections of particular tests, but many of us retain impressions of tests that appeared to be unfair or biased (Taylor & Nolen, 2008). One off-putting element of tests and quizzes is the notorious trick question. The following vignette describes a situation in which students are victimized by an instructor's thoughtless test item writing.

A vignette of a high school assessment experience:

Jermaine and Susan are talking together in the hallway before being allowed to enter Mr. Warren's classroom for the Honors Biology final examination. Both students are nervous about this important exam.

Susan asks, "Jermaine, did you review all the material we studied in genetics and evolution? I hope I can recall all the forms of inheritance presented in class."

"I spent a lot of time reviewing Punnett diagrams," answered Jermaine. "After all," he continued, "that's the area we spent a lot of time on in class."

Ten minutes later, Jermaine and Susan are sitting at their desks as the final exam for Honors Biology is given to each student. The first question on the exam is puzzling to both of them: "What do elephants have that no other animals have?"

Directly after the exam, Susan connects with Jermaine in front of the school. She states, "What on earth was that first question all about? I have no idea of the answer, and it bothered me for the rest of the test."

Jermaine responded, "I had no idea either. Perhaps we were expected to come up with something like, 'elephants have trunks.' "

Three days later, Susan is standing outside her Honors Biology class. The teacher has posted a copy of the exam with correct answers. She looks immediately for the answer to the first question, which the teacher has written just below the prompt: "baby elephants."

This vignette about Susan and Jermaine's negative experience with a final exam describes an assessment situation where a trick question has been introduced into a high-stakes assessment. In this instance, the question is unfair because it assesses student knowledge of a skill not included in Honors Biology. The skill is the ability to solve riddles. There is clearly no place for such a question in an unbiased and fair assessment of knowledge and skills related to genetics.

As teachers, we want to avoid this kind of experience for students. Our goal is to present students with assessment tasks that accurately measure skills and knowledge conveyed during instruction. When bias enters the assessment process, students do not have equal opportunity to succeed. In this example, students who are good at solving riddles have a good chance of getting the correct answer, even if their knowledge of genetics is far more limited than other students who are intimidated by the question and disturbed for the remainder of the test experience. As we explore essential principles of effective instruction in this chapter, we will be guided by a modification of the golden rule as it applies to schooling: Assess and evaluate others as we would like to be assessed and evaluated ourselves.

CLOSING THE DOOR ON BIASED AND OPPRESSIVE ASSESSMENT PRACTICES

One trait commonly observed in beginning teachers is a desire to reform teaching and learning (Kyriacou & Coulthard, 2000). Presumably, this noble purpose arises in some part from new teachers' own experiences in classrooms. Conversations held with aspiring teachers reveal both negative and positive prior classroom experiences (Holt-Reynolds, 1992). When conversations turn to issues of unfair practices, the topics under discussion are usually assessment and grading. The elimination of bias, unfairness, and oppression in student evaluation and grading is a central purpose of this book. Therefore, it seems appropriate to review the nature of bias and other forms of unfairness that may be found in testing, student work evaluation, and grade reporting.

When bias enters classroom assessment, certain students are advantaged based on other learner characteristics than knowledge, skills, or abilities—skills that should be evaluated in a fair assessment (Elder, 1997). Often, we hear of racial bias or gender bias in assessment practices (Cole, 1981). For years, the Scholastic Aptitude Test (SAT) has been used as a predictor of student academic success in college.[1] College admissions officials have relied on this test to predict successful academic performance in college, and they have used this property of the testing program as a justification for making admission and rejection decisions.

Research shows that female students, as a group, are performing better in college than their male counterparts (Aitken, 1982). More women are graduating from college than men, and women are gaining proportionately in the number of students admitted to postbaccalaureate study in medicine and law. These accomplishments are occurring despite the persistent trend for women to achieve lower scores, as a group, than men on the mathematics portion of the SAT. Is the SAT biased in favor of male test takers who may not perform as well in college as female students? This question and related ones involving racial and ethnic backgrounds of affected students are frequent topics of discussion in academic circles as well as in the popular press (Pallas & Alexander, 1983). Other factors that may influence assessment results include

- ▶ Luck
- ▶ Test-wiseness
- ▶ Prior experiences or learning not provided by the teacher
- ▶ Time allocated to complete the assessment
- ▶ Student vocabulary acquired as a benefit of privileged upbringing
- ▶ Mastery of English or any other language used in the assessment items
- ▶ Emotional response to the appearance or structure of a test
- ▶ Favored communication with the teacher prior to assessment and the teacher's opinions and perceptions about student abilities based on prior assessment experience
- ▶ Stereotypes about various learner groups to which students belong
- ▶ Unfair student access to information that is assessed (Nitko & Brookhart, 2007)

In testing and educational measurement, lucky students benefit from chance working in their favor during an assessment exercise. The common use of true-false items on short quizzes provides an opportunity for chance to favor outcomes for fortunate students and unfairly penalize other less-fortunate ones. Imagine for a minute that a teacher provides a quick, 5-minute quiz at the start of the day just to check that students are doing assigned reading as part of homework. The teacher writes 10 quick statements followed by the letter "T" for true and "F" for false. Let's also assume that there are only 10 true-false items on this short quiz. What are the chances that a student who did not do the reading and has no understanding of any of the items will nevertheless pass the quiz with 7 out of 10 correct items? If our hypothetical student makes random guesses over the course of many such quizzes, the student will guess half of the items correctly, or 5 out of 10 items will be correct with no need to apply relevant knowledge. But what is the chance that the student, still with no knowledge of any of the items, will get 7 of 10 items correct on any one quiz? A simple statistical concept called the **binomial distribution** applies to this situation, and a simple calculation will reveal that if no student had any knowledge of the quiz material in a class of 30 students, 5 of the students would pass the quiz on any given occasion, even if all of them used coin flipping to arrive at the answers (Diebold & Mariano, 1995). In this hypothetical situation, 5 students would pass, and 25 students would fail, even though they all had identical understanding—or lack of understanding—of the tested subject matter.[2]

Previously we introduced **test-wiseness**, a term used by Airasian (2000) and other assessment experts to describe how some students can use knowledge of test construction tendencies, unintended clues, and logical reasoning to find correct answers to test items. Students who use test-wiseness to score high on exams are attempting to infer teachers' intentions and expectations that were not intended to be conveyed to students. Teachers will want to minimize the effect of these skills and abilities if they want students to be evaluated on the content and skills taught in the classroom to the exclusion of general ability on test taking. One test preparation company, Princeton Review, incorporates test-wiseness training in its test preparation curricula (Powers & Rock, 1999). The author of this book was able to score high on the **Miller Analogies Test** by simply learning about a variety of commonalities that may appear among seemingly different items presented in analogy format. Prior to reading a booklet about scoring high on the test, I had not considered analogies taking on word forms as well as word meanings. For instance, in the analogy statement, "Rat is to Bat as Sun is to A: Planet; B: Star; C: Fun; D: Moon," the possibility that "C: Fun" could be the correct answer because it is a word with three letters with a common vowel (*a* in *rat* and *bat* and *u* in *sun* and *fun*), as appears in the prompt ("Rat is to Bat"), had not occurred to me. As a result of this reading experience, I was able to score higher on the exam than other students who had not prepared through the use of a test preparation strategy. My good fortune in finding the little book about analogies may have contributed to my admission to graduate school, even though the underlying trait intended to be measured by the exam, verbal reasoning ability, was supposed to be a by-product of my prior academic achievement and general learning aptitude, not a 1-hour review of a test preparation booklet.

We will explore test-wiseness closely as we discuss test construction, test item writing, and test item selection in Chapter 7. Some students who have years of experience taking examinations, even well-constructed multiple-choice exams produced by testing companies, are able to identify clues to the correct answer by eliminating possible wrong answers and increasing their chances when they must choose from four alternative answers. Effective test item writing and assessment practices can minimize differences in student test-wiseness as an unwanted factor leading to the assignment of grades and class marks (Thorndike, 2005).

Prior learning or background knowledge not conveyed by the teacher can benefit some students in comparison to others during testing. Years ago, when many students studied Latin as a foreign language, they learned about word prefixes and suffixes derived from Latin that are commonly used in English. Today, many students pay close attention when learning about prefixes and suffixes because they know these parts of words give clues to word meanings. These students have an advantage in certain science classes, notably biology, where much of the scientific vocabulary includes Latin prefixes and suffixes. For instance, a student who knows that the prefix *an-* means "without" will be able to distinguish between anaerobic respiration and aerobic respiration.

The rate at which students can complete test items can contribute to differences in student test outcomes, which may not be appropriate for tests that assess student content knowledge. On occasion, some students will perform well on a test where the grades have been curved, and many students were not able to answer all test items in the time provided. A common complaint of many college and high school students after an important exam is, "If only we had a little more time." The students who did not have sufficient time to answer several questions may also be sorted into two other categories: those that guess on all remaining items and those that leave them blank. When examinations are administered in this fashion, the rate at which students can solve problems and their varied strategies for dealing with remaining unanswered questions become characteristics of learners that are measured by the test. Exams that require students to perform tasks at a uniform and high rate, sometimes called **speeded tests**, are appropriate for measuring certain skills, such as repetitive task performance on an assembly line or typing speed, but may not be appropriate in general assessments of student knowledge and academic skills (Mead & Drasgow, 1993). For instance, if we administer a quiz to elementary school students calling for them to solve a set of long division problems, do we want to measure their ability to do so, or both their ability to do so and the rate at which they can do the task (Turner & Fischler, 1993)? Either speed or **accuracy** in performing computations may be important skills to measure, but typically speed is an important skill only when repetitive tasks are to be performed (e.g., keyboarding skills for a data entry position). Accuracy, on the other hand, may be relatively more important when issues of safety or health are important, as in making computations in a pharmacy.

One common problem with testing in our multicultural society is the practice of writing test directions and items in English. If the purpose of a course of study is to convey knowledge of English, this may be appropriate. On the other hand, English language learners as students in other subjects (e.g., social studies or mathematics) may not be able to understand directions or interpret the meaning of test items due to limitations in vocabulary or experience communicating in English. In these circumstances, tests that include complex or unfamiliar procedures and conceptually dense and complex vocabulary may present special challenges to English language learners, even if the learner has the knowledge or ability to perform the task required by the test item in their own language.

Another problem involving differential student responses to tests can involve the test structure itself. Some students develop test anxiety when they encounter certain test item formats, including multiple choice. These anxieties may arise as a general response to an item type that appears commonly on high-stakes tests. When students with test anxiety encounter exams that are entirely multiple choice, and the first few items on the test are particularly challenging, the exam may provoke fear and feelings of inadequacy in the test taker. Although other students in the class are perfectly comfortable and able to concentrate on the exam questions, these unfortunate students become anxious and unable to focus, even if they have the skill and knowledge to answer the question during regular classroom activity. This issue becomes more complex when teachers prepare students for standardized tests or standards-based tests that are administered in multiple-choice format. In these circumstances, it may be appropriate to use some multiple-choice items on most unit exams to prepare students for the multiple-choice items they are likely to encounter on a high-stakes test administered at the end of the course.

Other issues of fairness in testing and assessing student work arise from possible relationships between the teacher and certain students or the teacher's personal characteristics (Airasian, 2000). Although we all recognize that students should have the right to equal access to the curriculum that is to be tested, we can lose sight of this principle during the chaotic experiences common to daily teaching. Often schools use pullout programs to provide students with enrichment or remediation experiences (Madden & Slavin, 1987). Students in the general classroom are identified for these programs and are called out of the classroom at various times during the school day. On these occasions, pullout students do not have access to the instruction the remaining students are receiving. It would be wrong to hold students accountable for content they missed due to their participation in supplementary or compensatory educational experiences.

And how should teachers address the issue of extra help? If students stay after school or after class for additional academic assistance, should they benefit from these experiences when other students may not be able to access extra instruction due to other commitments? More important, these students should not be given access to information out of class that appears on an exam if students in the regularly scheduled class have not been provided the same information. Of equal importance is the teacher's response to students who seek clarification of directions or validation of possible answers from the teacher as the test is under way. Students will often approach the teacher or test proctor to ask confidential, private questions that, if answered, will provide the students with an advantage over the rest of the class, which is not privy to the conversation.

Ultimately, the most serious concern regarding the teacher's influence on assessment practices relates to perceptions teachers have of their learners. Negative stereotypes about English language learners, Title 1 learners, and poor and minority students have not only led teachers to believe certain students are less able to achieve, but they have also led teachers to provide lower scores and grades, as bias has influenced subjective assessment of student work (Farkas, Grobe, Sheehan, & Shuan, 1990).

Consider a situation in which a teacher is grading student essays. As each essay passes before the teacher's eyes, what is the likelihood that expectations about the quality of work that may be submitted by various learners will affect the evaluation of actual work samples submitted? Several landmark studies of the role of teacher bias and perception about different students' abilities have described this important issue (Alvidrez & Weinstein, 1999; Rosenholtz & Rosenholtz, 1981), and perhaps most famous among these is *Pygmalion in the Classroom* (Rosenthal & Jacobson, 1968). The tenet of their argument is that teacher expectations for student performance may actually influence how students perform. For our purposes concerning classroom assessment, we are most concerned about teachers' perceptions of student understanding or ability preceding and following instruction. When teachers hold students in low regard with respect to their abilities, they limit the kinds of learning activities provided to perceived underperformers to less-challenging and easily performed tasks. As students perform these tasks, they acquire less knowledge and fewer skills than if they had been presented tasks with richer cognitive challenges. These actions set the stage for the assessments that will follow. If teachers believe their students have limited capacity to learn, this belief will affect assessment in one of two ways: Either the assessment planned for the students will not be challenging enough to provide an opportunity for students to score high, or the teacher will conclude that students will be unable to perform well on challenging assessments and fulfill this unfortunate prophecy by not giving them the chance to meet high expectations (Jussim & Eccles, 1992).

The former situation is likely to unfold when a teacher, following the provision of un-challenging and simplistic instruction, follows these activities by administering a quiz or test with simple selected response items. The assessment might include some true-false and multiple-choice items with simple knowledge recall and lots of hints or cues that lead students to select a correct answer. Even though students have not learned much, they score high on this unchallenging test because it was written to ensure their success. Students are led to believe they have done well in school, parents are proud, and the teacher appears successful because students are getting good grades.

Conversely, a teacher in another setting has finished teaching a history or literature class to a group of students of varied abilities and ethnicities. Although the instruction provided was enriching and challenging, the teacher held negative beliefs about certain students and concluded by their seemingly disinterested behavior that they were bored with the material and not working hard to understand it. At the end of the unit, the teacher administers a challenging essay exam and provides scores on each essay based only on a subjective evaluation of the quality of each response. As the teacher encounters essays written by students who seemed disinterested in classroom activities, they receive low scores relative to those received by students displaying a more positive attitude and who happen to share the same ethnic status as the teacher.

Clearly, some causes of unfairness and bias in assessment are more disturbing and entrenched than others. Bias is usually difficult to overcome when compared to unfair elements in test construction or administration (e.g., including too many items to be reasonably answered in the allotted testing time). As professionals, we want to provide all students an equal opportunity to perform well on classroom assessments, just as we want to provide all students with the skills and knowledge needed to lead rewarding and fruitful lives. How shall we proceed, then, in planning instruction and assessments that lead to these outcomes without favoritism and selective advantage? In the following section we will explore the qualities we want to see in classroom assessment practices, and we will explore a few concepts and principles of assessment that can help us plan and evaluate instruction in the classroom.

 WHAT RESEARCH CAN TELL US...

- ### About Standardized Testing

  What is a promising new researcher from England to make of the use of standardized tests in America? One, Professor Jo Boaler of Stanford University, described her concerns for the use of standardized tests in California. In "When Learning No Longer Matters: Standardized Testing and the Creation of Inequality" (2003), Dr. Boaler suggested that one test score of a student's performance on a standardized test in mathematics is just that—one test score. When students are categorized in groupings labeled "basic" or "below basic" as a result of only one test administration, it is impossible to assess the extent of the student's learning just prior to the test administration. Dr. Boaler described the lessons learned in England about the need to assess student growth and development of knowledge through multiple forms of assessment. Only in this way can a school's performance be truly measured.

WHAT ARE THE QUALITIES WE SEEK IN GOOD ASSESSMENT PRACTICES?

Historically, terms like *assessment* and *testing* have conjured images of the power relationship between teachers and students. Assessment is something that teachers do to students to sort them into various categories with important social values. When students become teachers, they carry this notion with them, viewing their students as the next generation to be evaluated through classroom assessment methods. Fortunately, attention is now being paid to a new message that suggests assessment should be for students and not just about students (Stiggins, 2008). This section presents some principles about classroom-based assessment and how to use it to the best possible advantage for students. The following principles are useful guides for teachers as they plan assessments and evaluate student work for grades.

Design Assessments That Are Helpful to Students

Classroom assessment, when broadly conceptualized and well designed, should benefit students and their learning efforts. Classroom assessment can motivate students, arouse interest in subject matter, stimulate persistence to succeed, teach students new ways of thinking, and inform their work and study skills. Ideally, each classroom assessment should lead students to perform at a higher level on a subsequent assessment. Assessments come in many forms, and they can be used before, during, and after instruction. When used as part of the daily instructional routine, classroom assessments can guide student efforts and help them succeed. Moreover, classroom assessments can be focused on informing students about their understandings and their progress, as well as informing the teacher about student achievement. When teachers understand the current level of student understanding, they can use strategies and choices that will guide students to higher levels of understanding. Students as well as teachers can benefit from understanding their own achievement, and they can be guided to take action on their own behalf.

Provide Students of Varied Backgrounds and Expressive Abilities the Opportunity to Experience Success

Students vary in their expressive and responding abilities. These differences have an effect on student learning outcomes. When assessing student learning, we seek to minimize the effect of item formats and assessment design as restrictions on student opportunity to perform well on tests and quizzes. Too often, instructors focus on a limited set of methods to evaluate student performance. A teacher in a science department might discover the wonders of machine grading. The correct answers for many multiple-choice items can be entered on a preprinted form and loaded into an inexpensive machine that will subsequently grade all student performances in just a few seconds. Because of this timesaving use of technology, the teacher uses only multiple-choice items and the technology aid to grade all quizzes and tests in class. Although the use of technology in this instance is beneficial to the teacher, it may not be at all helpful to the students. The technology may lead teachers to use machine-graded multiple-choice items to the exclusion of other test item formats. Students who can interpret multiple-choice items will benefit from the emphasis on this kind of test item, whereas other students may be at a disadvantage. Teachers may legitimately consider ease of grading when selecting and arranging test items, but concerns for students' opportunity to perform at their very best should predominate as tests and quizzes are planned.

Successful student performance on multiple-choice items depends on more than student knowledge of subject matter. When students are required to read prompts thoroughly and make distinctions between finely crafted alternatives, they are heavily dependent on their literacy skills to succeed. Moreover, the ability to select among choices that may include "a and b above, but not c," or "none of the above" depends on logical reasoning skills that may not be important outcomes of the course and may favor students with privileged backgrounds in comparison to other students, particularly English language learners. When determining how knowledge will be assessed, the student as a successful learner should be the paramount consideration.

Assessment Practices Are Fair to the Student

Bias and favoritism are unpleasant but inevitable factors in student evaluation and grading. It is unlikely that any person exists today who is so pure of heart and innocent of mind that they would be unable to generalize in any negative way the abilities or characteristics of any individual on the basis of group association. To be fair to our students, it is better to assume that we harbor some elements of bias and that we are vigilant in our self-regulation to minimize the influence our bias will have on any individual student or group of students. Every time we construct a test, administer it to our students, measure student performance on the test, and assign grades, we are making value judgments about student achievement. Our perceptions about relative abilities of groups of students, based on their gender, ethnicity, or national origin of background, can and will intrude on our decision making in student performance evaluation. A commonly used phrase in public education is "the subtle bigotry of low expectations" (Weiner & Weitzman 2005). Teachers regularly encounter colleagues who can describe at length what their students can't do, while finding little opportunity to express surprise or admiration for student learning when expectations are not only set high, but are met at that level (Muller, 1997). To the extent that varied forms of student expression are used to assess student knowledge, we provide our students with opportunities to succeed. Projects, essay writing, creative productions, and varied item types on conventional tests provide students with opportunities to succeed. Most important, it is essential that we remain mindful of one overarching principle for reducing bias: We make judgments about performances and products, not people.

Assessment Assists the Learning Process

Effective and fair assessment of student learning requires the frequent application of many skills. These include

► Choosing from a variety of assessment tools

► Using assessment of varied purposes in the classroom

► Knowing the relative merits of assessment item types

► Writing good test items

▶ Constructing the test or other assessment

▶ Administering the test fairly

▶ Scoring and evaluating student efforts

▶ Assigning grades

To the extent we as educators constantly hone our assessment skills in each of these areas, we increase the likelihood that our students will have successful learning experiences, that they will grow in knowledge and skills, and that we will have fairly distinguished between performances of both low and high achievement. Moreover, we develop our own instructional skills as we analyze and reflect on our assessment experiences and assessment outcomes.

In our current reform environment, assessment is melding with instruction as never before (Stiggins, 2008). We find it threaded through the classroom daily routine along with instructional activities. As our knowledge of assessment practices deepens and we gain deeper understanding about our students and their learning needs, we inevitably gain new perspectives and insights into our instructional abilities, curriculum plans, and curriculum resources.

Assessments Are Tools for Teacher Learning

On almost a daily basis, teachers administer assessments, evaluate student forms or products to assign grades, record grades for later use in determining marks for reporting periods, and return forms and products to students. Unfortunately, these limited practices fail to provide the teacher with insights regarding the effectiveness of their teaching or the areas of student performance that are most troubling. When teachers take the time to apply analytical skills to the data that results from their assessment practices, they gain important insights into areas of difficulty regarding their ability to convey knowledge and skills and/or their students' ability to construct meaning from what they have observed in the classroom (Stiggins & Conklin, 1992). After teacher have graded a set of papers or tests, they can take time to look at patterns in the responses. If a test is carefully constructed to elicit data reflecting student misconceptions or mistakes in performing procedures, these problems can be identified after the test grading process to determine the extent to which the students exhibit the misconceptions or procedural errors. Teachers can then take measures to remedy these problems if they are evident.

HOW DO WE KNOW IF OUR ASSESSMENTS ARE MEASURING STUDENT LEARNING ACCURATELY? AN INTRODUCTION TO RELIABILITY

Measurement errors can result in undesirable outcomes. A consumer may be overcharged for a purchase; a construction design or engineering proposal may fail at the project site. In public education, measurement errors can result in misrepresentations of student learning and achievement, which can negatively affect the futures of the students we intend to serve. We as educators hold the same values as physicians helping their patients, hence the Hippocratic oath has relevance to assessment: "First, do no harm." If we are to use assessment practices for the benefit of student learning and the benefit of our teaching, we need to understand error in educational measurement and reduce the likelihood of its occurrence. The following situation, drawn from daily life experiences, may help in understanding how universal principles of error identification in measurement can be related to educational assessment practices.

A measurement scenario:

It is Monday morning following a long weekend of parties and lavish dinners. Janet Oberdorf has discovered to her dismay that several items in her closet just don't fit anymore. With trepidation, she steps on the bathroom scale and sees the reading: 142 lbs. "That can't be," she says to herself. Janet steps off the bathroom scale, lets the indicator return to "0," and steps back on again: 145 lbs. Perplexed by the different results, she steps on the scale one more time: 140 lbs. Janet concludes that there may be something wrong with the scale, but reaches the conclusion that she probably weighs somewhere between the lowest and the highest values observed.

Later that day, Janet dutifully goes to her doctor's office for a simple blood test. As always, the nurse takes her vital measurements prior to meeting with the doctor. "Step right up here so I can see what we have," the nurse says, as Janet puts both feet on the platform of the seemingly more accurate triple-beam balance connected to a platform by a long rod. Janet is curious to know the measurement because of her recent experience with the bathroom scale. "153 lbs.," states the nurse. Janet immediately responds, "Yes, but that's with all my clothes on." The nurse responds, "True, but that's how we always do it. Why don't you step off, I will reset the weights to '0,' and then you can step on the platform one more time to see what we get." Janet steps on the platform of the doctor's office scale one more time. After adjusting the weights, the nurse says, "153 lbs., just like before." At the end of the visit, Janet stops by the pharmacy to buy a new digital bathroom scale.

Clearly, Janet's bathroom scale is no longer functioning well. If Janet were a math or science teacher, her approach to the three different measures on her scale might have been to simply estimate a number about halfway between the most extreme values, perhaps 142 or 143 pounds in this instance, and accept that average of three different measures as a good approximation of her "true" weight. But her experience at the doctor's office provided information that suggests her scale not only provides inconsistent results, but it also provides results that do not correspond with a seemingly more precise, and probably more accurate, instrument: the doctor's triple-beam balance with moveable standard weights.

The properties of accuracy and **precision** in measurement tools, seen here as relatively well established for the doctor's balance when compared to the poor accuracy and imprecise measures of Janet's bathroom scale, are related to properties of assessment tools called reliability and validity. If we pass 30 student multiple-choice answer forms through an electronic scoring machine and obtain different kinds of scores for different pupils, can we be confident that the same scores will come up again if we pass the answer sheets through the machine one more time? Perhaps. If, on the other hand, we grade

30 student paragraphs written in response to an essay question administered as a "pop" quiz, is it likely that each student would be given the same numerical score, between 0 and 20, if the essays were graded again by another teacher? Probably not. The electronic machine's ability to render the same scores for the same students over and over contributes to the reliability of the multiple-choice test. The consistent machine scoring is similar to the consistent results that Janet observed when she was weighed in the doctor's office. It is possible, however, that many students in the class, perhaps students who have an after-school job, might have answered more items correctly if they had one or two more hours of sleep, or they simply may have been lucky in choosing "b" rather than "c" when they didn't know the answer to a particular prompt. The inability of multiple-choice questions to generate, in all instances, a wrong response from a student who does not know the answer to the question and a correct response from all students who do know the answer is a shortcoming of the test itself. This shortcoming in the test is similar to the inability of Janet's bathroom scale to produce values for her weight that are similar to the results seen in the doctor's office.

The **reliability** of an assessment process relates to properties of the assessment instrument itself, the setting in which the assessment takes place, the nature of the learner at the time of the assessment, and the means by which the assessment is scored (Stiggins & Conklin, 1992). If any of these conditions, or a combination of these conditions, would cause test administration at a different time to result in a different set of outcomes, then they diminish the reliability of the assessment. Clearly, it is impossible to design an assessment experience that is completely reliable. As classroom teachers, we seek to maximize reliability by minimizing variation in certain aspects of the assessment experience and enhancing other aspects.

INCREASING RELIABILITY IN CLASSROOM ASSESSMENTS

We may be confident in the reliability of a measurement to the extent that it is conducted repeatedly with consistent results. Scientists practice this principle when they take three or four measures of the same phenomenon and average the results. When we doubt the results we see on our bathroom scale, we could take three or four different measures and average the results as is done in scientific procedures. If we introduced several bathroom scales and took measures on each of them, we could add further to a reliable final result. This last method can be approximated by teachers when they use several different measures to assess the same kind of student knowledge or skill.

Teachers who use many quizzes, short tests, performance tasks, and observations of students to assess understanding or skill in a given area are looking for confirmation from one measure to the other regarding a student's ability. As each form of assessment provides feedback that is consistent with other forms of assessment of fundamentally the same skill or ability, the reliability of the teacher's appraisal of student knowledge increases. University professors who provide only a midterm and a final exam to arrive at a student's course grade are assessing student knowledge with low reliability. In our legal system, we seek corroborating evidence before reaching judgments of guilt or innocence.

When we seek corroborating data or information about student abilities or knowledge, we add to the reliability of our measures of student performances.

Teachers can improve reliability of their assessment measures by using different methods to measure the results of a learning experience. This process is generally referred to as triangulation, the process of using different methods and tools redundantly to measure a phenomenon (English & Keshavarz, 2002). When a teacher uses student reports, quizzes, and focused questioning to obtain a more informed perspective on student understanding of density in a physical science class, the teacher can be confident that student understanding of this difficult concept has been reliably measured.

A FIRST LOOK AT VALIDITY

Recall for a moment the assessment scenario at the beginning of this chapter involving two students, Jermaine and Susan. They were upset when the first question on their test turned out to be a riddle about elephants and the kind of offspring elephants produce. We characterized this test item as a trick question. Well, what's wrong with trick questions and why is there no place for them in classroom assessment practices? The primary reason is that they do not measure in a fair way the student understandings that we wish to evaluate. We might say that the question about elephants on the genetics test was not valid. What, then, is validity? **Validity** is a property of the assessment process that has been difficult for assessment experts to explain to teachers without using circuitous reasoning. One commonly seen definition of validity is "the ability of a test or other assessment tool to measure what it is intended to measure" (Thorndike, 2005). Perhaps an analysis of a commonly experienced assessment scenario might help us understand at least one form of validity.

A scenario of assessment at the department of motor vehicles:

It is a typical autumn day in California, and a new resident to the state enters the local office of the Department of Motor Vehicles (DMV). Following the completion of some paperwork and an eye exam, the new resident takes a 25-item multiple-choice test that includes several questions involving recognition of traffic signs, stopping distances of cars traveling at various speeds, and the future driver's understanding of California's unique color coded curbs that indicate various times permitted for roadside parking. If the exam is passed (20 out of 25 correct items), the new resident drives through some residential streets in the area of the DMV office under the watchful eye of an examiner sitting alongside the driver. If the new resident observes proper speed limits, comes to a full stop at stop signs, signals appropriately for turns, and checks the rearview mirror from time to time, chances are a new California driver's license will be issued for five years.

Suppose a new assessment entrepreneur approaches the authorities in charge of the DMV and proposes an alternative form of test. In this assessment, the written exam includes only items pertaining to parking regulations and certain important, but infrequently encountered road signs. The performance part of the test takes place in an automobile simulator that requires the driver to maintain a proper interval and handle precarious situations that appear on the screen. The precarious situations were developed from simulations of 15 of California's top 100 accident-prone traffic intersections and other settings. If a California resident performs well in the simulator, he or she moves on to the final stage of the assessment process. This final portion calls for the new resident to drive a personal vehicle for a two-week probationary period with a DMV-programmed video recorder mounted on the car's visor. The video recorder monitors the following distance the car experiences behind other cars during the 2-week surveillance period. At the conclusion of the probationary period, the new resident returns the video monitor to the local DMV office for analysis. If all goes well, a driver's license is issued.

Most readers of this scenario would judge the entrepreneur's assessment to be a more "valid" assessment of driving knowledge and skills than the conventional assessment process. If the entrepreneur could demonstrate that the new assessment process, when used in a pilot program, passed people who subsequently had far fewer accidents and violations than drivers who passed the conventional method, the entrepreneur might be able to convince the DMV official to adopt the new assessment program. This case would be made even more compelling if the new assessment method failed people who passed the conventional process and nevertheless had a relatively high incidence of accidents and violations.

Although there may be reasons to deny our entrepreneur the new assessment contract at DMV (feasibility, costs, invasions of privacy, failure of applicants to return the video-monitoring devices), the test's ability to distinguish between drivers who would perform very differently behind the wheel speaks favorably to the criterion-related validity of the test. If the criterion of assessment in this case is its ability to screen out bad drivers and accept good drivers, and the proposed assessment system does so with a reasonably large number of applicants in a pilot study at a high success rate deemed to be desirable by the officials at DMV, then the assessment system can be described as valid for these purposes.

What, then, is validity? Definitions found in some textbooks describe it as a property of a test or other assessment tool used to reach conclusions about learners or other test takers (Airasian, 2000; Thorndike, 2005). Other textbook authors (McMillan, 2004) have suggested that validity arises from the inferences made from assessment evidence. For our purposes, validity depends on how a measurement tool is used. If the measurement tool can help us obtain important measures of some learner attribute, then its validity is high. In our depiction of the entrepreneur who has invented a new assessment system to identify safe and unsafe drivers, a field test of the system may demonstrate that it is able to predict which examinees will have safe driving records and which will have accidents. If the system functions well for this purpose, we may conclude that it has high **predictive validity** when used to identify examinees that will subsequently have bad driving records. The system, on the other hand, may have little or no ability to identify courteous drivers.

Predictive validity is a term used by measurement experts to describe the relationship between certain test outcomes and the examinee's future performance at some task. If high test scores correlate with high performance on the task that follows and low performance correlates with unsatisfactory performance, then the test has good predictive validity.

Predictive validity is an important issue for colleges and universities that rely on certain kinds of examinations to make admissions decisions. For years, the Scholastic Aptitude Test (SAT) has been used to identify or predict which applicants will be more successful in college. The Law School Admissions Test (LSAT) is another examination marketed to law schools on the basis of its ability to predict student success in the first year of law school. These tests are also controversial because examinee test scores can be affected by test preparation programs. Colleges and universities have relied on these tests to measure some stable property of the examinee that will lead to success in college or law school. If short-term test preparation courses can result in higher scores, then the properties of examinees assessed by the test may not be relied on to last through the entire college or law school experience.

Another form of test validity speaks to the ability of an assessment to measure some attribute or quality in a subject that derives from theories about abilities, aptitudes, and perceptions. **Construct validity** describes an assessment's ability to measure some important characteristics or property developed from theory and research (Gullickson, 2003). Often, the construct in question is difficult to define and can be controversial. Art aptitude and intelligence are constructs that are measured by different kinds of tests. People differ in their understanding of the critical performance attributes of intelligence that can be assessed by an exam. In recent years Howard Gardner of Harvard University (1983) proposed that there are many forms of intelligence and that people may have a form of intelligence that is quite developed in comparison to other forms. Yet another controversy concerning intelligence is the stability that it demonstrates in people over time. In the past, researchers thought intelligence was determined early in life and stayed the same for any one individual throughout their lifetime. Other investigators believe that enriching experiences and education, particularly during the early years in one's life, can affect intelligence (Sameroff, Seifer, Baldwin, & Baldwin, 1993).

Classroom teachers are most interested in **content validity**, or the relationship between the content and tasks of an assessment and the content and skills taught prior to examination (Kubiszyn & Borich, 2007). A quiz, test, or other form of assessment used to measure prior student learning will attempt, in a relatively short period of time, to measure what students have learned over a longer period of time, perhaps a week, a month, or an entire semester.

Because assessment tools can only measure a sample of the content and skills taught, it is important that the tasks asked of students on the assessment be a fair sample of what has been taught. The Venn diagrams in Figure 2.1 show the nature of problems that arise when a teacher develops a test that does not have a proper sampling of the content that has been taught. The Venn diagram on the left demonstrates two types of error evident when test items do not correspond fully with information and skills conveyed during the period of instruction under measurement. One circle is intended to circumscribe all the content and skills conveyed during the period of instruction. The other circle circumscribes the content and skills included on the exam. Note that the test content circle partially overlaps the circle containing the content taught in class, and that the shaded area "B" represents content on the exam that was conveyed during instruction. Unfortunately, content in area "A" was taught, but is not assessed on the exam. Furthermore, content in area "C" appears on the exam, but it was not conveyed during instruction. Apparently, the test represented by the diagram on the left failed to sample content and skills that were conveyed during instruction, and of greater concern to the students, it did include test

FIGURE 2.1 Venn Diagrams

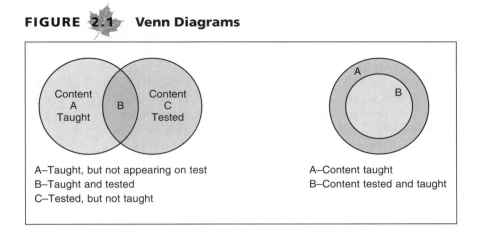

A–Taught, but not appearing on test
B–Taught and tested
C–Tested, but not taught

A–Content taught
B–Content tested and taught

items assessing content and skills that were not taught. These shortcomings contribute to low content validity in classroom-based tests. The failure of the exam to include content not tested is of substantial concern and less likely to occur than the relatively more common problem of item distribution.

In the diagram on the right, we see the circle circumscribing content taught completely enclosing the circle circumscribing content tested. If we compare it with the pair of circles on the left side of the figure, we can see that the domain of knowledge taught is larger than the domain of knowledge tested. In this representation, we see that much of what was taught may not appear on the test, but we need not be concerned that students will see items for content they did not encounter in class. However, the Venn diagram on the right reveals that much of what was taught remains untested, which is the case for any practical assessment. Assessments that have high content validity effectively sample from all areas of content covered in instruction and expected from students at the varied levels of cognitive challenge taught in the period of instruction covered by the test. The failure of the assessment to provide good coverage of the content and skills tested is yet another source of poor content validity in educational measurement. Clearly, content validity is an important consideration in preparing classroom tests and assessments. We want to provide students with tests that measure what we have taught.

VALIDITY AND STATE CURRICULUM STANDARDS

However, another form of validity has become increasingly important in the current reform environment, and it is criterion-related validity. Criterion-related validity, as defined by most textbooks on measurement (Linn, Gronlund, & Davis, 2000; Thorndike, 2005) is a test's ability to obtain results similar to results obtained from a different measure of the same property. For example, we could have two forms to assess safe student manipulation of a laboratory microscope. We could ask students to write a brief essay describing how they would safely carry a microscope from its storage area to a lab table, or we could have them demonstrate the skill by doing so. To the extent that high-scoring written tests correlated with observed safe procedures, we could conclude that the written exam has high criterion-related validity in relation to the actual performance of some safe microscope procedures.

Now that grade level and subject-specific curriculum standards have been adopted by all states, we are not only concerned about the extent to which a classroom test covers what was taught (content-related validity), but we are also concerned that the test measures content and skills to be assessed on high-stakes tests of the standards usually administered in the spring (criterion-related validity). In today's classroom, we need to construct assessments that answer two questions: (a) How well have my students mastered the content and skills I taught them during the period of time assessed by my test, observations, or other instrument of assessment? and (b) How well have I conveyed to the students, and they have mastered, the content and skills that are included in my state's curriculum standards that will be tested on state exams?

The following vignette, typical of a conversation that might be heard in progressive school districts today, illustrates the extent to which classroom assessment practices are addressing criterion-related validity with respect to the skills and content that are found in state curriculum standards. In the vignette, two teachers discuss their ongoing efforts to prepare their students for common assessments, the practice of administering a test to all students in the school taking the same course.

A vignette of a classroom experience in New Jersey:

William Brown, a teacher of middle school science in Paterson, NJ, was looking over his teacher's edition of the science textbook, his New Jersey core curriculum standards, and the directory of test specifications in science for the Grade Eight Proficiency Test (GEPA).[3] He was thinking about the upcoming unit on the human circulatory system to begin next week when Sandra Hollingsworth, another science teacher, interrupted his thinking.

"Oh, hi, Sandra. I was just thinking about our next unit. Will you be starting circulation next week?" William asked.

"I certainly hope so," Sandra replied. "Right now I'm worried about how my students will do on the test for the current unit that all our students are taking this Friday. Because we decided last year to use common assessments with embedded test questions similar to last year's GEPA, I have been concerned about how my students will perform in comparison to other eighth-graders."

"I'm always concerned about that," answered William. "When I start planning for a new unit, as I am now for the human circulatory system, I refer to my science standards and the GEPA test information available at the New Jersey Department of Education website to be sure I'm including information in the new unit that is likely to appear on our common unit assessment."

"I should be more mindful about that," responded Sandra. "Just today I remembered that last May, Bill Kelly, our department chair, said that one third of this year's common assessment test items would consist of released test items from the GEPA given in prior years."

Sandra's concern is well founded. In the current reform environment focused on adequate yearly progress of student achievement, state standards have become the core curriculum in all subject areas that are tested under No Child Left Behind (NCLB) requirements.

In the spring of each year, students across the country are tested on their understanding of skills and knowledge of their state's standards. If a teacher continues to develop tests from a textbook without recognizing the importance of the standards in the curriculum, the resulting test may have content validity in relation to the skills and knowledge conveyed by the text, but lack content validity with respect to the skills and abilities included in the state standards. In New Jersey, one test used statewide to measure adequate yearly progress of student achievement is the GEPA. The criterion for standards achievement in Grade 8 is a performance on the GEPA that is deemed "proficient" by state officials.

ENHANCING VALIDITY IN CLASSROOM-BASED TESTS

If validity describes the relationship between an assessment experience and the inferences or judgments to be made from the assessment outcomes, then it is important to think about the purposes to be served by the assessment experience. If we expect an assessment to evaluate some learner attribute in relation to the curriculum we are teaching, then it is important that the assessment experience provides each learner with an opportunity to display the desired attribute to their full advantage. In so doing, we want to keep the interests of the student foremost in out minds. Figure 2.2 includes a set of questions that serve as guideposts to establish valid relationships between assessment experiences and conclusions reached on the part of the assessor.

FIGURE **2.3** **Guidelines for Enhancing Validity in the Assessment of Student Work**

Did I provide my students with an opportunity to learn everything that will appear on this test?
Have I used a variety of test items, so that students will be assessed on what they know, rather than their ability to respond to certain types of questions?
Have I used clear, direct vocabulary in my test instructions and questions that prevent students with larger, more sophisticated vocabularies (unrelated to the content to be tested) from having an advantage on the test?
Will I be providing students with sufficient time to respond to all items, while minimizing student anxiety about test performance?
Is the variety and amount of material in the test reflective of the variety and amount of material that was taught?
Did I inform students that certain content and skills that were taught were of relatively greater importance, and if so, is this reflected in the distribution and nature of test item types on my assessment?
Will I be using a variety of measurement tools, including observation checklists, student written and oral reports, and practical examination of abilities, to corroborate the conclusions I reach with my exam?
Is the information collected from my assessment activities relevant to the decision to be made?
Can I justify a judgment or value I am placing on student work on the basis of the evidence I have from assessment?

Using a Table of Specifications to Plan an Assessment

Assessment experts have devised a tool that helps them construct valid assessments. This tool is called either a table of test specifications or, less frequently, a test blueprint. A table of specifications consists of a matrix that can be used to guide the development and appropriate distribution of test items to ensure a test or quiz under construction has a valid relationship to content and skills taught in the classroom. Table 2.1 lists the specifications of content to be covered by the teacher in a unit of instruction in elementary school science.

After the teachers have constructed a table of specifications, they can consider the kinds of student performances or responses that can be used to evaluate student understanding or skills included in each cell of the matrix. In addition, they can select types of test items that lend themselves to evaluating the performance situation in a given cell. Typically, low levels of challenge for students are described in the top rows of a table of specifications, and more challenging expectations are described in the bottom rows. Therefore, upper-row tasks and responses lend themselves to simple methods of recall and recognition such as matching exercises and sentence-completion items. For example, student recognition of the vocabulary could be assessed by asking students to match an appropriate term to a given description of matter. In this instance, several examples would need to be provided because students have a one in three chance of using the appropriate term for a given situation. Multiple-choice and essay responses are effective at measuring student performance of more complex tasks found in the bottom rows of the matrix. For instance, students might be asked to describe the events that take place as bubbles rise to the surface in a boiling liquid.

TABLE **2.1   Specifications for a Test in Elementary School Science Content Areas**

Process and Skill Objectives	States of Matter	Atoms and Molecules	Changes in states of Matter	Chemical and Physical changes
Understands vocabulary	Solids, liquids, and gases	Parts of atoms and molecules	Evaporation, condensation, melting, boiling	Defines examples changes
Recalls facts	Relates particle behavior to state of matter	Identifies and labels parts of atoms and molecules	Labels example changes	States rules that distinguish types of change
Applies rules and generalizations	Relates common states to given conditions	Balances charge with appropriate particles	Describes changes in particle motion	Given a change, provides example
Recognizes applicable principles	Relates states of matter to particle motion	Relates bonding to kinds of particles	Uses principles of bonding in explanations of changes	Describes changes in particle behavior
Solves problems		Constructs models from simple formulas	Describes a process for effecting a desired change	Given a situation, applies a method for changing a substance

Tables of specification can be used to monitor the distribution of items that will appear on a test. Each cell of the matrix should be represented by at least one related task on the test. Some cells, however, may be assessed by more items than others if the teacher has given proportionately more time to the development of content and skills of a given cell. Under these circumstances, students should see a close connection between test items and the content and skills taught in the classroom.

In our current reform environment, tables of specifications can serve another valuable purpose. They can evaluate student progress toward a successful performance on high-stakes standards tests used to measure adequate yearly progress of student achievement required by No Child Left Behind legislation. Teachers, working collaboratively, can use the Internet to find released and sample test items of their state's standards exams. Often, states release some test items that appeared in previous years. Hopefully, some released test items will assess the content and skills described in the table of specifications. When these test items are identified, they can be included in the unit exam as marker items to assess student progress toward a successful outcome on the test that will be administered at the close of the academic year. Of course, the assumption here is that released test items will bear a close relationship in content and skills assessment to exam questions likely to appear on subsequent state tests. If this assumption holds, and released test items can be found that assess the content and skills of the table of specifications, then the unit test can be judged to have good criterion-related validity with the anticipated state test. Students who perform well on the unit test should be well prepared to perform well on the state test for the same subject and grade level.

Summary

In today's reform environment high-stakes assessments are leading to significant consequences in communities where schools are not making adequate yearly progress. The testing programs required by NCLB are affecting daily classroom practice. The variety and frequency of student assessment has increased in response to NCLB accountability measures. More than ever before, we want students to benefit from assessment experiences and not suffer from faulty assessment practices. As teachers, we are concerned for our students, and we want them to perform at their best unaffected by prejudice, bias, or faulty assessment practices. It is important to understand the factors that contribute to quality assessment and avoid practices that disadvantage students in their efforts to learn.

Reliability and validity are powerful components of assessment that contribute to accuracy in educational measurement. They also contribute to fairness in assigning grades and marks for student work. Reliable assessments minimize the possibility that chance and circumstances unrelated to student learning will play a role in the score students obtain for their work. Valid assessments assure students that they will be evaluated on what they know and can do related to instruction that they received. Principles of fairness and equity require that we give all our students the same opportunities to succeed, and these principles, supplemented by knowledge about reliability and validity in assessment, assure our students that they are fairly and justly treated in our classrooms.

Exercises

1. Reflect on the first vignette in the chapter describing an incident of unfair assessment experienced by two students in a genetics class. Consider a similar event in your life, where you were unfairly assessed or graded. How was the incident similar to, or different from, the one described in the vignette? Were you a victim of bias, unfairness, or poor knowledge of assessment principles by the instructor?

2. Find an article on cultural bias in assessment. This has been an issue in the media with particular respect to standardized testing. Prepare a position statement on cultural bias in assessment. Are certain students at a disadvantage in assessment that constitutes discrimination? Defend your position with a citation from a relevant article or text.

3. Presume that each of us harbors bias toward a particular student group in terms of gender, ethnicity, or other socioeconomic status. What steps would you take in the construction of classroom assessments to eliminate or minimize bias of this nature from entering into your assessment and grading activities?

4. Try an exercise at home in the determination of percentage of error in a simple measurement. Record several trials (more than five) of measuring your weight using a bathroom scale. Calculate the average of your measures. Use the following expression to calculate your empirical error of measurement:

    Most extreme scores − average score/average score × 100 (If the extreme score is below the average, calculate the difference as an absolute value, or positive number.)

    Determine your percentage of error. Was it more than 3%? Do you have confidence in your bathroom scale? Compare your result with others and determine whether you need a new scale.

5. Two people are wearing watches, and each asks the other for the time. One person's watch is 2 minutes faster than the other. One person declares, "Well, mine is likely to be more accurate, because it's the only watch we are looking at that is digital." Comment about the extent to which the digital nature of the watch can account for its accuracy. Is it reasonable to conclude that the digital watch is the "correct" watch?

6. Think about the documents you submitted in your college applications and the information they conveyed. Grade point average, class rank, SAT scores, and letters of reference are possible documents you submitted. Based on your college performance, do you believe any of these data sources was an accurate predictor of your college academic performance? Which documents, in retrospect, had the greatest predictive validity with respect to your college education experience?

7. Intelligence, as a construct of measurement, has been controversial ever since efforts have been made to measure it. Do library research on the stability of intelligence. Do you believe education and experience can affect intelligence? Can intelligence be an achievement as well as an aptitude?

8. You have just finished teaching a 2-week U.S. history unit on the expansion of the American west after the Civil War. Students read the relevant chapter, heard your presentations, worked on some exercises from the text and the Internet, and watched a documentary on pioneer experiences. What steps would you take to assure students that the unit test you are writing is content valid?

Hint: Apply some guideline for enhancing validity that can be found in Figure 2.2.

Resources and Suggested Reading

Pygmalion in the Classroom (Rosenthal & Jacobson, 1968) is a classic study of a classroom phenomenon often referred to as a self-fulfilling prophecy. In this 40-year-old study of teacher expectations with respect to anticipated student achievement, the public was exposed to a controversy regarding teachers' exercise of judgment in the classroom. To what extent do teacher bias and first impressions about student potential set a threshold for achievement by students of color, students from poverty, or students of any group long associated with academic underperformance? The issues raised in *Pygmalion* are no less valid today. Teacher-generated classroom-based assessments, generated in the context of the busy lives of teachers, are less likely to undergo preliminary examination for fairness typically associated with standardized tests. As such, they may result in student measures of performance that include subjective interpretations of student ability, particularly when student written responses are included in the assessment instrument.

Peter Airasian's widely used textbook on classroom-based assessment (2000) includes an extensive discussion of test-wiseness, or student capacity to perform well on tests without having particular skills or abilities related to the content of the course of study. As students, many of us have wondered about the capacity of certain students to score consistently higher than their peers with no apparent profound understanding of skills and concepts as displayed in classroom discussion or presentations. Educators often encounter students who express great anxiety about tests, due to a record of low performance. Students who experience abnormal fear responses to test circumstances may themselves be experiencing a self-fulfilling prophecy of low expectations, which may result in a continuing cycle of underperformance on exams due to their assessment anxiety.

References

Airasian, P. W. (2000). *Assessment in the classroom: A concise approach* (2nd ed.). New York: McGraw-Hill.

Aitken, N. D. (1982). College student performance, satisfaction, and retention: Specification and estimation of a structural model. *The Journal of Higher Education, 53*(1), 32–50.

Alvidrez, J., & Weinstein, R. S. (1999). Early teacher perceptions and later student achievement. *Journal of Educational Psychology, 91*(4), 731–746.

Boaler, J. (2003). When learning no longer matters: Standardized testing and the creation of inequality. *Phi Delta Kappan, 84*(7), 502–507.

Cole, N. (1981). Bias in testing. *American Psychologist, 36*(10), 1067–1077.

Diebold, F. X., & Mariano, R. S. (1995). Comparing predictive accuracy. *Journal of Business and Economic Statistics, 13*(3), 253–263.

Elder, C. (1997). What does test bias have to do with fairness? *Language Testing, 14*(3), 261–277.

English, N. B., & Keshavarz, M. H. (2002). Assessment of achievement through portfolios and teacher-made tests. *Educational Research, 44*(3), 279–288.

Farkas, G., Grobe, R. P., Sheehan, D., & Shuan, Y. (1990). Cultural resources and school success: Gender, ethnicity, and poverty groups within an urban school district. *American Sociological Review, 55*(1), 127–142.

Gardner, H. (1983). *Frames of mind: The theory of multiple intelligences*. New York: Basic Books.

Gullickson, A. R. (2003). *The student evaluation standards: How to improve evaluation of students*. Thousand Oaks, CA: Corwin Press.

Holt-Reynolds, D. (1992). Personal history-based beliefs as relevant prior knowledge in course work. *American Educational Research Journal, 29*(2), 325–349.

Jussim, L., & Eccles, J. S. (1992). Teacher expectations II: Construction and reflection of student achievement. *Journal of Personality and Social Psychology, 63*(6), 947.

Kubiszyn, T., & Borich, G. (2007). *Educational testing and measurement: Classroom application and practice*. New York: Wiley.

Kyriacou, C., & Coulthard, M. (2000). Undergraduate's views of teaching as a career choice. *Journal of Education in Teaching, 26*(2), 117–126.

Linn, R. L., Gronlund, N. E., & Davis, K. M. (2000). *Measurement and assessment in teaching*. Upper Saddle River, NJ: Merrill/Prentice Hall.

Madden, N. A., & Slavin, R. E. (1987). *Effective pull-out programs for students at risk*. Baltimore: Center for Research on Elementary and Middle Schools, Johns Hopkins University.

McMillan, J. H. (2004). *Classroom assessment: Principles and practice for effective instruction*. Boston: Allyn and Bacon.

Mead, A. D., & Drasgow, F. (1993). Equivalence of computerized and paper-and-pencil cognitive ability tests: A meta-analysis. *Psychological Bulletin, 114*(3), 449.

Muller, C. (1997). The minimum competency exam requirement, teachers' and students' expectations and academic performance. *Social Psychology of Education, 2*(2), 199–216.

Nitko, A. J., & Brookhart, S. M. (2007). *Educational assessment of students* (5th ed.). Upper Saddle River, NJ: Merrill/Prentice Hall.

Pallas, A. M., & Alexander, K. L. (1983). Sex differences in quantitative SAT performance: New evidence on the differential coursework hypothesis. *American Educational Research Journal, 20*(2), 165–182.

Powers, D. E., & Rock, D. A. (1999). Effects of coaching on SAT I: Reasoning test scores. *Journal of Educational Measurement, 36*(2), 93–118.

Rosenholtz, S. J., & Rosenholtz, S. H. (1981). Classroom organization and the perception of ability. *Sociology of Education, 54*(2), 132–140.

Rosenthal, R., & Jacobson, L. (1968). *Pygmalion in the classroom: Teacher expectations and pupils' intellectual development*. New York: Holt, Rinehart and Winston.

Rothman, R. (2002). *Benchmarking and alignment of standards and testing*. Los Angeles, CA: Center for the Study of Evaluation, Graduate School of Education and Information Studies, University of California, Los Angeles.

Sameroff, A. J., Seifer, R., Baldwin, A., & Baldwin, C. (1993). Stability of intelligence from preschool to adolescence: The influence of social and family risk factors. *Child Development, 64*(1), 80–97

Stiggins, R. J. (2008). *Student-involved assessment for learning*. Upper Saddle River, NJ: Merrill/Prentice Hall.

Stiggins, R. J., & Conklin, N. F. (1992). *In teachers' hands: Investigating the practices of classroom assessment*. Albany: State University of New York Press.

Taylor, C. S., & Nolen, S. B. (2008). *Classroom assessment: Supporting teaching and learning in real classrooms*. Upper Saddle River, NJ: Merrill/Prentice Hall.

Thorndike, R. M. (2005). *Measurement and evaluation in psychology and education* (7th ed.). Upper Saddle River, NJ: Merrill/Prentice Hall.

Turner, C. W., & Fischler, I. S. (1993). Speeded tests of implicit knowledge. *Journal of Experimental Psychology, Learning, Memory, and Cognition, 19*(5), 1165–1177.

Weiner, K. G., & Weitzman, D. Q. (2005). The soft bigotry of low expenditures. *Equity and Excellence in Education, 38*(3), 242–248.

Endnotes

1 The SAT website, www.collegeboard.com/splash/, provides information about the SAT, "Sex Differences in the Academic Performance of Scholastic Aptitude Test Takers," College Board Report No. 84-8.

2 Additional information about binomial distribution is available at a number of websites. Properties of binomial distribution are described at www.guilio.com/pdf/stats.pdf. Practical examples of binomial distribution in common events are described at www.mentor.lscf.ucsb.edu/course/winter/eemb146/lecture/ABasics.doc.

3 Information about New Jersey's Grade Eight Proficiency Assessment is available at www.nj.gov/njded/assessment/ms/.

Chapter 3

The School Year Begins: Setting Instructional Goals and Objectives

LEARNER OBJECTIVES

At the conclusion of this chapter the reader will be able to

▶ Distinguish between educational goals and objectives.

▶ Identify distinguishing features of educational objectives.

▶ Describe the influence of state standards on setting goals and objectives.

▶ Write a standards-based educational objective.

GRAPHIC ORGANIZER

> Educational Goals

> Educational Objectives

Then:	Now:
• Curriculum guides	• State standards and frameworks
• Conventional texts	• Standards aligned text
• Content to be covered	• Performance descriptions
• Skills to be conveyed	• Criteria of proficiency

ASSESSMENT VOCABULARY

Behavioral outcomes: Student performances or products that can be observed or measured. Behavioral outcomes demonstrate to the instructor that learners have acquired knowledge and skills through their actions and products.

Educational goals: Major purposes and expectations for educational systems, which may include learning goals for students and economic and social goals for families, communities, and other organizations.

Educational objectives: A description of instructional targets and outcomes that will result from a plan of instruction, often consisting of descriptions of knowledge and skills students are to acquire.

Educational outcomes: Particular abilities, knowledge, skills, and dispositions to be demonstrated by students as a result of instruction.

Frameworks: An explication of disciplinary content and skills, along with pedagogical suggestions, assessment methods, and resources for teaching the skills and content. A resource guide for teachers.

Transitive verb: A verb that has a subject and an object. Transitive verbs typically describe actions, and they are used in describing student products or performances in behavioral objectives and outcomes of instruction.

INTRODUCTION

Any discussion of educational goals and objectives must begin with a definition of terms, because *goals* and *objectives* are often used interchangeably. For our discussion, we will define **educational goals** as broadly inclusive purposes of public education that serve the needs of students as individuals and the needs of society in our pluralistic democracy.

Although goals may include desired outcomes for specific disciplines and may be achieved through a course of study, they are generally achieved over substantial periods of time. Examples of educational goals include:

Prepare youth for a life of civic engagement and social participation.

Students will understand essential principles of descriptive statistics.

Students will understand the role of the U.S. Constitution in shaping public life.

Educational objectives, on the other hand, describe a set of outcomes to be achieved within more broadly written goals (Gronlund, 2004). Objectives are usually written as descriptions of student skills, dispositions, or knowledge that result from a planned experience. Typically, several objectives will be achieved within a semester or academic year. Objectives are often subsumed under educational goals that relate to them.

Educational goals link large segments of the curriculum to essential purposes of public education. Objectives focus on the skills, knowledge, and dispositions teachers want their students to achieve through daily instruction. In a well-developed curriculum, the achievement of objectives leads to the attainment of larger instructional goals. Figure 3.1 includes some examples of objectives that fall within the goals just provided.

The preparation of effective educational objectives is a challenging task. When planning education objectives, the writer needs to envision outcomes of instruction and describe them in language that is useful to the learner. Essential components of objective statements include an active voice **transitive verb** that leads to the production of

FIGURE  **Educational Goals and Objectives**

Goal statement:
Prepare youth for a life of civic engagement and social participation.

Related objectives:
Students will identify the typical characteristics of community-based organizations.

Students will attend a public meeting of a governing board for a community-based organization and prepare a report that describes the contributions of the organization to the citizens of the local community.

Goal statement:
Students will understand essential concepts of descriptive statistics.

Related objectives:
Given a set of data, students will identify the proper values for the mean, median, mode, and range of the data set.

Students will define quartile and percentile rank.

Students will accurately describe a score distribution as normal, positively skewed, or negatively skewed.

Goal statement:
Students will understand the role of the U.S. Constitution in shaping public life.

Related objective:
Students will describe the public debate that gave rise to the Bill of Rights.

Students will describe the historical significance of *Marbury v. Madison*.

Students will identify the civil rights implications of *Plessy v. Ferguson*.

an observable product or performance. Well-crafted objective statements describe a vision of the student product or performance that will be observed by the reader, who may be either the author of the objective or a colleague on a collaborative planning team. Finally, the objective should include criteria that can be used to identify proficient productions. An example objective statement follows:

> *Students will write a one-paragraph autobiography of their life growing up to become a butterfly. The paragraphs should form a chronological narrative that includes, in proper order, the following terms:* egg, larva, pupa, chrysalis, *and* adult butterfly.

The performance expectations within the objective include the description of the paragraph, "a chronological narrative," and the specification of terms to be developed sequentially, "includes, in proper order, the following terms: *egg, larva, pupa, chrysalis,* and *adult butterfly.*" A reader of this objective statement can use it to evaluate work that students produce after instruction. By contrast, the typical learning expectation of a standards statement, "Children will know the life cycles of some common animals," lacks these features and is not useful for evaluating student work.

SELECTING EDUCATIONAL GOALS AND OBJECTIVES: THEN AND NOW

As new teachers embark on their first year of teaching, they have little time to consider important goals and purposes of their teaching efforts. Typically, a teacher is hired for a specific teaching assignment, perhaps a third-grade classroom in an elementary school or a set of history classes in a high school social studies department. The principal or department chair provides a quick introduction to the classroom where textbooks and curriculum resources are available for use. Usually the new teacher begins the school year teaching from these resources, page by page and chapter by chapter, with little guidance from school leaders until the academic year is well under way. Sometime professional development is provided in the use of specific textbooks adopted by the school district, but these workshops are typically conducted later in the school year.

At some point in time, after experienced teachers have arrived and classes have started, new teachers meet with experienced colleagues to review expectations for the quarter, the semester, or the year. How have these conversations between teachers changed as educational reforms have found their way into classrooms during the last decade? Let us look into classrooms of the past and the present to reveal the extent to which the selection of instructional goals and objectives have changed in this relatively brief period of time.

A vignette of goal selection in the past:

> In late summer 1994, Carol Moscone joined the faculty of Taft Elementary School in the rural town of Bishop, Iowa, as a new third-grade teacher. Carol was recruited to the Bishop schools at a teacher recruitment fair held in May of the same year, and during the summer she entered an alternative teacher training program sponsored by a college in Iowa that provided her with "classroom survival" skills. In this program, she learned quite a bit about

classroom management and the essentials of lesson planning. In late August she attended 3 days of orientation with a small group of teachers new to the Bishop schools, and during the last day of the orientation, she met with Gretchen Dawson, the third-grade teacher leader in Bishop. Gretchen understood the urgency of many tasks Carol had to complete before students returned for the new school year, so she got right to the point during her first opportunity to discuss the third-grade math curriculum.

"Two years ago we started our review of the math curriculum under direction provided to us by the curriculum committee of the Board of Education," Gretchen explained. "We were pleased with our mathematics textbook from a major publisher until we noticed that standardized test scores were beginning to decline, so we looked into other possibilities, including math textbooks that other school districts seemed happy with. Ultimately, we settled on this new book because it scored highest on a rating checklist recommended by a math curriculum expert in the state department of education. We all thought that it was a little more challenging than our prior text, and it came with good support materials including test generation software and supplementary workbooks for the children. I think you will find it works well for you," she concluded. With Gretchen's advice in mind, Carol began the school year with page 1, Chapter 1 of the text and moved through the teacher's edition in chapter order for the remainder of the year. On occasion, she would check with Gretchen and other teachers about challenges she faced in her efforts to make mathematics meaningful to her students. For the most part, she relied solely on the text to prepare students for tests that she wrote for her own students from the test generation software provided by the publisher.

Given the process of textbook selection described, we may ask how instructional goals and objectives are established in the Bishop School District. Several years ago, local boards of education had complete authority to adopt curriculum and declare to their teachers the scope and sequence of content to be conveyed at each grade level and in all core curriculum courses. Following these curriculum decisions, teachers selected instructional resources such as textbooks that were recommended for adoption by the board of education as the primary tools for conveying the content of the curriculum. In this environment, teachers could largely determine the areas of the curriculum they would emphasize as long as their instruction adhered to the goals and objectives of the district curriculum guide, and the curriculum resources provided to teachers were used as a resource to achieve goals and objectives. Once the classroom door was closed, teachers were free to interpret broad district goals as they saw fit. They could develop their own instructional objectives and use their textbooks independently of others (Erickson, 1986).

As educational reform gained momentum following the publication of *A Nation at Risk* in 1983 by the National Commission on Excellence in Education, international studies comparing the quality of the U.S. school curriculum with curricula of other countries suggested that the lack of uniformity and standards led to uneven quality of educational experiences for children and youth (Lee, 2002). During the last 20 years, states have written curriculum standards intended to form the minimum expectations of learning for all students.

The reauthorization of the Elementary and Secondary Education Act as No Child Left Behind (NCLB) sought to rectify perceived inequity in school curriculum practices. Many national reports and studies about the state of public education in the United States revealed that disadvantaged students and underperforming students were not getting access to the same rigorous curriculum experienced by students in more advantaged settings (Schmidt, 1999). States adopted curriculum standards to provide all students access to a rich curriculum, hoping that this new policy direction would close the achievement gap between rich and poor students. In this new environment, teachers share common instructional objectives when they have common teaching assignments. This new opportunity has led to increased teacher collaboration and accountability for student achievement of state standards (Gable & Manning, 1997), as seen in the following vignette.

A vignette of contemporary goal and objective setting:

In early June 2006, Irma Rodriguez was delighted to obtain her first teaching position in a seventh- and eighth-grade English and language arts position at Sunrise Middle School in the town of Barefoot, California. Two months later she reported for new teacher orientation. Following completion of paperwork, a tour of the school district, and a review of district policies for new teachers, Irma met with Joyce Waterston, chair of the English department at Sunrise, who had volunteered to serve as Irma's mentor as part of the professional induction program offered locally for new teachers. Following a brief introduction, Joyce began to describe to Irma the resources she would use for planning instruction to meet state standards.

"Irma, I have a number of documents here for your review prior to the start of classes," Joyce said. "They include the English/Language Arts Curriculum Frameworks for California Public Schools, the district's pacing guide that identifies the critical English standards that need to be achieved within the first 9 weeks of classes, our standards-aligned textbook approved by the state curriculum authority, and some important California Department of Education websites that explain the standards, the frameworks, and the California Standards Test your students will take in spring," she explained, concerned that she was overwhelming her new colleague. "For now," Joyce continued, "it's important for you to identify the district's critical standards that your students will be achieving. During the week of October 23 we will be administering our common benchmark assessment to measure student achievement of state standards included in the pacing guide for the first nine weeks of school. Your seventh- and eighth-grade English classes will be taking the exam at that time. I just want to be sure you are fully aware of this accountability measure before you begin instruction," Joyce concluded.

"Well thank you," Irma said in response to this surprising amount of information. "I will look into these resources and get started with my planning just as soon as I can," she said with a slightly forced expression of enthusiasm.

Joyce, sensing Irma's growing anxiety, concluded their brief conversation by stating, "I am sure you are feeling a little overwhelmed by all this emphasis on the standards, but you won't be alone. Our district's induction program provides me with time during the course of the school day to check in with you and support your planning efforts. We know that these new assessment expectations may come as a surprise to new teachers. Your seventh- and eighth-grade colleagues with the same teaching assignment will meet with you weekly to plan lessons and assessments targeted for a successful outcome on the first benchmark test. You won't be alone with this," she said with sincerity.

The conversation between Joyce and Irma reveals the extent to which state boards of education have asserted influence over the curriculum taught in schools in the form of curriculum standards that are assessed annually as required by NCLB regulations. The events in Bishop, Iowa, by contrast, took place when the school district curriculum guide and the district's selected textbooks were provided to the teachers with the expectation that they would teach from these resources. The state had little influence over local curriculum. By contrast, our second vignette portrays a standards-based teaching environment in which state curriculum standards guide instruction. In contrast to the first vignette, coverage of the curriculum is ensured through the provision of a common assessment derived from state standards and administered to all students in the same subject, during the same week, following 9 weeks of teaching that are focused on the achievement of locally selected state standards.

State standards have emerged in the center of the curriculum (Darling-Hammond, 1999). Student achievement of selected state curriculum standards are assessed by federally mandated state standards tests in language arts and mathematics for Grades 3 through 8. Recently, science has been added to the short list of subjects to be tested. Instructional planning, teaching, and classroom assessment are essential activities that teachers perform to effect student learning. In the last few years these activities have undergone adjustment to address state curriculum standards (Linn, Baker, & Betebenner, 2002). What, then, are the new practices and expectations for teachers who are working in public schools to achieve the standards?

STATE CURRICULUM STANDARDS INFLUENCE THE SELECTION OF INSTRUCTIONAL GOALS AND OBJECTIVES

Now that state curriculum standards are mandated by federal laws that require high-stakes standards tests, local school districts must include them in the development of their curriculum goals and objectives. In some states too many curriculum standards have been written for teachers to achieve in one academic year, so districts have been forced to choose some standards to include while neglecting others. A typical school district may charge curriculum committees with the task of identifying critical state standards to be achieved by students in their district. The selected critical standards are then sequenced for their orderly and coherent development through the academic year. As the standards reform movement continues to unfold from state to state, school districts are adopting pacing guides for the achievement of selected state standards in an orderly and coherent fashion (Jacobs, 2004). Courses of study in core content area have been reorganized to achieve state standards by following standards pacing guidelines.

HOW DO TEACHERS MEET EDUCATIONAL GOALS AND OBJECTIVES?

Across the country, teachers are adjusting to new roles and responsibilities in their efforts to address the standards. What new changes in teaching and learning are implied by the provisions of the NCLB law? How have lesson and unit planning, teaching, and classroom assessment changed under the influence of state standards? The following developments characterize teaching and learning to the standards that are fully developed in some locations, but just emerging in others (Spillane, 2003).

In years past, many factors were considered in the selection of textbooks because no external authority determined the content to be conveyed at specific grade levels and in particular subjects. In the current reform environment, state standards are the dominant factor guiding the selection of textbooks and other instructional resources. Textbooks are purchased by school districts if they are aligned to the state standards, and other factors, including the readability of the text, become secondary. In many elementary school classrooms across the country, language arts and reading text materials are tightly aligned with standards, and teachers are expected to use these standards-aligned resources to the exclusion of other materials that may be available. Teachers refer to texts that must be followed by rote as "scripted" curriculum (Atkeison-Cherry, 2004). School districts provide specialized training in the use of these materials to new teachers and expect adherence to explicit directions for the use of the materials with "fidelity."[1]

Secondary school teachers are also affected by state standards. The introduction of high school exit exams based on state standards has influenced teaching and learning in middle and high schools. Although most of these tests focus on student mastery of basic skills, teachers of other subjects are addressing standards in mathematics, reading, and writing to ensure student success with these new exams. From kindergarten through Grade 12, the learning expectations of state standards determine the resources to be used in core subject matter classrooms.

Standards and Related Resources Guide Instructional Planning

In the past, a locally selected textbook was used to determine the topics and skills conveyed in daily teaching. Now, state standards are used to select textbooks and to identify instructional goals and objectives. State standards resources include frameworks, the standards, information about the state standards tests, and sample tests or released test items. Teachers are learning to use these resources to guide their instructional planning and to develop classroom assessments.

State standards are the primary resources of the standards reform movement, but they are rarely used by teachers as resources for teaching (O'Shea, 2005). A standard may describe a skill, a body of knowledge, or even a disposition. Some standards describe particular skills, abilities, or knowledge that students should acquire with enough clarity and specificity to be used. The following statement is an example of a clear and unambiguous standard that can guide classroom instruction.

California Science standard for Grade 6:

> Students know lithospheric plates the size of continents and oceans move at rates of centimeters per year in response to movements in the mantle. (Reprinted by permission, California Department of Education)

This science standard is quite limited in scope. It is an expectation that students acquire knowledge of a very specific fact concerning the size and rate of movement of tectonic plates.

By contrast, the following language arts standard is so broadly written and so vague that it takes on the appearance of an educational goal. As such, it is not useful in shaping instruction in the classroom.

2.2 Write responses to literature:

> a. Demonstrate an understanding of a literary work (Reprinted by permission, California Department of Education)

State standards differ in specificity and usefulness because of the manner in which they are written. Committees of scholars in each discipline are typically selected to determine the content and skills children are to acquire. A committee of English and language arts scholars may write standards quite differently than those prepared by a committee of geologists.

Although standards are highly influential in determining course content, curriculum **frameworks** are more useful tools because they guide instructional planning. Curriculum frameworks include teaching suggestions, resources that help students understand a given standard, and classroom activities that can help students understand topics and skills of the standards. Unfortunately, most state frameworks do not include useful resources for helping teachers set expectations for student learning nor do they include resources for assessing standard achievement. Useful resources would include descriptions of student products or performances that meet the standards, including quality indicators for evaluating student work. They do not include sample assessment instruments teachers can use to assess student achievement of the standards through the year. The following excerpt is from the History-Social Science Framework for the California Public Schools.

> Children are now ready to consider those who came into this region and the impact each new group had on those who came before. To organize this sequence of events, children should develop a classroom time line by illustrating events and placing those illustrations in sequence with a caption under each. Depending on the local history, this sequence will include the explorers who visited here; the newcomers who settled here; the economy they established; their impact on the American Indians of this region, and their lasting marks on the landscape. . . . (Reprinted by permission, California Department of Education)

This excerpt from the frameworks about California's early settlers, the Native Americans that preceded them, and the impact these groups have in the present day is rich with teaching suggestions, including the development of a classroom timeline with clearly specified elements. However, the framework would be more useful if it included a reference to a website where sample timelines are shown, complete with commentary about the quality of the timelines and guiding information for evaluating timelines and related student work.

Frameworks are useful instructional tools for interpreting the meaning of the standards. Some teachers continue to use their locally adopted textbook to guide their teaching, but increasing numbers of teachers are turning to curriculum frameworks to identify the learning expectations for students. New teachers should become familiar with these resources as their primary source for setting instructional goals because they set state expectations for higher levels for student achievement. In addition, they are the source material for state tests of student achievement required by NCLB.

Using Standards and Frameworks to Plan Instructional Objectives

If state curriculum frameworks and standards are primary resources for setting expectations for student learning, how do we use them to plan instructional objectives? In a process referred to as curriculum translation, teachers use the content and skill statements found in standards and frameworks to describe student products and performances that will meet the standards' learning expectations. These descriptions of student products and performances become the instructional objectives of a standards-achieving lesson (O'Shea, 2005).

The process begins with teacher analysis of the content and skill statements in standards documents. For example, the excerpt about the life of pioneer settlers includes the suggestion that students develop a timeline of events that unfolded in their region, complete with captions and dates for key events. Although teachers are expected to include Native American groups, explorers, and early settlers on their timeline, the exact content to be included will depend on the specific events in their local region. These historical events would be different for students in San Francisco compared to those in Los Angeles. It would be up to teachers to decide on the specific events and individuals students should identify and properly place on the timeline. Most important, teachers would need to describe the characteristics they expect to see in a properly developed timeline if they are to judge the quality of the work and deem it standards achieving.

For example, students in central California might be expected to include the dates the area was occupied by specifically named Native American groups, their local economy, cultural features, and sites where their settlements have been found. Students would be expected to identify early explorers who came to the central California region, including Juan Cabrillo and Gaspar de Portola, the role of Father Junipero Serra in establishing the missions on El Camino Real, and the establishment of early ranchos in the region. Finally, they would identify when Japanese and Sicilian fisherman arrived to exploit the ocean resources in the area.

As teachers deliberate about these historical events and choose some as more important than others, their shared vision of a high-quality timeline would emerge. They would prepare a list of items that students should include on the timeline and the quality features it should possess, such as accuracy of events, proper spelling of names and places, and the dimensions of the timeline. Perhaps their concluding statement about the timeline would be something of this nature: "Each class will construct a timeline that shows in proper proportions the length of time certain groups lived in this area, including the Ohlone Indians and other indigenous peoples, the missionaries under authority of Spain, the rancheros, and ultimately various national groups that came to exploit the resources of the sea, including Japanese shell divers and Sicilian sardine fishermen. Key historical events and individuals should also be noted, including the arrival dates of Juan Cabrillo, Gaspar de Portola, and Farther Junipero Serra, the dates of the establishment of the missions in Carmel and San Juan Bautista, and the establishment of early ranchos."

The Role of Instructional Objectives in the Assessment Process

When teachers engage in describing student **behavioral outcomes** as the important characteristics of products or performances that students will display, they anticipate the assessment process that will follow. When student work is collected, teachers can evaluate the quality of the work submitted by comparing it with the descriptions of student work in their instructional objectives. For instance, teachers who expect students to produce a timeline of historical events in central California can produce a checklist of the elements and qualities they expect to see in the timeline and use that checklist to evaluate student work after it is collected.

The link between good instructional planning and high-quality assessment practices is well-written **educational outcomes** that result from the planning process. The outcomes are described before teaching begins because the desired student outcomes are the targets of the teaching process. After a lesson, the teacher can evaluate student achievement of the teaching target by comparing the resulting student work to the student outcome descriptions from lesson planning. If a small group of teachers were to evaluate student timelines they had collected, they could use the descriptions of the timelines they wrote in their objectives as evaluative criteria to assess student work. If their expectations for student work are written with explicit descriptions of quality indicators, then the student work can be compared to the objective statements. For instance, teachers could look for the proper spelling and temporal placement of each explorer name on the timeline (e.g., Juan Cabrillo, Gaspar de Portola) and could inspect each timeline to see that the chronological lengths of time periods or events are proportionally represented by segment lengths on the timeline.

Different scoring tools can be used to evaluate student work in relation to expectations in lesson objectives. We have already referred to checklists as one instrument that is useful for this purpose. In Chapter 8 we will examine tools that can be used to evaluate student work with some detail, particularly student written statements and student projects that require subjective judgment of quality. At this juncture, it is important to note that well-written student performance descriptions include measurable or observable quality and quantity elements that result in a mental image of the expected student work.

COLLABORATIVE DEVELOPMENT OF INSTRUCTIONAL OBJECTIVES

The uniform learning expectations of state curriculum standards provide for consistency in teaching and learning from one classroom to the next. Teachers with the same instructional assignment are expected to convey the same standards to all their students. In this new environment, it makes sense for teachers to collaborate to achieve the same instructional goals and objectives. The following vignettes illustrate new collaborative practices found in a growing number of schools across the United States.

Standards-Based Curriculum Materials Are Reviewed to Find Learning Expectations

We meet Mrs. Elena Carlson before she joins her colleagues in a grade-level team meeting to plan a standards-based lesson. As she gathers materials for the meeting, she can be seen flipping through her district's curriculum guide. She is looking for the curriculum pacing tables that will guide her planning group's efforts. These tables inform teachers in Mrs. Carlson's grade level when specific standards are to be achieved. She turns to the tables to find science standards and corresponding language arts standards that third-grade teachers are expected to achieve during the next 2 weeks

Mrs. Carlson finds the relevant tables in the pacing guide. One table identifies science standards, and a second table identifies language arts/reading standards. The tables can be seen in Tables 3.1 and 3.2. School districts bring administrators and teachers together to plan these tables. Although district pacing calendars and tables may vary in appearance from location to location, they include information about the standards to be covered and the period of time allocated to each. Typically, an exam is planned to assess student comprehension of the paced standards after they have all been conveyed. In the examples provided, the identification of standards and the date by which they should be covered is augmented with information about learning expectations for students related to each standard. These are included under the heading,

TABLE 3.1   **Component of District Pacing Guide Related to a Life Science Standard**

Science Standard set	Specific Standard	Sample Content Statements of Framework	Sample Performance Expectations	Resources	Pacing Guide Achievement Dates
Life cycle standard set 3: Adaptations in physical structure or behavior may improve an organism's chance for survival.	**3a: Students know plants and animals have structures that serve different functions in growth, survival, and reproduction.**	External structures of plants and animals serve important functions. This standard can be taught in conjunction with standard 3b: adaptation of organisms to oceans, deserts, tundra, forests, and grasslands.	**Students match body parts of different animals to an appropriate life function: nutrition, protection, reproduction, (cactus thorn, kangaroo pouch, crab shell).**	Text reading: Animal and plant structures and their functions. pp. 67–74	February 2nd week 3rd grade team to evaluate student work by Feb. 21. Benchmark Test: March 3

TABLE **3.2**   **Component of District Pacing Guide Related to Writing Standard 1.1**

Language Arts standard Addressed	Specific Standard	Sample Content Statements of Framework	Sample Performance Expectations	Resources	Pacing Guide Achievement Dates
Writing strategies: Students write clear and coherent sentences and paragraphs that develop a central idea.	1.1 **Create a single paragraph** **Develop a topic sentence.** **Include simple supporting facts and details.**	Students write compositions that describe and explain familiar objects. Provide a context in which action takes place. Demonstrate use of research and draft writing.	**Students write one paragraph that starts with a topic sentence related to a concurrent science or social sciences standard. Student identifies text used as a reference for writing.**	Provide students with sample paragraphs drawn from science or social **science** discipline.	February 2nd week 3rd grade team to evaluate student work by Feb. 21. Benchmark Test: March 3

"Sample Performance Expectations." Specific standards and related student performances that meet the standards are highlighted in bold.

Focusing on the Content to Be Conveyed

Mrs. Carlson pays special attention to the performance expectations column in each table. She is already thinking of student performances that might meet the standards when she is greeted by her colleagues, Mrs. Garcia and Mr. Chandler, who remind her that it is time for their grade-level team meeting. During their short walk to an adjoining classroom, the teachers discuss various animals, the places in the world where they are found, and the parts of their bodies that are involved in various life functions.

When they arrive at their grade-level meeting with other colleagues, we find that they, too, were thinking about the same topics. Mrs. Garcia and Mr. Chandler have also been thinking about the skills of the corresponding language arts standard. Mrs. Rice suggests that they examine the science frameworks that describe learning expectations for the students associated with the selected standard. The teachers find the following information that appears on page 51 of their science framework:

> Students have learned about the roots and leaves of plants in grade one and the functions of flowers and fruit in grade two. Many other external structures of plants and animals (e.g., cactus thorn, porcupine quill, crab shell, bear claw, and kangaroo pouch) serve important functions, and students in grade three will recognize many common examples through reading and observing examples from nature. (Reprinted by permission, California Department of Education)

Additional information from the related standard, 3b, is also on page 51:

> The organisms that live in oceans, deserts, tundra, forests, grasslands, and wet-lands are different from one another because their environments are different. For example, animals with thick fur are able to survive a cold habitat. Gills allow fish to obtain oxygen from water, whereas lungs allow mammals to obtain oxygen from the atmosphere. . . . (Reprinted by permission, California Department of Education)

The teachers look at these statements to identify important facts and ideas that students should know. The identification of content and skill statements in the standards is the first step toward the development of standards-based instructional targets. Mrs. Carlson, having noted that the framework statement focuses on body parts and how they help animals adapt to their surroundings, begins the group conversation by stating, "Perhaps students should know, for example, that polar bears are protected from the cold by their fur and body fat."

The descriptions of student performances that Mrs. Carlson and her colleagues derive from standards and frameworks content statements become the targets of their instruction and the basis for developing assessments to measure student achievement of the standards. We will see how performance descriptions establish a foundation for standards-based assessment in the next vignette.

Translating Content Statements into Student Performance Descriptions

Additional statements about the content and skills to be learned by students help the teachers frame the content and skills to be conveyed. After the content has been developed and agreed to by the teachers, the more difficult process of curriculum translation follows. The teachers need to propose student work products that will demonstrate that they have met the standards' learning expectations.

Following Mrs. Carlson's lead, the other teachers begin to discuss possible student performances that would show knowledge of the standards. Mr. Chandler suggests an idea. "Let's think of different animals that live in different climates and have students describe their adaptations." Mrs. Garcia suggests another idea. "Let's have students work with one life function at a time to make it easy for them." She makes a quick drawing based on her idea (Figure 3.2). As everyone looks over her drawing, they begin to envision students writing about specific body parts that adapt animals to live in their biome conditions. Ideas develop in discussion related to students matching an animal and its biome to a particular life function (e.g., locomotion, taking in food, protection, or escape). After students match the animal to a given life function, the students will be expected to describe the adapted body part that helps the animal perform the life function in its particular biome.

Mrs. Garcia closes the discussion about this central activity in the lesson by explaining her chart to the other teachers. "The children will place their cards with an animal name and where it lives under a given life function. They will then describe in the space below how the animal's particular body part is well

FIGURE  **3.2**   **Mrs. Garcia Suggests a Student Product that Meets a Life Science Standard**

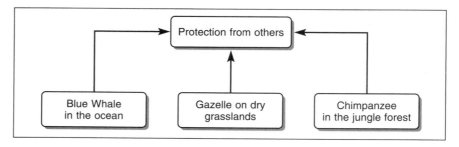

adapted to protecting the animal in the biome where it lives," she states with some satisfaction.

Mrs. Carlson adds, "That's a real good idea, but how do we get them to the process of writing paragraphs using a topic sentence?" Mr. Chandler makes the suggestion, "Perhaps the students can practice writing topic sentences that state the name of their animal, the biome in which it lives, and that the animal has body parts adapted for living in that biome. After the topic sentences are completed, they can write paragraphs with sentences that describe three of the animal's body parts that are adapted to its biome." The conversation quickly turns to the development of a list of possible activities that would lead to student understanding of animals, their adaptations, their body parts, and important life functions.

Ensuring That Outcome Statements Are Observable or Measurable

Mrs. Garcia makes the observation that the team should move beyond a discussion of possible activities to a discussion of the essential outcomes students should exhibit to demonstrate achievement of the selected standards. Mrs. Carlson suggests that students should demonstrate new understandings through processes that include writing, as suggested by their selected language arts standard. The teachers start to write a list of possible outcomes for a lesson on animal adaptations:

1. Students will write, with correct spelling, the name of a favorite animal and the biome in which it lives on a large note card.

2. Students will place the note card under a description of a life function and write a phrase that describes a body part of the animal and how it is adapted to the life function

3. After reading about their favorite animal, students will write a topic sentence that names the animal and states that it is adapted to the animal's correct biome.

4. Students will complete a paragraph that includes the topic sentence and three supporting sentences that include three different body parts of their favorite animal and how the body parts are adapted to a life function.

As the teachers continue their conversation, they remain mindful of their goal: By the end of the planning session they will craft a lesson plan with clearly stated objectives derived from their science and language arts standards. The objectives describe student products or performances that would demonstrate achievement of the selected standards. Near the end of the planning session, they reach agreement on the lesson's objectives and a sequence of activities that would hopefully give rise to the objectives. Their lesson plan appears in Figure 3.3.

FIGURE **3.3** **Lesson Plan for Animal Adaptations**

Rationale
Students should know that animals have body parts that help them perform important life functions including nutrition, escape from predators, reproduction, and shelter from extreme weather conditions. Animals have adapted body parts that help them survive in different climatic regions or biomes of the world. In the third grade, students should be able to write a paragraph, derived from their own research, that begins with a topic sentence.

Science Standard Set 3 Life Sciences:
Adaptations in physical structure or behavior may improve an organism's chance for survival. As a basis for understanding this concept:

3a: Students know plants and animals have structures that serve different functions in growth, survival, and reproduction.
3b: Students know examples of diverse life forms in different environments, such as oceans, deserts, tundra, forests, grasslands, and wetlands.

Language Arts/Reading Standard:
1.1 Cards with animal names
Create a single paragraph. Develop a topic sentence. Include simple supporting facts and details.

Resources
Posters for student descriptions of life functions (e.g., "Protect and support," "Movement/mobility," "Take in information," "Take in food/water")
Poster paper for posting life functions
Writing paper for student essays
Textbooks and reference books on animals, where they live, and their adaptations for life functions

Lesson objectives

1. Students will select a favorite animal, identify the biome where it lives, and research the body part adaptations that help the animal fulfill life functions in its biome.
2. Students will write the name of their animal on a large note card, along with a brief description of the biome where the animal lives.
3. Students will place their note card with the animal name beneath a life function for which the animal has special adaptations.
4. Students will write brief statements identifying body parts that adapt their animal to fulfill the life function they have identified.
5. Students will write a topic sentence stating that their favorite animal has a specified number of adaptations for fulfilling life functions in its biome.
6. Students will write a draft paragraph beginning with their topic sentence that includes supporting sentences for each adapted body part identified.

(continued)

FIGURE 3.3   Lesson Plan for Animal Adaptations (*continued*)

Suggested Lesson Activities:

As an introduction to the lesson, read *Wolves* by Karen Dudley to the students and use discussion to identify key wolf body parts. Model the development of a topic sentence and paragraph that describes the body parts of wolves and their adaptive functions.

Have students read about animals, the biomes where they live, and particular body parts of the animals that are adapted to life functions (e.g., obtaining nutrition, protection, and escape).

Students will write the name of an animal and where it lives on a large note card.

Have each child place the note card beneath a life function that they want to write about, as illustrated in Mrs. Garcia's drawing.

Students will then write brief statements on the lines under the note card that describe their animal's body part adaptation that fulfills the special life function.

Following the teacher's example, students write a topic sentence that includes the name of the animal, its biome, and a particular body part that is adapted to a particular life function.

Students will participate in a writing workshop, developing paragraphs that describe how their animal is adapted to at least three life functions.

Assessment:

Teachers will bring student work samples to a collaborative work evaluation session for their grade level. At the session, they will score student-produced note cards, topic sentences, and draft paragraphs by comparing the student work with the quality indicators that appear in the lesson objectives. Student error patterns in paragraph construction will be noted for corrective actions during subsequent instruction.

After the teachers reach agreement on the essential features of their lesson plan, they end their session and return to their classrooms. They will teach their new standards-achieving lesson within the next 10 days as the culminating lesson on biomes and diversity of animal life on earth. They have also agreed to teach to the same set of instructional objectives. After their lessons have been taught, they will conduct a collaborative student evaluation session to compare student work products to the expectations they set in their lesson objectives. As for the rest of the unit, the teachers will pursue student understanding in ways that may vary according to their own plans.

Prior to teaching their collaboratively planned lesson as a culminating activity of a unit of instruction, one or two of the teachers may place special emphasis on the diversity of life in various biomes, asking for students to develop special understanding of one particular animal, the biome it lives in, and the adaptations it has for meeting its life functions within its biome. Yet another teacher may emphasize the diversity of life within biomes. In this instance, the teacher may ask students to select a particular biome to study, including the variety of plants and animals in the biome and the adaptations of the various animals. The teachers retain their autonomy in developing student knowledge and skills related to animal adaptations to different biomes. They have agreed, however, to teach the culminating lesson the same way, because this particular lesson will show evidence that students have achieved the standards selected for their unit. During the lesson on animal adaptations in biomes, collaboratively planned student work products are expected to emerge that show the standards have been met.

This first vignette displays new instructional roles and responsibilities appearing in schools as part of the curriculum standards reform movement. Teachers are learning to work together as they plan instruction to achieve state standards. At some point in time, however, each teacher must return to the classroom to work independently with students.

TEACHING TO STANDARDS-BASED INSTRUCTIONAL OBJECTIVES

During these lessons instructional objectives prepared with other teachers emerge as student products and performances that manifest achievement of objectives derived from curriculum standards. In our next vignette, we eavesdrop on the classroom of Mr. Chandler, who is the first person in the third-grade planning team to teach the collaboratively planned lesson about animal adaptations.

A vignette of standards-based teaching in a third-grade classroom:

As we arrive in Mr. Chandler's classroom, we see that he has chosen to write certain student expectations on the whiteboard, including (a) the standards to be achieved, (b) the related knowledge content statements from the frameworks, and (c) the lesson objectives developed by his grade-level team. He decides to have students read *Wolves* silently at their seats as he prepares a follow-up activity. At the front of the classroom he has displayed a large diagram of a wolf, with lines indicating various body parts. Following the reading, Mr. Chandler asks several students questions about the passages they read.

Mr. Carlson scans the students toward the back of the classroom and asks, "What is an essential life function we read about in *Wolves*, Jana?" After some consideration, she replies, "Getting away from predators and other animals that could be harmful."

Mr. Carlson replies, "That's a good one, Jana. We can write that one here on the board: 'Escape and Protection.'"

We note that Mr. Carlson is careful to use the words found in the standards and frameworks. He is interested in building student understanding of the academic language of the standards. After he writes "Escape and Protection" on the board, he points out the same word in the standards statements written elsewhere on the board, turns to the students and asks the question, "I need someone to tell me what 'protection' means in their own words, William?" Mr. Carlson knows that the important vocabulary of the standards needs to be acquired and used by students.

As the lesson proceeds, Mr. Carlson elicits each of the four life functions identified in the grade-level team planning session. Soon, the whiteboard includes the categories "Protect and Support," "Move/Mobility," "Take in Information," and "Take in Materials." He and his students have read the book *Wolves* by Karen Dudley, and from this reading students are able to identify the wolf body parts that can be sorted under each of the four functions.

Billy says, "The wolf uses his eyes to see other animals that may be food."

Mr. Carlson asks, "Under which life function should we write 'eyes'?" Latisha raises her hand, and following a nod from Mr. Carlson, she responds, "Under 'Take in Information.'"

Soon Mr. Carlson is asking students to identify two of their favorite animals they researched during lessons he taught earlier in the unit. He asks each student to write a list of body parts of their favorite animal and the life functions that the body parts fulfill. It is evident that Mr. Carlson is working toward the achievement of the language arts objective selected by his grade-level team: "Students will write brief statements identifying body parts that adapt their animal to fulfill the life function they have identified with their favorite animal."

As the lesson proceeds, Mr. Carlson continues to provide examples, demonstrate sentence composition, and guide students to the development of topic sentences for their paragraphs. He seems to be mindful of the need to elicit, or evoke, student writing efforts that demonstrate achievement of the objectives he developed from the standards with assistance from his grade-level colleagues. At the conclusion of the lesson, Mr. Carlson collects student work in anticipation of the next phase of activity in his standards-focused instructional setting. Mr. Carlson will meet with his planning group to review student work samples and compare them to the instructional targets they described in their lesson plan objectives.

INSTRUCTIONAL OBJECTIVES AND CLASSROOM ASSESSMENT

Two aspects of teaching that have undergone the most change in response to the standards movement are teacher collaboration and assessment practices (Murnane, Sharkey, & Boudett, 2005). Now that teachers at the same grade level or subject assignment are expected to plan instruction together from the same set of standards, more school districts are expecting teachers to collaborate in planning common assessments (Carr & Harris, 2002).

After teachers plan lessons that are designed to achieve well-crafted objectives, they develop assessment procedures for evaluating student work in relation to the objectives. Various scoring tools can be used to compare features of student work to the instructional objective expectations. A checklist is one tool that can be used quickly when reviewing student work samples. We will close this chapter by looking in on an assessment meeting of our three third-grade teachers, Mrs. Carlson, Mrs. Garcia, and Mr. Chandler. In later chapters, we will examine a variety of assessment methods that have become common in the environment of standards-based reforms.

A vignette of collaborative assessment activity:

Mrs. Carlson, Mrs. Garcia, and Mr. Chandler meet again after each of them has had an opportunity to teach the collaboratively developed lesson on animal adaptations. They will evaluate samples of student work in comparison to their lesson plans' objectives. As they sit down to discuss the outcomes of their lessons, Mr. Chandler describes some of the activities that took place during his lesson

"I decided to focus my lesson on the specific part of our standard that includes the statement, 'Animals have structures that serve different functions in survival.' I then looked over the pages of our frameworks and the pages of our local textbook that address this standard to be sure I was providing my students with everything they should know to meet the standard. The textbook and the framework citation identified four essential life functions that are met by various animal body parts. These life functions include 'escape and protection,' 'move/mobility,' 'take in information,' and 'take in materials,'" he said.

Mr. Chandler continued his description of the events of his lesson. "In class we read the relevant text pages. I then listed the four main life functions on a poster that the students could read. After students wrote their favorite animal name and its biome features on note cards, they placed their cards under a particular life function on the poster. This was our first exercise in matching life functions to the body parts of a specific animal. We discussed a variety of animals, their body parts, and the role of those body parts in fulfilling one or more of the essential life functions that appeared in our textbook and the frameworks. I wanted to hear my students offer oral descriptions of animal adaptations while using the science terms we encountered in the framework citation. These included 'body part,' 'life function,' and most important, 'adaptation,'" Mr. Chandler added animatedly as he described activities he felt would lead his students to produce standards-meeting work.

He continued, "Following this discussion, I wanted to see students use these terms properly as they wrote brief paragraphs about their animal. In these paragraphs, students were to identify a favorite animal and name the body parts of the animal that fulfilled each of the life functions they described on their poster. For the most part, my students demonstrated success with this lesson. I felt they had a good handle on the kinds of adaptations animals need to survive in their various biomes," he concluded.

Mrs. Carlson spoke next while placing a number of student work samples on the table for all to see. "I'd like to talk about my students and the paragraphs they wrote," she said. "After looking over these papers from my class, I'm not sure they could develop a topic sentence for a paragraph without a lot of assistance from me," she concluded.

"I agree," said Mrs. Garcia. "I would like to continue to work on the language arts standard in our next lesson," she concluded.

Mrs. Carlson returned everyone's attention to the task at hand. "Let's take a look at each of our students' paragraphs first and see how they responded to the expectation of writing a paragraph with a topic sentence," she said.

The teachers examined each of their objective statements in their collaborative lesson plan as they prepared a checklist of expectations for the student paragraphs that were derived from the objectives. Their checklist expectations are included in Figure 3.4.

Using copies of the checklist, the teachers evaluated several paragraphs submitted by the children in their classes. After 15 to 20 checklists were completed, they examined all of them to identify commonly missed items. They also looked for the use of the academic language of the standards and correct spelling of important terms, including "adaptation," "protect," "function," and "materials." As a result of the analysis, the teachers reached the conclusion that their students met most, but not all, of the lesson objectives they had set during their collaborative lesson planning session. They were quite happy with the

FIGURE 3.4   Characteristics of a Proficient Paragraph

Topic sentence:
_____ Animal name stated as subject of sentence
_____ Includes the following terms: "body parts" and "adaptations"

Supporting sentences
_____ One sentence for each adapted body part
_____ Minimum of two sentences

Supporting sentence structure
_____ Body part identified
_____ Its adaptation included
_____ Life function served is also concluded

Note: Proficient performance equals five or more elements checked as present.

outcome, knowing that the expectations of their state standards were largely met and their students were likely to perform well on state standards assessment items related to paragraph writing and topic sentences.

Summary

We began this chapter with an overview of educational goals and objectives. Educational goals are intended to achieve major purposes of the curriculum and frame the curriculum taught in schools. Educational objectives are expressed as student products, performances, or dispositions we expect to see as outcomes of instruction. In the past, instructional objectives were developed from school district curriculum guides and adopted curriculum resources.

State curriculum standards have affected the identification and development of instructional objectives in two substantial ways. State standards documents, frameworks, and standards-aligned instructional programs are new resources to identify content, skills, and dispositions to be included in today's instructional objectives. The emergence of state standards tests, largely as a result of NCLB, has led teachers to construct instructional objectives that prepare students for success on these exams. Pacing guides and benchmark assessment programs affect the order and rate for achieving standards-based instructional objectives. The programs also raise expectations for teacher collaboration in setting instructional goals and objectives.

Our vignette of teacher collaboration through a cycle of planning, teaching, and student work evaluation provides insights into the professional lives of teachers who work together to achieve curriculum standards. It is a manifestation of the vision held by educational reformers who believed teachers should work together to set higher expectations for their students. The activities of collaboration for the achievement of curriculum standards include

- Identifying the standards to be addressed in their lesson following school district guidelines.

- Selecting content statements from standards, frameworks, and other official state documents that describe student expectations for achieving the standard.

- Translating selected content statements into student performance descriptions, and using the performance descriptions to prepare a list of lesson objectives.

- Using curriculum resources to select instructional activities designed to give rise to student outcomes identified in the lesson objectives,

- Teaching the lesson and analyzing student work samples to find evidence that students achieved the lesson's objectives.

Instructional objectives describe our targets for teaching. The targets are student outcome behaviors, products, or performances. In today's reform environment, these outcomes are often developed from standards resources. Well-written student outcomes form the foundation for assessing student academic achievement. If our instructional objectives describe student outcomes with sufficient detail to form a vision of a high-quality student product or performance, the objectives can be used to develop assessment tools for evaluating student work. Assessment will be easy to plan after we have prepared thoughtful and explicit instructional objectives because we will know what we expect to obtain from our students after instruction is completed. In the chapters that follow, we will identify methods of assessment for measuring student achievement of our instructional objectives.

Exercises

1. The History-Social Science Framework for California Public Schools guides teachers in the selection of state standards to be achieved by California's children and youth. Some of the standards are written as goals, and other standards are instructional objectives. State two rules that you will apply in sorting the statements into separate categories labeled "learning goal" and "instructional objective."

Rule #1: _____

_____

Rule #2: _____

_____

Apply your rules to the following statements from the History-Social Science Framework for California Public Schools. Place a "G" beside apparent goal statements and an "O" beside apparent objectives.

Our Local History: Discovering Our Past and Our Traditions

_____ Students describe the American Indian nations in their local region long ago and in the recent past.

_____ Students demonstrate an understanding of the economy of the local region.

_____ Students differentiate between primary and secondary sources.

_____ Students identify geographic features of their local region.

_____ Know the histories of important local and national landmarks.

_____ Understand the three branches of government, with an emphasis on local government.

2. State standards statements may meet some criteria of effective instructional objectives, but one or more of the following criteria are frequently missing: use of an active voice verb to describe a student action, description of a product or performance that results from student action, and quality indicators that will be used to evaluate the resulting product or performance.

Note the first example:

Students identify geographic features in their local region.

#1: Specific geographic features need to be provided (e.g., Willard's Creek).
#2: The verb *identify* fails to describe an observable student action.
#3 A specific number of geographic features has not been stated.

Examine each of the following statements and describe one or more properties of the statement that need enhancement to be used effectively as an instructional objective.

Describe some goods or services that are produced by the local economy.

#1 _____
#2 _____
#3 _____

Students understand major events preceding the founding of our nation.

#1 _____
#2 _____
#3 _____

State two causes of the Civil War and describe for each cause the position taken by the Southern states regarding the issue.

#1 _____
#2 _____
#3 _____

3. Imagine that you are Carol Moscone, the new teacher hired at Taft Elementary School in Bishop, Iowa, as described in the first vignette of this chapter starting at page 55. Following your conversation with the experienced teacher, Gretchen Dawson, what resources would you obtain to begin planning your long-term goals and instructional objectives? Describe the relative importance of each of these resources. Which of them would you examine first? Which resource would probably be used most frequently in planning daily instruction?

4. Re-read the second vignette of this chapter, which takes place in early June 2006. Imagine that you are Irma Rodriguez, and you have just finished your conversation with Joyce Waterston, chair of the English department. Which of the following documents would you review first for an understanding of the curriculum you are responsible to

teach? Which of the documents is likely to contain information that will lead you to be either anxious or assured about your assignment? Which of these would be most likely to be relatively familiar to use? Which resource would you be most likely to examine later when you have more time?

English/Language Arts Curriculum Framework for California Public Schools

The school district's pacing guide, which identifies critical standards to achieve in 9-week intervals during the school year

The district's standards-aligned textbook

California Department of Education websites that explain the standards and frameworks

5. You are a member of faculty committee charged with responsibility for selecting critical "essential skills" standards to be developed at your grade level (fourth grade). Review the following essential skills, and then decide on a rule or priority consideration that will allow you to identify the six essential standards you will develop during the course of your academic year. Apply your rule or priority consideration in selecting the six essential standards, and list them, from 1 to 6, in order of importance according to your rule or priority consideration. Write the rule(s) or principle(s) used in making your decisions, then indicate the priority order of your standards under your rule statement.

Chronological and Spatial Thinking

_____ Students place key events and people of the historic era they are studying in a chronological sequence and within a spatial sequence; they interpret timelines.

_____ Students correctly apply terms related to time, including *past, present, future, decade, century,* and *generation.*

_____ Students explain how the present is connected to the past, identifying both similarities and differences between the two, and how some things change over time and some things stay the same.

_____ Students use map and globe skills to determine the absolute locations of places and interpret information available through a map's or globe's legend, scale, and symbolic representations.

_____ Students judge the significance of the relative location of a place (e.g., proximity to a harbor on trade routes) and analyze how relative advantages or disadvantages can change over time.

Research, Evidence, and Point of View

_____ Students differentiate between primary and secondary resources.

_____ Students pose relevant questions about events they encounter in historical documents, eyewitness accounts, oral histories, letters, diaries, artifacts, photographs, maps, artworks, and architecture.

_____ Students distinguish fact from fiction by comparing documentary sources on historical figures and events with fictionalized characters and events.

Historical Interpretation

_____ Students summarize the key events of the era they are studying and explain the historical contexts of those events.

_____ Students identify the human and physical characteristics of the places they are studying and explain how those features form the unique character of those places.

_____ Students identify and interpret the multiple causes and effects of historical events.

_____ Students conduct cost-benefit analyses of current events.

Selected standards provided courtesy of the California Department of Education, _History-Social Science Framework for California Public Schools._

6. Consider the following statement, which might be found in a state science framework. It possibly includes content statements, skill statements, general curriculum expectations, resource descriptions, and suggestions for teaching. Identify the content and skill statements that might be used to write an instructional objective.

> (a) Students can develop an understanding of scientific principles by working with models. (b) Simple electric circuits serve as models for students to understand electricity and magnetism. (c) They can construct simple series and parallel circuits that include some features found in complex wiring systems. (d) Obtain some batteries, battery holders, alligator clips, bell wire, various resistors, small 1.5-volt lightbulbs, and switches that students can work with. (e) They should begin by drawing a diagram of a simple series circuit. (f) It is important that students identify the source of electrical power, electrical conductors, and resistors. (g) Students should be able to draw a simple circuit and arrange electrical components with wires guided by their drawing.

Using the letter that precedes each sentence in the paragraph from a hypothetical science framework, identify the statements that are:

Content statements:

_____

Skill statements:

_____

Teaching suggestions:

_____

Curriculum expectations:

_____

7. In our third vignette, we introduced Mrs. Elena Carlson, who worked with her colleagues to develop instructional objectives from state standards resources. Before

going to her meeting, Mrs. Carlson gave consideration to the life science standards to be achieved:

> Students know plants and animals have structures that serve different functions in growth, survival, and reproduction.

She thinks of the polar bear and its adaptations for life in the arctic, including its fur, its large paws, and its large amount of body fat. She then considers animals that have special features for protection, including the porcupine with its quills, the skunk with its scent, or the deer and its ability to run away quickly. She then looks at the language arts standard that calls for students to write a descriptive paragraph that includes a topic sentence. Write one or two instructional objectives that might be written by Elena Carlson for an in-class writing activity. The instructional objective calls for students to write a paragraph that contains features that address both the science standard statement and the language arts standard.

Possible answers:

Students will write a topic sentence that includes a specific animal, describes the habitat where it lives, and states the body parts that help it function in its environment. Students will practice writing sentences that include the name of an animal, a body part, and how the body part helps it survive.

Students will complete the prompt: "_____is a(n) animal
                                                    (name of animal)
that lives in the_____. It has_____that helps
                          (name of habitat)   (body part)
it survive by_____."
                    (function of body part)

Resources and Suggested Readings

The reauthorization of the Elementary and Secondary Education Act as No Child Left Behind (NCLB) has placed a new emphasis on school reform along with accountability measures. The public has recently become accustomed to read about local school test scores as part of the new law. A lesser known feature of NCLB has been an emphasis on teacher quality. Research by Stanford University Professor Linda Darling-Hammond (1999) has revealed the significance of high-quality and well-prepared teachers for student learning. Her research findings reveal that students who experience poor-quality instruction due to the bad luck of having an underqualified teacher for two or more consecutive years are often irreparably harmed intellectually and never recover full command of essential skills of computation and communication that are at the heart of the school mission. NCLB has sought to remedy this problem by requiring schools to hire teachers who are highly qualified and competent, particularly in their area of certification.

References

Atkeison-Cherry, N. K. (2004). *A comparative study of mathematics learning of third-grade children using a scripted curriculum and third-grade children using non-scripted curriculum.* Jackson, TN: Union University.

Carr, J. F., & Harris, D. E. (2002). Succeeding with standards: Linking curriculum, assessment and action planning. *Harvard Educational Review, 72*(4), 561–563.

Darling-Hammond, L. (1999). *Teacher quality and student achievement: A review of state policy and evidence.* Seattle, WA: Center for the Study of Teaching and Policy, University of Washington.

Dudley, K. (1996), *Wolves.* Calgary, Albert, Canada: Weigl Educational Publishers.

Erickson, F. (1986). *Tasks in times: Objects of study in a natural history of teaching.* East Lansing, MI: Institute for Research on Teaching, Michigan State University.

Gable, R. A., & Manning, M. L. (1997). The role of teacher collaboration in school reform. *Childhood Education, 73*(4), 219–227.

Gronlund, N. E. (2004). *Writing instructional objectives for teaching and assessment.* Upper Saddle River, NJ: Merrill/Prentice Hall.

Jacobs, H. H. (2004). *Getting results with curriculum mapping.* Alexandria, VA: Association for Supervision and Curriculum Development.

Lee, J. (2002). Racial and ethnic achievement gap trends: Reversing the progress toward equity? *Educational Researcher, 31*(1), 3–12.

Linn, R. L., Baker, E. L., & Betebenner, D. W. (2002). Accountability systems: Implications of requirements of the No Child Left Behind Act of 2001. *Educational Researcher, 31*(6), 3–16.

Murnane, R. J., Sharkey, N. S., & Boudett, K. P. (2005). Teacher response to NCLB. *Journal of Education for Students Placed at Risk, 10*(3), 269–280

O'Shea, M. (2005). *From standards to success: A guide for school leaders.* Alexandria, VA: Association for Supervision and Curriculum Development.

Schmidt, W. H. (1999). *Facing the consequences: Using TIMSS for a closer look at U.S. mathematics and science education.* Boston: Kluwer Academic Publishers.

Spillane, J. (2003). *Standards deviation: How schools misunderstand educational policy.* Cambridge, MA: Harvard University Press.

Endnote

1. The Reading First program, a part of NCLB, includes provisions that federally identified programs be followed by teachers with fidelity to the text. Further, provisions of the guiding regulations strongly advise that other resources should not be included unless they are tightly aligned with the locally implemented literacy program.

Chapter 4

Assessment Before the Year Begins

LEARNER OBJECTIVES

At the conclusion of this chapter, learners will be able to

► Distinguish between conventional preinstructional assessment and new assessment practices in standards-based settings.

► Identify preinstructional assessment tools and describe their use and limitations.

► Identify the characteristics and uses of standardized tests and state standards tests and their use in assessing student knowledge.

► Develop a professional perspective toward preinstructional assessment that precludes the possible influence of bias, prejudice, or inappropriate information when making inferences about learners and their instructional needs.

GRAPHIC ORGANIZER

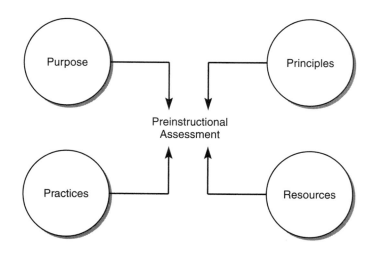

Then:
- Standardized tests
- Student records
- Prior performance
- Teacher comments

Now:
- Standards test results
- Special needs assessment
- Cumulative progress records

ASSESSMENT VOCABULARY

Criterion-referenced test: Exams or other assessment instruments designed to measure a student's achievement in relation to an established body of knowledge, often state curriculum standards.

English language learners: Students who have a first language other than English, which may be spoken at home. Sometimes referred to as limited English proficient learners.

Grade equivalent score: A score resulting from the use of a norm-referenced exam that describes a student's performance in comparison to an average student of a given grade level. Scores are typically reported with two digits, with the first representing a grade level and the second representing one of the 9 months in a 9-month academic year. If a student scores 5.8, then the score is representative of the performance of student in April of Grade 5.

Individuals with Disabilities Education Act:	A federal law stipulating the rights and resources to be accorded to individuals with disabilities. In its current form, the law is grounded in the belief that students with disabilities should have as much access to the general education curriculum as possible.
Individualized Education Program:	A legally required plan prepared by educational specialists for a student with disabilities. It describes educational goals and means for achieving them. These plans and their preparation, including the rights of parents and students with regard to their development and implementation, are described in the 2004 reauthorization of the Individuals with Disabilities Education Act.
Norm referenced:	A description of exams and other forms of educational assessments that result in scores that compare the performance of a student, or group of students, with a reference group demonstrating a normal distribution of scores. The normal distribution is the more widely known bell curve, which places one half of student scores above the average performance and one half below. Student scores are often reported as percentile ranks within the distribution of scores of the reference group.
Permanent record card:	A cumulative report of a student's progress through school, which will include scores on large-scale assessments, diagnostic assessments, course or subject grades, and teacher comments. Other information may appear, depending on the format of the card used in a given school district.
Special needs:	Defined broadly, a student who has a learning disability, physical disability, or other condition that may impede learning progress. Schools have a legal and ethical responsibility to provide accommodations that give the student with special needs an equal opportunity to learn.
Standards test:	State-administered exams intended to measure student achievement of content and skills included in state curriculum standards.
Standardized test:	Any large-scale assessment administered to large groups of students, typically in different locations, under tightly controlled and equivalent circumstances. The controls and circumstances are intended to maximize the reliability of the assessment process.
Triangulation:	The use of multiple methods and perspectives to measure a given phenomenon for the purpose of ensuring the accuracy or reliability of the measurement.

INTRODUCTION

Across the United States, classrooms are becoming increasingly diverse. Our immigrant nation continues to provide classrooms with new students who need to acquire essential literacy skills in English. These students may arrive in the school system at any age. Federal laws that protect persons with disabilities require that all students be placed in the least-restrictive environment that maximizes their access to the general education curriculum.[1] Segregation in all forms has been under attack since the middle of the last century. In sharp contrast to teaching in the post–World War II era, new teachers in our public schools today should expect to teach in classrooms populated with students from various racial, ethnic, or ability groups, and new teachers should understand that this diversity is a resource for teaching and enriching the classroom experience. But with diversity come learning differences and the need to determine students' instructional needs through assessment activities. Student diversity includes differences in student family and cultural experiences, exposure to prior learning, and student mobility in and out of the school district. Student differences imply the need for individualized learning plans and individualized instruction. The varied nature of student diversity means assessment of students' prior learning and student readiness for instruction is more important than ever (Tomlinson, 1999).

In this chapter, we will explore assessment from the perspective of teachers planning for the beginning of a new school year. We will look at conventional practices in preinstructional assessment as they might have unfolded for an elementary school teacher approximately 10 years ago. We will take note of the teacher's special interest in the 32 students who populate a general education classroom and the concern the teacher expresses for conducting a fair and unbiased evaluation of prior student learning so that improper assumptions are not made about student capacity or motivation to learn. As we look into this elementary classroom, we will note the particular nature of preinstructional assessment that arises in general education classrooms where a relatively small number of students work with the same teacher for the entire academic year.

We will then move forward in time to an urban middle school in the process of developing a preinstructional assessment system within the context of the current standards-based reform environment. We will observe preinstructional assessment as it takes place in a departmentalized curriculum where teachers instruct more than 120 students in groups of 25 to 30 learners. In these settings, teachers work with their students for relatively brief periods, typically less than 1 hour, and they have less opportunity to observe their students deeply to engage their complete intellectual and social development, when compared to an elementary school teacher. In secondary schools, teachers place a priority on student development of discipline-bound knowledge, and their preinstructional assessment activities reflect this focus (Lortie, 1975).

Through this analysis, we will see how effective assessment prior to teaching can go a long way toward ensuring student success through the school year. When students start school fully engaged in learning experiences that are appropriate to their abilities and well integrated with prior learning, they make a comfortable transition to a new learning environment with the promise of experiencing success from the first day of school. If, on the other hand, students find themselves in an unfamiliar environment where learning expectations are confusing and unrelated to the skills and knowledge they bring to the new classroom, inappropriate behavior and low motivation to learn can soon follow (Bohn, Roehrig, & Pressley, 2004). Routines and practices of preinstructional assessment are an important part of the repertoire of teachers who experience the joy of student learning throughout the school year.

ESSENTIAL PURPOSES OF PREINSTRUCTIONAL ASSESSMENT

As late summer arrives, teachers begin to think about the upcoming school year and the new students who will fill their classrooms. First-year teachers may wonder in general about students they will soon encounter, but experienced teachers have more specific questions in mind that arise from their prior experience. Typical questions that an experienced teacher may consider include:

▶ Will I have large numbers of students with **special needs**?

▶ How many of my new students will be English language learners?

▶ Will my students display substantial variety in their abilities and background knowledge, or will my students be relatively uniform in abilities and scholastic achievement?

▶ Will my students be motivated?

▶ How many students are new to my community, the school district, or the country?

▶ Are my new students at grade level and ready to learn what I will be teaching on the first day of school?

Preinstructional assessment has been part of the American schooling experience for decades, and it forms the stereotypic image of the first day of class in any school (Airasian, 2000). This simplistic view of preinstructional assessment is as well known to the general public as it is to teachers. At the beginning of the school year, students are asked to take out a sheet of paper and write a page or two describing what they did during their summer vacation. Strangely, no one seems to ask why teachers of the past gave such an assignment and what they learned by reading the essays.

What are the purposes of preinstructional assessment, and how can they benefit teachers and students at the start of the school year? How have preinstructional assessment practices changed in light of the current reform movement that focuses on state curriculum standards and intensive accountability for their achievement? How are large-scale assessments, including **standardized tests** and the new state **standards tests**, used appropriately in preassessment activities? What precautions are necessary when making inferences about student capacity to learn prior to getting to know them as individuals? What differences are we likely to see in the preinstructional practices of elementary school teachers or other teachers of relatively few students when compared to departmentalized secondary school teachers who work with more than 100 students in a day? What kinds of preassessment activities are used in diverse classroom settings that include **English Language Learners** and students with special needs? To explore these questions, we will examine the procedures teachers have used to learn about their students at the beginning of the school year and how these practices have changed with the times.

WHAT RESEARCH CAN TELL US ...

- ### About Teachers' Opinions of Motivating Factors for Adolescents

  Are adolescent students similarly motivated to succeed in school from one country and one culture to another? In "Teachers' Beliefs about Student Motivation: Similarities and Differences across Cultures" (Hufton, Elliot, & Illushin, 2003), three international researchers attempted to discern teacher opinion, which could affect attitudes toward contemporary youth prior to instruction. Certain factors did appear consistent among American, English, and Russian teachers' beliefs about factors affecting student motivation to learn, and these included parental expectations, parent communications, and certain peer interactions. Conversely, teachers are concerned about the growing influence of media on student motivation in school, and these concerns seem to cross national and cultural boundaries. The researchers in this study also concluded that conducting comparative intercultural research into opinion formation is fraught with methodological problems. Do teachers form opinions about their students' motivations based on their understanding of family structures and communications? Evidence suggests that this may be so, but cultural differences may limit our ability to generalize about student motivations in all cultures.

PREINSTRUCTIONAL ASSESSMENT: THEN AND NOW

The work that teachers perform in the waning days of summer and during the first few days of school has changed substantially since the advent of state curriculum standards (Craft & Bland, 2004). These changes have resulted in part from the new forms of assessment required by federal law and the emergence of teacher collaboration to improve student learning (DuFour, Eaker, & DuFour, 2005). In the following vignette, we will examine preinstructional assessment as it was performed a little more than a decade ago in an elementary school located in the mid-Atlantic coast. During this time states were developing and implementing curriculum standards to guide student learning at each grade level and in important core subject areas, but annual testing of state standards achievement was only beginning to appear in the United States. Assessment practices at this time were generally planned by teachers working in relative isolation, and one teacher's test or final unit assignment might have very different learning expectations than that of another teacher at the same grade level or common assignment (Yinger, 1980). The one common assessment experience of the time was the standardized test administered every few years to measure student achievement in a school or district in relation to a reference population of similar students across the state or the entire country (Berliner & Biddle, 1995).

A vignette of preinstructional assessment in 1998:

> It is late summer, and we find ourselves leaving the fourth-grade classroom of Mrs. Holyfield, a veteran teacher in a suburban community in St. George's County, Maryland. She is heading toward the principal's office on this early September day before the start of the school year. Mrs. Holyfield just received a copy of her student roster for the academic year. She will be teaching a class of 26 students, and she already wants to know all about them. As we enter the principal's office, we hear an exchange between Mrs. Holyfield and Mrs. Johnson, the principal's secretary.
>
> "Well, good morning, Mrs. Johnson, I hope you had a pleasant summer and that we are all ready to start off another school year," Mrs. Holyfield said pleasantly.
>
> "Well, good morning to you, Brenda, and yes, we are most certainly ready. I have all the student records you asked for right over here where you can look at them for as long as you may wish and without interruption," said Mrs. Johnson, who had gathered student permanent record folders and standardized test scores as requested by Mrs. Holyfield.
>
> During the summer, Brenda Holyfield gave considerable thought to the preinstructional assessment tasks she would undertake prior to the first day of school. The first of these would focus on a review of student records on file in the principal's office. Using a data recording form of her own design, Mrs. Holyfield began to review the materials prepared for her. On the table was a **permanent record card**, grade reports from the third grade, commentary about student classroom performance by third-grade teachers, and standardized achievement test scores for each of the students.
>
> As Mrs. Holyfield went about consolidating student information on her data form, she asked Mrs. Johnson for other information that she did not see.
>
> "Mrs. Johnson," she called out, "has information been provided concerning any special education students that may be included on my roster? I'm looking for information from student IEPs."
>
> "I don't believe we have that information at this time, but I will certainly provide it as soon as it becomes available," said Mrs. Johnson.
>
> "Well, Mrs. Johnson," said Mrs. Holyfield, as she concluded consolidating student information on her recording forms, "I think I have what I need, so I will get out of your way now so that these materials can be secured in their proper place. Thank you so much for your help." Mrs. Holyfield gathered her forms and returned to her classroom for additional preparations.

At the conclusion of our vignette, Mrs. Holyfield returns to her classroom with important information about each of her students consolidated on a record sheet that she will be able to access throughout the school year. To use this information, Mrs. Holyfield needs to understand its significance, its limitations, and how to make inferences from both the quantitative information provided (e.g., standardized test scores) and the qualitative data she obtained (e.g., teacher commentary about student effort or learning problems).

At this juncture, we will consider the variety of student information Mrs. Holyfield reviews in her preinstitutional assessment practices, beginning with the information that was not provided concerning students with special needs.

Recall that Mrs. Holyfield requested information regarding students with special needs by looking for federally required **Individualized Educational Programs (IEPs)**. These instructional plans are written by teams of educators, including special education teachers, counselors, school psychologists, and general education teachers, depending on the needs of the student involved (Pretti-Frontczak & Bricker, 2000). The IEPs that Mrs. Holyfield expects to review will specify learning goals for special-needs students coming to her fourth-grade classroom. IEPs are federally mandated learning plans for students identified as having disabilities, including cognitive disabilities that may include learning disabilities such as dyslexia (Bateman & Linden, 1998). Federal law limits Mrs. Holyfield's access to only the portion of IEP information that she needs to know to meet a student's learning needs in her classroom. This information will include instructional goals, statements describing student academic strengths and weaknesses, and the criteria that Mrs. Holyfield should apply in making a determination of whether the IEP goals have been met. When Mrs. Holyfield receives this information, she will review it with special education professionals, who will guide her efforts in helping each of the students for which an IEP has been written. Often, IEPs call for special accommodations or adaptations in a teacher's instructional plans to meet the special needs of certain students in the classroom. Students with special needs are assessed through different means than conventional tests or quizzes (Overton, 2003). On occasion, additional time or special circumstances are provided for special-needs students during assessment activities. These special circumstances will be described in the IEP information Mrs. Holyfield will receive.

One important source of student achievement information Mrs. Holyfield obtained was student standardized test scores for language arts and mathematics. The interpretation of standardized test results depends on the nature of the scores provided. In Mrs. Holyfield's school, standardized test scores in language arts and mathematics are reported as **grade equivalent (GE) scores**. The grade equivalent scores will tell her how each student was performing in language arts and mathematics when the test was administered in the third grade. Student achievement reports on the language arts portion of the test are reported as a series of subskills (e.g., word recognition, grammar conventions), and each student's results appear as two-digit numbers for each skill area. The numbers, which might appear either with or without a decimal (i.e., 3.8 or 38), stand for a year and month of academic school year achievement reflecting the median performance of a nationally normed group of students. For instance, a student score of 3.8 in vocabulary development would lead Mrs. Holyfield to infer that the student understood vocabulary equivalent to the midrange of students across the nation who are in the third grade and eighth month of their language arts education (Thorndike, 2005).

After returning from the principal's office, Mrs. Holyfield noted that William McHenry, a student who would be in her class, received a GE score of 4.5 in the vocabulary development subtest of the language arts achievement exam taken in the eighth month of the third grade. Mrs. Holyfield understood the score to mean that William performed at the median level of a nationally developed large sample of fourth-grade students in their fifth month of a 9-month academic year. Given that William took the test while he was in the eighth month of the third grade, Mrs. Holyfield correctly infers that William is reading somewhat above his grade level. By examining and recording the GE scores of all her students, Mrs. Holyfield is able to identify the relative performance of all her incoming students in terms of grade-level equivalence. She intends to use the GE scores from the district's standardized testing program and corroborating information in the form of grade reports, prior teacher commentary, and her own assessment to be administered in the first week of class to form reading groups.

Mrs. Holyfield knows that some students do not perform well with standardized tests, and she wants to be sure that other sources of information corroborate the achievement test measures of her students' reading abilities. Moreover, she understands that students mature at different rates, and that developmental changes over the summer might be identified by administering a language arts assessment shortly after the Labor Day weekend. Mrs. Holyfield enters the information she has obtained at the principal's office into electronic files that she will maintain for each of her new students on the computer she recently received.

The vignette of Mrs. Holyfield and her preparations at the start of the school year reflect conditions in public schools of just a few years ago. Technology in the form of student information management systems and computer networks were just beginning to appear in schools. We note, however, that sensitive student information was kept in the principal's office, and Mrs. Holyfield went there to obtain important information about her students' prior academic performance and standardized test scores. We should also note that Mrs. Holyfield did not rely solely on GE test scores of students or any other single source of information to reach conclusions about student abilities. She sought corroborating information such as grade reports and teacher commentary from the prior year. Last, Mrs. Holyfield was mindful that young students can mature quickly in short periods of time, and that additional timely assessment would be needed to support her opinions about student basic skills made from data collected several months earlier.

School-Based Information for Preinstructional Assessment

Let's consider for a moment the variety of conventional assessment measures that Mrs. Holyfield relied on to ascertain student abilities in core fourth-grade subjects. We will also consider other kinds of information she may use in to develop her estimations of student learning needs at the beginning of the school year.

It is evident that Mrs. Holyfield uses standardized testing information from tests taken by students in their prior grade to evaluate student readiness to learn basic skills. **Norm referenced** standardized tests can provide a teacher with important information about student skills and abilities that the tests have been designed to measure. When a student receives a score from a norm-referenced standardized test, the outcome can be used to compare the student's performance to a large national sample of students who responded to the same or similar test items. The test serves to compare one student's performance, or the average performance of a group of identified students (e.g., all third-grade students in a given school), with a measure of the performance of a large group of students drawn from the nation, hence the use of the term *nationally normed standardized test* (Stiggins, 2001).

A student score may be compared to the performance of the nationally developed pool of students through a variety of means, including the grade equivalent scores discussed earlier or a percentile rank, which states the percentage of students that achieved a score below that of the student score reported. If William McHenry's achievement score had been reported as a percentile rank, perhaps Mrs. Holyfield might have encountered a value such as "78th percentile." This score would tell Mrs. Holyfield that William McHenry's score in vocabulary development is higher than 78% of the students across the nation who took the test as part of the test development activities of the test publishing company.

How might Mrs. Holyfield use this information in planning lessons in the future? She might begin the school year by planning supplemental reading and writing exercises for William that will help him build on his substantial language arts skills. If Mrs. Holyfield places her students in reading groups, she will probably include William in an advanced group. She will monitor his progress to see if the information relied on for preinstructional assessment is valid. Mrs. Holyfield has noted in the past that some students perform quite differently than expected when they start the school year. There are always occasions when preinstructional assessment fails to identify factors that contribute to an unexpected student performance.

Often a testing company can report student percentile ranks in comparison to other populations of students, including the students in a school district. For instance, William McHenry's test data may reveal that his performance in vocabulary development is in the 78th percentile nationally but in the 68th percentile in his local school district. This additional information may lead Mrs. McHenry to form inferences about William's response to the local curriculum, presuming that William attended schools in the district for a substantial portion of his educational experience. Standardized achievement tests are not as frequently used now as they were in the past, largely because regulations of No Child Left Behind (NCLB) have tended to displace standardized testing programs with a different kind of exam, standards-based examinations. (Do not be confused by the appearance of the stem "standard" in *standardized tests* and *standards-based tests*. These are different kinds of examinations and should be interpreted differently, as we will discuss later.)

Our vignette suggested that Mrs. Holyfield also relied on information provided by former teachers to evaluate current students' reading abilities. The vignette disclosed that student grade reports and teacher commentary about student performance were available to Mrs. Holyfield, along with a summary document of student cumulative performance measures in the form of a permanent record card. These additional forms of information consist of assessments of student ability and performance made by prior teachers. As such, they may reflect other factors that come into play during assessment, including (a) inconsistencies in teacher ability to observe and interpret student behavior, (b) the nature of the relationship between the student and the teacher, and (c) bias that the teacher may hold against a student either as an individual or as a member of a group.

In the late 1980s the author was invited to model an interactive mathematics lesson in a class of first-grade students. As students engaged in learning tasks, two eager young boys kept coming up to the teacher to show her the work they had done. During the course of the activity, the teacher confidently assured me that the two boys were by far the most able math students in her class. Her observations missed the substantially more sophisticated performance done by one precocious girl, whose more reserved nature failed to attract the teacher's attention.

The principle of **triangulation** should be applied when examining student performance data (Butler & McMunn, 2006). In triangulation, several different measures of the same phenomenon are conducted using different methods. If a measurement of one phenomenon leads to similar results when compared to other measures of the same phenomenon performed with different methods, confidence in the accuracy of the data increases. Triangulation can lead to improved reliability in assessment practices. When two or more measures of the same phenomenon corroborate, the reliability of the overall assessment process is increased. If in William McHenry's case the second-grade teacher noted that William's vocabulary development was above grade level and the third-grade teacher noted independently that William's vocabulary development continued to progress nicely, these two confirmations of William's performance on the standardized achievement test could lead to the reasonable conclusion that William is likely to perform well in reading tasks presented at grade level during the fourth grade.

Finally, Mrs. Holyfield may take note of other information on the permanent record card that could affect the conclusions she reaches about student abilities, prior achievement, or prior motivation to learn. Often permanent record cards reveal attendance information or a history of student mobility from one school setting to another. If a student experienced abnormally high absences or underwent a great deal of change, these events may explain anomalies in student academic performance, particularly if the anomalies took place concurrently with an extended period of absence due to illness, a family stressful event, or a relocation during the academic year.

Our vignette of Mrs. Holyfield working independently from other teachers in a classroom of the late 1900s portrays a concerned and conscientious teacher who uses preinstructional assessment practices to start the year well. She relies on available information and triangulates her data to make reasonable conclusions about student abilities relative to the curriculum she will be teaching. Her intention to administer her own assessment in the first week of the school year displays her understanding that young students can mature rapidly and that uncorroborated data obtained over a year earlier should be viewed skeptically.

ISSUES OF FAIRNESS IN PREINSTRUCTIONAL ASSESSMENT

Certain principles of preinstructional assessment are evident in Mrs. Holyfield's activities. These include a concern for bias that may be introduced in either the data collection or data interpretation activities. Bias often occurs when an educator applies general perceptions about groups of people to members of these groups in their classroom (Dusek, 1975). News reports constantly identify differences in academic performance between ethnic and economic groups in the United States. It is inappropriate, however, for teachers to use this information to judge the abilities or intelligence of individual students. For instance, family membership is often interpreted in a biased fashion when teachers speculate about the future performance of a new student based on prior experience with an older sibling.

Other concerns arise from limitations in the reliability and validity of observer reports (Vitaro, Tremblay, & Gagnon, 1995). Reports by a prior teacher are one professional's opinion about a learner. A single report lacks the reliability that would be provided by several observers reaching the same conclusion. On the other hand, classroom teachers have extensive opportunity to observe students during a school year, so their opinions are neither trivial nor poorly informed. Nevertheless, it is always valuable to obtain a second or third opinion where possible. Other professionals who can provide additional perspectives on student academic performance can be school counselors, paraprofessionals, or school psychologists.

Preinstructional assessment should not lead to hastily reached conclusions or first impressions that persist despite countervailing information from direct observations of students as they begin the new school year. Teachers need to remain open-minded and optimistic about students' likelihood to meet expectations and perform well, despite evidence to the contrary in past performance. Preinstructional assessments are expected to have predictive validity, but prediction is not as important as actual performance. When predictions fail to live up to reality, we need to dismiss our prior assumptions and value the performance of the students before us.

Finally, professionals should always be skeptical of casual conversation and anecdotal comments concerning students (Lyons, 1990). Comments that can be heard in the teachers' lounge, department offices, or school cafeteria about a student's behavior, disposition, or abilities should not be expressed in those settings. Principles of due process and fair dealing are certainly not evident on these occasions, for the students who are the subjects of these conversations are rarely present to defend themselves or provide their interpretation of events.

As we move our attention from preinstructional assessment as it took place a decade ago, we should be mindful of the principles of assessment practiced by Mrs. Holyfield, for these methods are as valid today as they were then. Furthermore, information about prior student achievement used by Mrs. Holyfield is still appropriate for use today with the possible exception of Mrs. Holyfield's reliance on standardized tests. As we step into the present, we will see that that teachers' use of large-scale assessment information has changed substantially (Darling-Hammond, 1998).

We now turn our attention to the present time, as teachers conduct preinstructional assessment in this reform era with its emphasis on state curriculum standards, increased use of assessment of all kinds, and attendant accountability for student success. Student assessment data is now used to guide student learning throughout the school year, and new assessment methods have emerged that build on the strategies we saw Mrs. Holyfield use in 1998.

Most important, teachers are working together to interpret assessment data and plan instruction in ways that would have been unfamiliar to Mrs. Holyfield.

A vignette of preinstructional assessment in a contemporary classroom:

> For this next vignette, we will eavesdrop on the classroom of Ms. Susan Richards, who teaches seventh-grade math in a middle school outside Birmingham, Alabama. It is late August, and returning teachers are now joining recently hired colleagues who had reported to the district for new teacher orientation a few days earlier. Following a half day of introductory remarks and a presentation of school district student achievement goals for the upcoming year, teachers reported to their schools for grade-level and subject-alike team meetings to prepare for the upcoming year. Ms. Richards, an experienced teacher in the district, is meeting Mrs. Anjette Greer for the first time. Mrs. Greer is a new teacher who has just arrived for her first meeting with a veteran teacher.
>
> "Welcome to North Arlington Middle School. I'm Susan Richards. Did you enjoy the orientation week for new teachers? When I first arrived here 7 years

ago, the orientation went on forever. I hope you had a better experience," Ms. Richards said.

"Well, hi, I'm Anjette Greer. It's a pleasure to meet you, Susan. Actually, I liked the orientation. It was very informative and considerate of our needs as new teachers. About a half hour ago we were directed to go to our schools for grade-level and common-assignment team meetings. Is this where the seventh-grade mathematics team meeting is to be held?" she asked.

"Yes it is, and I hope we won't overwhelm you with our rather busy agenda. We will be discussing student achievement on the Alabama Reading and Math Test (ARMT) to see how our incoming students performed with respect to sixth-grade math standards last year. We will be particularly interested in student foundational skills compared to the standards we need to achieve in the first 9-week period of our pacing calendar," Susan said.

"We learned about pacing calendars during orientation," Anjette said, "but I haven't reviewed any curriculum materials for my teaching assignment just yet."

"Have you received the new Alabama edition of our seventh-grade math text and a copy of the district curriculum guide?" Susan asked. "The guide includes the pacing calendar, the Alabama Math Standards we are to achieve in each 9-week assessment period, and information about the benchmark assessments we administer at the end of each period."

"Yes," responded Mrs. Greer. "I have all those items, though I am not too sure I understand the assessment system just yet."

"Well, first things first," answered Ms. Richards. "Our students start tomorrow, and Wednesday we will be administering a common assessment based on critical sixth-grade standards. This diagnostic test is designed to assess student readiness to achieve seventh-grade math standards. If students display a pattern of weakness on any of the critical sixth-grade standards, we know the essential material that must be reviewed before we move forward with the seventh-grade standards. We don't have much time for review because we also must achieve certain seventh-grade standards before the close of the first assessment period." She continued, "On Thursday of next week, we will all meet again to look at the results of the sixth-grade essential standards test and conduct our first planning session. At that time we will look at samples of student work from last year that demonstrated good understanding of the first two seventh-grade standards we are to achieve."

"This is all so new to me," said Mrs. Greer. "I didn't learn about standards assessment in my teacher training program."

"That's okay," responded Mrs. Richards. "Our system is still new, and many teachers are adjusting to it. We will all work together to figure this out. Don't worry about a thing. The district is very concerned about student performance on the ARMT, and we are getting a lot of support for collaborative planning and assessment in professional development sessions," she concluded, as other teachers approached her room for the start of the first seventh-grade math teachers' meeting of the year.

The distinctions between Mrs. Holyfield's preassessment activities in the first vignette and the activities described by Mrs. Richards in the second vignette should be evident.

Mrs. Holyfield worked in isolation as she reviewed student achievement data filed away in the principal's office. By contrast, Mrs. Richards describes a variety of activities that will be conducted by the seventh-grade math teachers working collaboratively. Additionally, Mrs. Holyfield focused her attention on individual students and their prior academic performance. As an elementary school teacher, she would get to know these students at a level not reached by secondary school teachers, who must teach many more students for relatively brief periods of time during the course of a school day. Mrs. Holyfield wanted to know the academic nature of each of her students, their achievement records, relative abilities, personalities, and any other attributes relevant to forming a healthy, motivated, and successful fourth-grade class.

Although Mrs. Richards cares for her students and wants to nurture their growth and development as young adolescents, she is primarily focused on their successful achievement of mathematics skills and principles for ultimate success in higher mathematics, especially algebra. Furthermore, Mrs. Richards teaches three classes of seventh-grade math and two classes of prealgebra for eighth-grade students for a total of 137 students. She does not have the time to get to know and understand her students as well as Mrs. Holyfield will know her students because she has five times the number of students to teach.

When Mrs. Richards examines student cumulative records, she attempts to identify differentiated learning goals for her students with special needs. One of her classes has many English language learners, and she will need to make accommodations for these students as well as those with disabilities. In some schools, information about special learning goals and recommended instructional strategies for students with special needs are communicated to teachers by a special education teacher or school counselor. For the most part, Mrs. Richards is concerned with students' mathematics achievement and does so by identifying patterns of relative strength and underperformance across all 137 students. She identifies the patterns through the use of a well-designed assessment system focused on the achievement of critical state mathematics content standards, in particular, and comprehensive readiness for algebra, in general. By the time Mrs. Richards concludes her preinstructional assessment, she will have identified the special-needs students in each of her classes. Furthermore, she will arrange meetings with special education professionals in her school or district who can tell her how she can best address these students' needs. She will also know those students in each class who have not met critical state content standards in the sixth grade. Finally, she will have identified areas of general weakness in the sixth-grade curriculum that need to be reviewed and developed prior to moving forward with the seventh-grade mathematics curriculum.

Another distinction between Mrs. Holyfield's circumstances and those of Mrs. Richards is the focus on student achievement of state curriculum standards as a key indicator of learning. The regulations of NCLB make schools and districts accountable for student achievement of state curriculum standards. Since the passage of this law, states have intensively assessed student achievement of the standards at the end of the year through state standards tests (Linn, Baker, & Betebenner, 2002). In recent years many school districts have installed other assessment activities in an effort to prepare their students for success with state exams. One of these activities is the use of assessment results obtained from the state testing program to improve the achievement of state standards in subsequent years.

In school districts across the country, administrators and curriculum leaders are analyzing test reports received in late summer (O'Shea, 2005). They provide teachers with this information at the beginning of the year for use in improving instruction for the incoming classes. Ms. Richards and Mrs. Greer will be examining the test results for incoming seventh-grade students to assess the extent to which those students achieved critical sixth-grade standards. The group of seventh-grade math teachers will also probably want to know how their students in last year's seventh grade performed to improve instruction from that perspective. In all this activity, Ms. Richards and Mrs. Greer are relying on the ability of the state standards exam to provide them with information they can use to adjust instructional planning, teaching, and student evaluation activities. What is the nature of these state standards exams, and how can teachers use the information they provide to guide their instructional planning? How do these exams differ from the standardized exam that Mrs. Holyfield used in her preinstructional assessment activities?

PREINSTRUCTIONAL ASSESSMENT AND STATE STANDARDS ACHIEVEMENT

Due to NCLB, all public schools must demonstrate adequate yearly progress in measures of student achievement on state standards exams. Federal law requires states and schools to track the progress of students from various ethnic and ability groupings from year to year. The goal is for all students to perform at a proficient level by 2014 (Nichols, Glass, & Berliner, 2005). To comply with the new law, each state adopted a testing program specifically designed to measure student achievement of state curriculum standards. Tests that measure student achievement of specified knowledge and skills described in the state-adopted curriculum standards are called standards tests. As stated earlier, the similarity in name between standards tests and standardized tests masks their differences. It is important to understand standards tests and how they can be used in preinstructional assessment because school districts are increasingly using them for these purposes. Teachers are playing a key role in using analyses of standards test results to plan their instruction for the school year (DuFour, 2004).

Standards tests may consist of a variety of item types, but multiple-choice questions are the dominant form. States with large economies and many students have contracted publishing companies to develop tests designed to measure student achievement of the state's standards. Company test experts are to write test questions designed to measure student achievement of the content and skills of the state's curriculum standards. Before test questions are written, decisions must be made regarding which specific standards will be tested in any given year. Most states have far too many standards to be assessed in one test session, so the publishing company, under state direction, must identify the particular standards that will be tested in any one year (Marzano & Kendall, 1998). In some states, information about standards likely to be tested is communicated on the state department of education's website. States vary in the extent to which they disclose information about standards likely to be tested. For instance, the Commonwealth of Virginia released entire test results from prior years and rather specific information about standards likely to be tested. The state board of education in California, on the other hand, insists that all standards are of equal value, and the board will not share information that would lead to the inference that some standards are more likely to be tested than others. In California only a few sample test items are released after testing is completed.

After the standards test is developed, it is evaluated for its effectiveness through trial administrations. A determination is made regarding the percentage of items students must answer correctly to demonstrate a proficient understanding of the standards. Often, other gradations of achievement are also labeled, which may include "far below basic," "basic," "proficient," and "advanced." The state uses a formula to determine if a school is making adequate yearly progress, which is usually dependent on the percentage of students in each of various ethnic or special-needs groups that are achieving a minimally acceptable level of performance, usually defined as "proficient." When test development is finished and states begin to administer standards tests in language arts, mathematics, and other subjects in grades 3 through 8, score reports are made available to school districts. These reports can be analyzed by a school district assessment coordinator to show teachers how last year's student performed in each of the standards, or sets of related standards, that were tested. With this information in hand, teachers like Ms. Richards and Mrs. Greer can make adjustments in their teaching to increase the number of students in their classes obtaining proficient and advanced scores. If the teachers in the school are successful in obtaining high scores, then the school can avoid sanctions for underperformance. State exams that are developed from content and skill statements of curriculum standards and for which a certain measure of correct items constitutes a proficient performance are examples of **criterion-referenced tests**. After the testing company and the state authority determine the percentage of correct items needed to meet a rating of proficient, then that percentage becomes the criterion measure of proficiency for students who take the test statewide.

It is important to note the distinction between state standards tests and norm-referenced standardized tests. Recall that norm-referenced tests compare one student's performance to that of a reference group. When norm-referenced tests are used by school districts, they identify each student's performance in relation to a national, state, or school district group. Students are declared to be above a certain percentile, above average, in the top 10% of all students, or in some other position relative to the reference group.

Criterion-referenced scores of state standards tests do not compare one student's performance with that of a group of students. They relate the student's performance to a predetermined level of mastery often expressed as a percentage of items correct in a given section of the exam. When criterion-referenced state standards tests are used to measure student learning, reports of student performance are stated in terms of student understanding of a body of knowledge, not in terms of a student's performance in relation to that of other students. This is an inherently more content-valid measure of subject matter achievement than is the case for norm-referenced tests.

Criterion-referenced state standards tests have a substantial advantage over more traditionally used standardized tests when measuring or predicting student achievement. State standards tests measure a student's attainment of mastery, or proficiency, in the subject matter of the standards that are presumably taught in the classroom. Under ideal circumstances, all students in a classroom will be expected to meet the criterion percentage of correct items deemed proficient or perhaps even advanced. There is no need to identify students who are below average when everyone is proficient or advanced. When criterion-referenced standards tests are used to assess student learning, students are not being compared in a competitive way to their peers, which is the case with standardized tests. As educators, we should be more interested in the specific knowledge and skills that our students attain in relation to the curriculum that is taught. If all our students learn the material that is expected of them, they should be rewarded for their efforts. Teachers who use comparative assessment, on the other hand, grade students on a bell curve, awarding students who perform relatively well with high grades and students who answer relatively fewer questions correctly with a low grade. The unfairness of this process becomes evident when students in a highly advanced class all score well on an exam. In this situation, it would be foolish to provide grades of "D" or "F" to students who happen to score below average simply because of their relative position in the distribution of test scores, when an analysis would reveal that they have impressive knowledge of the subject matter.

Benefits of a Standards-Based Educational System

The current focus on curriculum standards provides an opportunity to set student learning expectations and measure their achievement on the basis of what is taught. If the standards are taught in classrooms, then criterion-referenced standards tests inform teachers of their students' success in learning the content actually taught to them. Nationally normed standardized test items, by contrast, measure knowledge and skills that are thought to be covered in schools across the nation, and test items are written with the express purpose of discriminating knowledge among below average and above average performers. A nationally normed exam will likely include many items that were not taught in class and are not included in the standards of the state in which the test is actually administered. In these settings, advantaged students who have access to knowledge and skills not taught in class but likely to appear on a nationally normed test are at an unfair advantage over disadvantaged students who do not come from enriched backgrounds and are lacking broadly based life experiences. For this reason, nationally normed standardized tests identify student differences in learning both in and out of the classroom and perpetuate the achievement gap between rich and poor students. Standards tests, on the other hand, are intended to assess only the content that is conveyed in a standards-based curriculum. This limitation in the domain of knowledge tested provides all students who attend class regularly with equal access to the knowledge that appears on these high-stakes exams. Unfortunately, this idealized situation is only realizable in those states that contract with a publishing company to develop a test that includes only items that are developed from state standards. In many states with small populations and economies, funds are not available to develop a test from the standards. In these settings, a different method of assessing state standards is used that relies on nationally normed standardized tests that are available for purchase at relatively low cost compared to the development of a criterion-reference state standards test.

Some less-wealthy states use a different approach to assessing student progress with the standards that makes it difficult for teachers to identify the standards their students have mastered (Firestone, Monfils, & Schorr, 2004). In these settings, the state education authority asks a test publishing company to identify test items in an existing standardized test that seem to measure content and skills included in their state's standards. In some cases, the state may ask the publishing company to augment the test with additional items if the currently available standardized test does not have any items aligned with certain standards that need to be assessed. When students take these exams, they will be encountering test questions on the nationally normed test that are not derived from their state standards, items that are topically aligned to the standards, and others that may actually have been written from the standards. We can imagine that a student who has learned their standards content well will respond quite differently to these varied items. It is unfortunate that this practice persists, but limitations in funding for state testing programs lead some states to use a nationally normed standardized test to measure state standards.[2]

Today's teacher needs to be aware of the methods used to develop their state standards assessment because those methods substantially affect how the test is used to interpret student learning. Information about the standards testing program in any state can be found by reviewing documents pertaining to the system on the website of the state's department of education. A brief review will reveal whether the state's test is a criterion-reference exam derived from state standards or a standardized test with aligned or augmented items. If the state's standards assessment system is based on modified use of a standardized test, its effective use by teachers comes from understanding how students performed on aligned or augmented items, for only these items are linked to the content of the state standards. The state's website should provide information for identifying augmented or aligned items.

AN INTRODUCTION TO BENCHMARK ASSESSMENT

In many school districts, annual testing programs have been developed to guide students to success on the spring state standards exams. These programs expect teachers to administer common exams throughout the school year that include test items similar to those students will encounter on the spring exam. Often, the school year is divided into 9-week intervals that culminate with the administration of a standards-based common exam sometimes referred to as a benchmark exam (Rothman, 2002). Items on the test are intended to measure student achievement of skills and content of selected standards covered within the 9-week episode. The test items may include some questions that appeared on prior administrations of the state standards exam and were subsequently released on a state department of education web page. When teachers plan together at the start of the school year, they can review recently released test items from the prior administration of the state standards tests and select items they may wish to include on the common assessment at the end of the first 9-week period. The items to be identified should be derived from standards that will be conveyed during the first 9-week period (O'Shea, 2005).

Teachers will also be concerned about student retention of information taught in the prior grade. Recall from the second vignette that Ms. Richards expressed concern for student understanding of sixth-grade standards now that students were about to begin seventh grade. In that vignette, she explained to Mrs. Greer that assessment of student mastery of sixth-grade standards would help them identify the content and skills of the sixth grade that would have to be reviewed before students progressed into the seventh-grade curriculum. Given that each grade's curriculum sets the foundation for learning in subsequent grades, student mastery of sixth-grade standards is a prerequisite for student success with seventh-grade standards. In addition to concerns for student retention of sixth-grade standards, teachers will want to know how last year's seventh-grade students performed on the standards test. In particular, they will want to know the test items that large numbers of students missed and review the curriculum and teaching plans regarding standards that caused difficulty for students on the state standards exams. If some of the state standards test items assessed content taught in the first 9 weeks of the seventh-grade mathematics course last year and student performed poorly on one or more of the test items related to these standards, then the seventh-grade teachers should review their text, their teaching strategies, and the evaluation methods they used to assess these standards during the first 9-week period of the school year.

Our vignette of preinstructional assessment practices that are currently in development near Birmingham, Alabama, reveal the power inherent in a common curriculum and teacher collaboration that is harnessed for effective curriculum delivery. Certainly, the concerns about individual student performance expressed by Mrs. Holyfield in her elementary school classroom in 1998 are as important today as they were then, and teachers should continue to use student achievement data contained in student permanent record cards and other conventional forms of data as Mrs. Holyfield did then, exercising the proper due diligence she did at that time prior to the emergence of common assessments for the achievement of state curriculum standards.

PREINSTRUCTIONAL ASSESSMENT FOR TODAY'S DIVERSE CLASSROOM

We noted in our vignette of an elementary classroom in 1998 that the teacher, Mrs. Holyfield, was concerned for students with special needs and that she was aware of how the IEP was used to guide learning for students with various disabilities. We also noted that students with disabilities were part of the evolving contemporary classroom with its increased diversity when compared to public school classrooms in the prior century. Before we close this chapter on preinstructional assessment, we will develop a deeper perspective on specialized assessment procedures for students with disabilities and the rapidly growing student population of English language learners.

In our first vignette we presented an elementary school teacher's perspective on preinstructional assessment for students with disabilities. For the classroom teacher, this perspective focuses on the individualized educational program, or IEP. A new teacher, confronted with the expectation of using an IEP for each student in the classroom with an identified disability, may ask, "What is in an IEP, and how am I supposed to use it?" Other questions may include, "Who prepared this IEP, and what are their expectations of me?"

One year before Mrs. Holyfield conducted her preinstructional assessment activities in 1998, the government passed the **Individuals with Disabilities Education Act (IDEA)**. The central effect of this law was to mandate that students with disabilities be placed in general education classrooms and be provided with access to the general education curriculum to the greatest extent possible (U.S. Department of Justice, 2005).

The final amendments to the law include new requirements for the development of IEPs. The IEP is developed by a multidisciplinary team of individuals that has the skills and abilities to diagnosis learning problems and prescribe accommodations for learning on behalf of students who are referred by teachers, parents, or other concerned parties (Salvia & Ysseldyke, 2001). Additional legislation has also affected the way persons with disabilities will be provided educational services in public institutions. Section 504 of the Americans with Disabilities Act speaks to protections against discrimination and ensures that students with disabilities have access to assistive technologies that result in their engagement with the general education curriculum. These legal requirements place particular expectations on teachers who work daily with students needing accommodations in assessment practices, adaptations of materials and equipment to access the curriculum, and adjustments to instructional experiences that will include students with disabilities and give them equal opportunity to learn along with other students in the general education classroom.

Fortunately for beginning teachers, the IEP helps students with disabilities experience success in the general education classroom. A teacher will find important information in an IEP that will add significantly to other preinstructional assessment information obtained for other students in the general education classroom. This includes a description of the knowledge and skills of the student at the time that the IEP was written, learning objectives to be achieved by the teacher, annual goals to be achieved by all service providers who interact with the student, and most important for the teacher, a description of the evaluation procedures and the educational program for the student (Overton, 2003). Other important information may include the use of special equipment, including sound recording devices, vision enhancement technologies that help with reading assignments, and headsets that help students hear classroom discourse. The document may also specify learning goals to be achieved that are distinct from those of the rest of the classroom population. These goals are described as skills or abilities that a student with disabilities will be able to demonstrate at the end of a period of instruction. Demonstration of a skill may take the form of a written product, a labeled drawing, a selection of one alternative from among many, or the production of a specific behavior or expected performance in the form of a graphic representation, an utterance, or an accurate representation of a concept or principle.

Students with disabilities are best served when their general education classroom teachers work closely with special education professionals, including special education resource teachers, paraprofessionals assigned to classrooms where special needs students are taught, school counselors, school nurses and other health service professionals, and the school psychologist (Avramidis, Bayliss, & Burden, 2000). These professionals form a team to oversee the implementation of the IEP. Teachers can meet with team members who authored IEPs at the beginning of the school year. Professionals who wrote the IEP and will also be service providers to special-needs students enrolled in a teacher's general education classroom can help teachers interpret the IEP. They can clarify expectations regarding accommodations to instructional plans, accommodations for assessments, and adaptations in the instructional environment, including technology. Through partnerships with special service providers to students with special needs, general education teachers can lead special-needs students to successful achievement of the education program described in their IEP (Pretti-Frontczak & Bricker, 2000).

English language learners add to the diversity of the classroom, and they bring enriching dimensions as cultural and linguistic assets to the classroom community. Due to high mobility levels of English language learners who are children of migrant workers, it is likely that they will come to the school with few, if any, formal records from another setting (Lash & Kirkpatrick, 1990). For this reason, and the rapid proliferation of English language learners across all states, teachers should anticipate that English language learners may appear in their classroom without warning at the start of the school year.

English language learners, like students with special needs, benefit from federal protections. Federal law pertaining to English language learners derives in large part from a landmark court case, *Lau v. Nichols,* a 1974 Supreme Court decision that ultimately led to revisions of the Bilingual Education Act, which ensured equal access for all children to meaningful instruction in a language that they understand (Brisk, 1998). Preinstructional assessment for English language learners focuses on their ability to understand the content of the state curriculum standards that are to be achieved by all students. Special assessment tools, in the form of large-scale assessments that gauge the English language arts skills of these learners, are used to identify the setting where students will be best served. The Language Assessment Scales (LAS), published by CTB-McGraw-Hill, is an example of an assessment used by schools to determine the proper placement of students in various levels of bilingual education or English as a second language programs, to assess their growth and development in these programs, and to determine when a student is ready to advance to mainstream classrooms.

In states where English language learners constitute a large segment of the overall student population, standards for English language acquisition are established across the state that can be applied from setting to setting within the state and thereby address the student mobility problem. California's English Language Development Standards describe effective student use of the four English language arts at various grade levels where those skills will be applied. The standards grounded the development of the California English Language Development test, which is used to determine whether students are appropriately placed and making progress toward grade-level competency in the use of English language skills.

When teachers begin their school year preparations, they will want to know how to interpret assessments of language skills for their English language learners. This task calls for specialized training, not always offered in preservice programs. Typically, schools that enroll many English language learners have professionals on staff with expertise in the use of assessments of English language development and the use of instructional methods that help students understand instruction and grow in their English language skills. General education teachers should seek assistance from these professionals as they learn to interpret language proficiency assessments and modify their instruction to accommodate these learners.

Summary

Preinstructional assessment is an often-neglected component of preparations for teaching at the beginning of the academic year. If properly conducted, this activity can contribute significantly to student academic success during the first days of the year that can then be sustained until the close of the school year in June. Preinstructional assessment serves a number of important purposes that contribute to student success early in the academic year. These include

- Assessing student readiness for grade-level instruction
- Affirming student understanding of prerequisite information for content soon to be introduced
- Identifying students with special needs and the resources available to serve them
- Connecting with student prior experiences and finding other opportunities to motivate student learning
- Identifying class subgroups in need of remediation

Conventional resources that aid preinstructional assessment are often located centrally, perhaps in the principal's office, and they consist of student performance reports and achievement test scores. In the past, norm-referenced standardized tests were a primary source of information about student achievement. These tests would compare one student's achievement or abilities in relation to the achievement and abilities of a large population of similar students. In recent years, criterion-referenced state standards tests have dominated large-scale student assessment programs. Standards-based criterion-referenced exams compare a student performance within the curriculum to state-established learning goals derived from state curriculum standards. In recent years, the accountability measures associated with state curriculum standards have provided new forms of assessment that help teachers understand student mastery of the content and skills that form the foundation of the curriculum for the current academic year. A new teacher interested in preinstructional assessment might look for student achievement information by investigating the following data sources:

- Large-scale norm-referenced standardized achievement tests used by the school district

- State standards-based criterion-referenced examinations

- Student permanent record cards, including grades recorded in the prior academic year

- Teacher commentary about student abilities, motivations, and achievements

- Assessment of English language acquisition abilities for students who are English language learners

- Individualized educational programs (IEPs) of students with special needs

Teachers should take steps to avoid the influence of bias and inaccurate measures when interpreting preinstructional assessment information. Anecdotal information should be viewed skeptically, and teachers should recognize that student maturation can make student records obsolete. The principle of triangulation, or the use of multiple and different methods to measure the same phenomenon, can introduce greater reliability to preinstructional assessment exercises.

Teacher collaboration related to instruction and student progress monitoring have led to changes in the way teachers work together to understand student readiness for learning. In some settings, teams of teachers with the same instructional assignment learn about student readiness to acquire new information across all classes of a given grade level or secondary subject area as they prepare learning goals derived from state standards resources. Preinstructional assessment practices can be easily acquired and practiced. They can contribute to a good beginning of the academic year.

Exercises

1. You are a new teacher to your school, and you want to request information about your new students from the principal's office. You have heard from other teachers that preinstructional assessment is not commonly practiced in this setting. Prepare a brief statement that you would send as an e-mail to your new principal and his secretary asking for access to your students' permanent record cards. Let them know

your reasons for conducting a preinstructional assessment. Hint: To be persuasive, you should justify the need for the student information in terms of the benefits that preinstructional assessment will provide the students.

2. Consider some of the questions teachers have typically asked themselves about their new students before the start of the academic year. Which of these questions properly justify the time and effort involved in conducing preinstructional assessment?

3. In the first vignette, which described Mrs. Holyfield as she conducted preinstructional assessment in 1998, we noted that the teachers demonstrated certain precautions in obtaining and interpreting student information. These precautions were intended to protect students from misinterpretations of assessment information and bias that can enter poorly considered assessment activities. Describe some of the activities Mrs. Holyfield conducted to ensure that students were properly evaluated through valid and appropriate methods.

4. Compare preinstructional assessment conducted by Mrs. Holyfield in 1998 and that by Mrs. Richards in 2006. What new information is available to Mrs. Richards that allows her to understand her incoming students' learning needs in relation to the curriculum they will be taught that was not available for Mrs. Holyfield? How should Mrs. Richards use this information to understand her students' learning needs with respect to the curriculum that will be taught in her classroom?

5. In 1998, Mrs. Holyfield used grade equivalent (GE) scores from standardized tests to understand her students' readiness to learn in her classroom. By contrast, Mrs. Richards uses state standards tests to identify student learning needs. Prepare an explanation of the differences between these two types of assessments and their relative merits in conducting preinstructional assessment for students. As you prepare your explanation, decide which kind of exam you would prefer to use in your own preinstructional assessment activities.

6. Mrs. Richards and her colleagues conduct a number of assessment activities collaboratively. The main reason for their collaboration is their need to achieve the same state curriculum standards according to a pacing calendar. Describe some of the activities that Mrs. Richards and her colleagues conduct together to ensure that all their students achieve state standards as measured by common assessments.

7. State standards assessments vary from state to state, and the resources available to help teachers prepare their students for state standards tests also vary. View the state department of education website in your state and find the web page information on state assessment of student achievement as required by No Child Left Behind. After you have reviewed the contents of your state assessment website, respond to the following items:

   • Does you state provide a criterion-referenced state-developed test to measure student achievement of state standards, or does it use a modified version of a commercially available standardized test with augmentations? Commonly referenced standardized tests include the Stanford Achievement Test (SAT), the California Achievement Test (CAT), and the Iowa Test of Basic Skills (ITBS).

   • Does your state provide electronic copies of entire state standards tests, or does your state only release a sample of test items?

- Does your state provide a directory of test specifications or a test matrix to describe the number of test items used to evaluate achievement of each state standard?
- Examine guidelines provided to teachers to help them prepare students for state tests. What resources are available, and do they seem helpful?
- What evaluative criteria are applied to student outcomes? What constitutes a "proficient" test performance? What other categories of student performance are provided?
- What kinds of test items must students respond to? Are item types other than multiple choice provided on the exam?

8. All public schools are expected to comply with federal laws that protect the interests of special-needs learners, but fidelity with the law varies from setting to setting. Interview one or more special education professionals at your school to determine the extent to which general education teachers are provided with helpful information. Will you receive the complete individualized education programs of your students with special needs, or just partial information? What support will you receive as you work to meet achievement goals of special-needs students? Who are the support providers of your special-needs students, and which of the support providers do you interact with on a regular basis?

9. Investigate the assessment system used to identify the learning needs of English language learners in your school district. What is the name and nature of the test used to measure English language proficiency in your location? Are achievement goals set for your English language learners, and how are these goals to be measured? What information pertaining to English language learners is available to you for preinstructional assessment? Develop a preinstructional assessment plan for your English language learners based on available information.

Resources and Suggested Readings

Due to NCLB, assessment and accountability are now consuming much of the energy of teachers and school administrators as schools seek to demonstrate adequate yearly progress toward the goal of 100% student proficiency by the year 2014. This continuing school improvement effort may catch the new teacher off guard and unaware of the extent to which test data now drives the school improvement agenda. In some states, statewide test results are sent to school districts by late summer, and they are available to guide new teachers in identifying school performance goals before the school year begins. In other states, test scores don't arrive until midautumn. In these settings, teachers do not have the benefit of planning instruction in response to the prior year's student test performance.

The further development of policy that supports the use of data to improve teaching and learning is described in a number of periodicals available to teachers. Beginning teachers can keep in touch with new developments in the nation and in the state as the current school reform movement continues to mature. The state affiliate of the National Education Association will keep teachers aware of state policy changes involving statewide assessment practices. Another good source of information for teachers is the weekly trade journal, *Education Week*. This publication monitors the development of policy and regulations at the national level, and it reports on significant state developments where they occur. Information about *Education Week* can be found at the website for the publisher of this trade weekly: www.edweek.org/ew/index.html.

References

Airasian, P. W. (2000). *Assessment in the classroom: A concise approach* (2nd ed.). New York: McGraw-Hill.

Avramidis, E., Bayliss, P., & Burden, R. (2000). A survey into mainstream teachers' attitudes towards the inclusion of children with special education needs in the ordinary school in one local education authority. *Educational Psychology, 20*(2), 191–212.

Bateman, B. D., & Linden, M. A. (1998). *Better IEPs: How to develop legally correct and educationally useful programs.* Longmont, CO: Sopris West.

Berliner, D. C., & Biddle, B. J. (1995). *The manufactured crisis: Myths, fraud, and the attack on America's public schools.* Reading, MA: Addison-Wesley.

Bohn, C. M., Roehrig, A. D., & Pressley, M. (2004). The first days of school in the classrooms of two more effective and four less effective primary-grades teachers. *Elementary School Journal, 104*(4), 269–288.

Brisk, M. (1998). *Bilingual education: From compensatory to quality schooling.* Mahwah, NJ: Erlbaum.

Butler, S. M., & McMunn, N. D. (2006). *A teacher's guide to classroom assessment: Understanding and using assessment to improve student learning.* San Francisco: Jossey-Bass.

Craft, H., & Bland, P. D. (2004). Ensuring lessons teach the curriculum with a lesson plan resource. *Clearing House, 78*(2), 88–93.

Darling-Hammond, L. (1998). Teachers and teaching: Testing policy hypotheses from a national commission report. *Educational Researcher, 27*(1), 5–16.

DuFour, R. (2004). What is a "professional learning community"? *Educational Leadership, 61*(8), 6–11.

DuFour, R., Eaker, R., & DuFour, R. (2005). *On common ground: The power of professional learning communities.* Bloomington, IN: National Education Service.

Dusek, J. B. (1975). Do teachers bias children's learning? *Review of Educational Research, 45*(4), 661–684.

Firestone, W. A., Monfils, L. F., & Schorr, R. Y. (2004). *The ambiguity of teaching to the test standards, assessment, and educational reform.* Mahwah, NJ: Erlbaum.

Hufton, N. R., Elliot, J. G., & Illushin, L. (2003). Teachers' beliefs about student motivation: Similarities and differences across cultures. *Comparative Education, 39*(3), 367–389.

Lash, A. A., & Kirkpatrick, S. L. (1990). A classroom perspective on student mobility. *The Elementary School Journal, 91*(2), 176–191.

Linn, R. L., Baker, E. L., & Betebenner, D. W. (2002). *Accountability systems: Implications of requirements of the No Child Left Behind Act of 2001.* Los Angeles: Center for the Study of Evaluation, University of California, Los Angeles.

Lortie, D. C. (1975). *Schoolteacher: A sociological study.* Chicago: University of Chicago Press.

Lyons, N. (1990). Dilemmas of knowing: Ethical and epistemological dimensions of teacher's work and development. *Harvard Educational Review, 60*(2), 159–180.

Marzano, R., & Kendall, J. S. (1998). *Implementing standards-based education.* Washington, DC: National Education Association.

Nichols, S. L., Glass, G. V., & Berliner, D. C. (2005). *High-stakes testing and student achievement problems for the No Child Left Behind Act.* Tempe: Education Policy Research Unit, Education Policy Studies Laboratory, College of Education, Arizona State University.

O'Shea, M. (2005). *From standards to success: A guide for school leaders.* Arlington, VA: Association for Supervision and Curriculum Development.

Overton, T. (2003). *Assessing learners with special needs: An applied approach.* Upper Saddle River, NJ: Merrill/Prentice Hall.

Pretti-Frontczak, K., & Bricker, D. (2000). Enhancing the quality of individualized education plan goals and objectives. *Journal of Early Intervention, 23*(2), 92–105.

Rothman, R. (2002). *Benchmarking and alignment of standards and testing.* Los Angeles: Center for the Study of Evaluation, National Center for Research on Evaluation, Standards, and Student Testing, Graduate School of Education and Information Studies, University of California, Los Angeles.

Salvia, J., & Ysseldyke, J. E. (2001). *Assessment* (8th ed.). Boston: Houghton Mifflin.

Stiggins, R. J. (2001). *Student-involved classroom assessment* (3rd ed.). Upper Saddle River, NJ: Merrill/Prentice Hall.

Thorndike, R. M. (2005). *Measurement and evaluation in psychology and education* (7th ed.). Upper Saddle River, NJ: Merrill/Prentice Hall.

Tomlinson, C. A. (1999). *The differentiated classroom: Responding to the needs of all learners.* Alexandria, VA: Association for Supervision and Curriculum Development.

U.S. Department of Justice, Civil Rights Division, Disability Rights Section. (2005). *A guide to disability rights laws.* Washington, DC: Author.

Vitaro, F., Tremblay, R. E., & Gagnon, C. (1995). Teacher ratings of children's behaviors and teachers' management styles: A research note. *Journal of Child Psychology and Psychiatry, 36*(5), 887–898.

Yinger, R. J. (1980). A study of teacher planning. *The Elementary School Journal, 80*(3), 107–127.

Endnotes

1. Individuals with Disabilities Education Act, or IDEA, is described at http://idea.ed.gov/.
2. Achieve.org is a research and policy development organization sponsored by several state governors and corporate officers whose policy work has included the evaluation of state standards assessments. Reports on individual states are available at www.achieve.org.

Chapter 5

Formative Assessment: Guiding Their Learning Throughout the Year

LEARNER OBJECTIVES

At the conclusion of this chapter, learners will be able to

▶ Describe the value of formative assessment to the teaching and learning process.

▶ List several purposes of formative assessment.

▶ Distinguish between conventional formative assessment practices and new practices that have emerged in today's standards-based schools.

▶ Use methods of formative assessment that follow directly after instruction.

► Use methods of formative assessment that are congruent with instruction.

► Identify areas of likely student error in understanding and matching interventions used to address these concerns.

GRAPHIC ORGANIZER

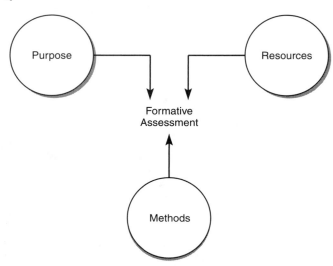

Then:
- Student observation
- Eliciting responses
- Questioning
  ○ Individual reports
  ○ Child responses
- Quizzes and exercise

Now:
- Collaborative methods
- Eliciting standards-based performances
- Standards-aligned proficiencies
- Student feedback

ASSESSMENT VOCABULARY

Affective response: A student-generated behavior or product that displays emotion or attitude in response to a teacher's question or behavior, or some other stimulus in the curriculum or the classroom.

Authentic task or authentic assessment: A curriculum activity or assessment experience designed to emulate application of skills and knowledge in formats or conditions found in daily life, business endeavors, artistic expression, or other forms of nonacademic human activity.

Benchmark test or assessment: A school- or district-administered assessment experience intended to prepare students for success on state standards

	exams or other high-stakes assessments. If rapid feedback is reported to teachers, benchmark tests can serve as formative assessment tools to guide further instruction before high-stakes tests are administered.
Choral response:	A simultaneous response by all students to a question or prompt, in contrast to sequential responses provided by one student at a time.
Elicit:	To evoke a response from students. Activities, questions, or directions can elicit desired behaviors or products from students.
Formative assessment:	Activities that elicit student responses that convey understanding of knowledge and skills as they are taught with the purpose of guiding further instruction to achieve instructional objectives.
Progress checking:	Activities teachers undertake in the course of instruction to evaluate student understanding of knowledge and skills as it is in the process of being conveyed. Examples are observation of student work as students are practicing new skills just taught.
Recitation:	A process of questioning students characterized by the teacher asking a question and selecting one student to answer. This process is repeated with the same question until a correct answer is obtained, or the teacher simply moves on to the next question.
Sponge activities:	Busywork and seat work exercises that do not intellectually engage the student. They are intended to preoccupy students during transitions or at the end of a period of instruction to consume allocated time not used to engage students intellectually.
Structured activity:	An activity intended to elicit student responses that can be formatively evaluated to guide instruction.

INTRODUCTION

In our overview of assessment in Chapter 1, we noted that **formative assessment** is used to guide student learning. Although it may be used at any time during the academic year, it takes on different forms and emphases as the school year unfolds. During the early weeks of the new school year, formative assessment builds on knowledge about learners gained during preinstructional assessment. When students assemble in classes for the start of the academic year, informal observations and responses to planned activities add to the teacher's perceptions of student abilities, motivation, and retention of content taught previously.

Each autumn, children and youth arrive in classrooms as mysterious young people with varied backgrounds, experiences, and histories of academic learning. Prior to the start of the year, teachers can use preinstructional assessment to obtain a general understanding of students' prior academic experiences, but this information offers only a limited insight into student understanding of facts, concepts, and skills that form the foundation of a unit of instruction or set of lessons soon to be taught. Formative assessment, by contrast, can guide the instructional process by informing the teacher about students' readiness to learn new material as it is being introduced. It can also be used to make adjustments to instruction in response to students' efforts to acquire new material. In this chapter, we will explore formative assessment as a powerful teaching tool that changes in purpose and methods as the school year advances.

FORMATIVE ASSESSMENT AS THE YEAR BEGINS: THEN AND NOW

When students enroll in classes at the start of the school year, teachers have an opportunity to observe them in their many roles as learners. Their responses to other students, to the teacher, and to the learning tasks put before them provide clues about their future performance in upcoming instruction and challenges they may present through the academic year. Teachers can arrange activities that **elicit** student responses for evaluation. The student responses form the data that, when analyzed, leads to inferences about student readiness to acquire new knowledge. Thoughtful consideration of student performances derived from formative assessments leads to decisions about the best course of instruction to meet students' learning needs (Sadler, 1989). The following vignette displays a teacher's use of formative assessment at the start of the school year as it might have been conducted only a few years ago.

A vignette of formative assessment in 1997:

We are visiting the classroom Mrs. Anna Whang, a third-grade teacher, as she begins a formative assessment exercise embedded in a mathematics activity at the start of the school year. She has decided to check on her students' retention of mathematics skills acquired during the final months of their prior school year. Her school district's mathematics curriculum guide describes the money handling skills students should acquire in the second grade. Presumably, her new students learned about the value of coins prior to their arrival in her classroom. As third graders, they will need this information as they learn to make change from a dollar bill in their first math unit of the school year.

Mrs. Whang has developed a task that will challenge students to use paper coins in response to her questions. She is interested in their ability to perform a variety of tasks, including (a) recognizing the value of different paper coins, (b) combining a specific number of coins of various types and determining their total value, and (c) using a specified number of coins to achieve a specified total amount of money. Her district curriculum guide indicates that students should be able to perform these tasks prior to making change for a dollar.

Mrs. Whang has created a checklist from her class roster that she will carry on a clipboard as she moves about the classroom. She will use the checklist to record observations as the children perform tasks with coins. The children are arranged in pairs to make the activity social in nature, and each pair has a bowl of paper coins to share. In addition, each student has a place mat consisting of the various coin denominations at the top of columns under which coins of the same denomination can be placed and counted. As Mrs. Whang moves about the room, she will and observe the individual students' ability to respond to her directions. If students are able to perform the tasks she gives them, she will place a checkmark next to the student's name. If students exhibit problems performing specific tasks, she will take notes about the observed difficulty. A portion of her checklist appears in Figure 5.1.

We observe Mrs. Whang's interaction with students as they become acquainted with the paper coins provided to each pair of students.

"In the middle of your table you will see a bowl of paper coins. Please take 4 quarters, 4 dimes, 5 nickels, and 10 pennies out of the bowl," says Mrs. Whang, as she moves about the room observing students.

"Now, place each coin in the proper column on your place mat, and count the total amount of money for each type of coin. I will be coming around to see how you are doing," she says, while stopping by pairs of students to record correct performances or make notes about observed difficulties. She makes notes next to students' names if they exhibit difficulty. She notes that Seth Bull is unable to find the total under each type of coin. He manages pennies and dimes correctly, but shows difficulty with nickels and quarters. As Mrs. Whang moves about the room, she looks for other instances of student difficulty with this task.

"Now please place each coin in the proper column on your place mat and count the total amount of money for each type of coin," she continues. Mrs. Whang is watching individual students handle the paper coins, and she is looking to see if they can place the proper coins in each column. She is also checking to see that they can count the number of coins in each denomination and determine the total amount of money that they have. As she moves about the room observing students and recording their accomplishments on her checklist, she continues to give them directions intended to elicit the behaviors she wants to observe.

"Place the following coins on your place mat under the columns showing each type of coin: two quarters, three dimes, one nickel, and seven pennies.

FIGURE 5.1 **Mrs. Whang's Checklist for Recording Student Responses**

Student Name	Identifies coin values	Can identify total value of a set of coins	Can produce a specific total from a certain number of coins	Comments
Alicia Adamo	_____	_____	_____	_____
Jerry Adams	_____	_____	_____	_____
Seth Bull	_____	_____	_____	_____
Sarah Cohen	_____	_____	_____	_____

After you have placed the coins in each column, write on your individual white-boards the total amount of money all the coins make together," she says, while moving among the pairs of students to make observations about as many students as possible and to record student understandings on her checklist. Mrs. Whang continues in this fashion until she is able to observe students complete the final task. For her last observation, she says to the children, "Now use no more than five coins to make a total of 57 cents. Please raise your hand when you think you have the right combination of coins to make 57 cents, and I will come by to check your work."

CHARACTERISTICS OF GOOD SUMMATIVE ASSESSMENT

We can see in our vignette that Mrs. Whang uses planned, formative assessment activities to gather information about her students' math understandings. We should note a number of salient features in her activity. The first is the power of the planned activity to evoke the specific student responses she wants to observe and evaluate. She knows that the unit she will soon be teaching rests on the ability of students to understand the value of particular coins, to add values of several coins to achieve a total sum, and to choose from coins to achieve a specified sum with a specified number of coins. Her assessment activity leads students to display specific behaviors that illustrate their understanding of these skills. Mrs. Whang has also planned an activity that provides her the opportunity to make observations and record data about student knowledge and skills.

Thoughtful planning of assessment exercises leads to student behaviors that are useful for evaluating subject matter understanding. But the use of **structured activities** is also needed to provide teachers with the time and opportunity to focus on student activities and make thoughtful observations.

It is difficult for a teacher to evaluate student understanding during a lesson if prior planning for this function has not taken place. As soon as a conventional lesson begins, the teacher must concentrate on the subject matter conveyed, immediate decisions regarding the implementation of activities, and the management of student conduct. How can a teacher make observations of student behavior and make a record of the observations in this hectic environment? If the teacher plans lessons that focus student attention on tasks they are to perform at their desks or in small-group interactions, an opportunity to observe students as individuals and in groups will arise. At these times the lesson is focused on student-generated activity rather than teacher-generated activity. During Mrs. Whang's assessment activity involving coins, students are focused on their own activity and not on what the teacher is doing. During these moments when students are preoccupied with tasks, either working alone or with other students, the teacher has an extended opportunity to observe student and group behavior and make a record of observations.

An additional feature of Mrs. Whang's activity is its relationship to learning expectations of the school district's curriculum guide. Mrs. Whang is interested in maintaining continuity in student learning from one grade level to the next. Her attention to the scope and sequence of the curriculum guide that describes what students should learn in mathematics at each grade level will result in the orderly accumulation of knowledge in a coherent fashion as students move from one grade level to the next. Prior to instruction, Mrs. Whang reviewed her district's curriculum guide to identify money skills that students were to acquire in the second grade. She then reviewed third-grade expectations with regard to money to identify the knowledge and skills she needs to teach to her students. Based on this review of the district curriculum guide, she was able to identify three specific skills, supposedly learned during the second grade, that formed the foundation of new skills and knowledge she was about to convey. Through her thoughtful interpretation and monitoring of her school district's curriculum guide, Mrs. Whang is making sure that her students are acquiring skills and knowledge at the rate and pace needed to ensure that students are keeping up with the learning expectations of the school district.

Finally, the coin activities that Mrs. Whang chose for her students are authentic tasks that ask students to display skills and abilities that can be used in everyday life. The tasks are authentic because real coins or facsimiles are handled by students, and they are expected to perform tasks with the coins that they would encounter in daily transactions (Valenia, 1997). In addition, students are responding to oral prompts provided by the teacher, which reflects what they might encounter when making a purchase.

Authentic tasks and assessments stand in contrast to conventional test or quiz questions that ask students to read a written prompt, select from alternative choices to find a correct answer, or provide a written description of a correct action, rather than performing the action (Butler & McMunn, 2006). Although reading prompts, selecting choices, and writing statements are appropriate means for expressing understanding, teachers should not rely on these methods to the exclusion of student performance tasks.

Real-life challenges do not consist of responding to multiple-choice items, filling in a blank space to complete a sentence, or drawing lines between one word in a column of words and its matching term found in an adjacent column of words. **Authentic tasks** and **authentic assessment** activities prepare children for future life and responsibilities because these tasks are either similar to, or identical to, tasks they will perform in daily life or in future responsibilities. When Mrs. Whang asks her students to identify their coins and determine their value, or when she asks them to add up the value of all the coins they have, she is challenging them with tasks they are likely to encounter when making a purchase.

The third task in her activity, by contrast, is not authentic. It is unlikely that students will be asked to make a purchase using a specified number of coins. Although this task is not authentic, it serves an important educational purpose by challenging students to solve a problem to meet two criteria simultaneously. This kind of challenge is referred to as a higher-order reasoning task (Chinn & Malhotra, 2002). This task requires students to use reasoning skills that include algebraic thinking. In the task, students are to use a certain number of coins to achieve a sum, and they are to achieve the proper sum with coins of specific values. They use reasoning skills to meet two conditions simultaneously, an expectation that anticipates reasoning called for in higher-level mathematics classes. In later chapters that focus on writing test items and constructing tests, quizzes, and other kinds of assessment instruments, we will keep in mind our goals that involve the use of authentic tasks and higher-order reasoning tasks.

We should be impressed with the thoughtfulness and care Mrs. Whang put into planning an activity that evoked specified student performances. As students generated the expected performances, Mrs. Whang recorded her observations on a form she prepared for this purpose. She moved about the room, asking questions and examining student responses as she wrote descriptions of student behavior, checked behaviors she was specifically looking for, and made note of student learning problems as she encountered them. The value of this effort, however, is only realized when she uses the assessment information to plan instruction for her students.

At the end of the day, after students have left and Mrs. Whang has the opportunity to review documents closely and carefully, she will examine the record of observations on her checklist to identify patterns of student mathematics knowledge. If several students seem challenged by an important foundational skill, she may choose to review these specific skills with the entire class. If, on the other hand, only a few students demonstrate problems with a particular skill, she may arrange a specific intervention for just the students who need it. Often, teachers' guides to text materials and supplemental resources provide skill building and concept building activities that can be used with small groups of children who need additional assistance.

In Mrs. Whang's situation, several students may have forgotten skills during the summer break. If this is the case, she may simply conduct a whole-class review to shore up student understanding of specific skills identified as concern areas during the assessment activity. As a result of the review, students with a poor foundation in the use of money will reacquire skills lost over the summer, and students who retained the skills will have them strengthened as a result of additional practice.

After Mrs. Whang determines the nature of interventions or supplemental instruction to be provided to students, one important outcome remains in the formative assessment process. Each student should learn from the assessment process along with the teacher. Therefore, steps should be taken to provide students with feedback about their performance on the assessment task. Each student will want to know if they performed the task well, but it is unlikely that they will understand the implications of their performance on their future learning efforts. Students who need additional instruction or a special intervention should know why these experiences will be valuable for them and how the assessment task performance relates to the decisions to provide them supplemental instruction as needed. If a student needs supplemental instruction to be ready to progress with the rest of the class, the student should be informed of the particular skill or knowledge to be addressed so that student effort is focused and effective (Stiggins, 1997).

In closing, we should note that Mrs. Whang's use of authentic tasks to evoke student understanding of specific operations involving money is a fine example of instructional practice that was current at that time. Further, her planned activity, her use of a recording checklist, and her reliance on authentic and higher-order reasoning tasks are as effective and appropriate in classrooms today as they were in 1997. In this new century, additional considerations have been added to the assessment process that reflect the reforms brought about by the standards movement, and we will examine these considerations in our next vignette.

FORMATIVE ASSESSMENT IN A STANDARDS-BASED SETTING

Formative assessment at the start of the school year or at any time during instruction has undergone substantial modification as state curriculum standards have emerged. It has also been affected by the emergence of teacher collaboration as a widely recognized component of the reform movement (Gable & Manning, 1997). Our vignette of Mrs. Whang in

1997 featured a teacher working alone to assess student learning in relation to expectations established by the school district's curriculum guide. In other settings, the teacher might assess student learning in relation to expectations described in the teacher's edition of a textbook. Today's teacher, by contrast, is likely to measure student retention of prior learning that is described in state standards and frameworks. A teacher starting the school year will want to know that the students have retained essential content and skills included in the school district's selected state standards (O'Shea, 2005).

Teachers with a common instructional assignment can plan their instruction together. They can collaborate on the development of assessment activities that measure skills and abilities essential to the achievement of their standards (Stiggins, 2001). In our next vignette, we will observe two fourth-grade teachers as they examine their state standards resources to identify skills and abilities to be measured through a formative assessment exercise they will each administer in their respective classrooms.

A vignette of formative assessment in a contemporary setting:

Janet Carlson and Olivia Guardino teach at La Canada Elementary School in Via Las Flores, California. As the only two fourth-grade teachers in the school, they share responsibility for the achievement of California's curriculum standards in language arts, social sciences, mathematics, and science. Both participated in the selection of critical content standards in California history for their school district. California history is a subject they teach at their grade level. Both teachers share a concern for student readiness to achieve fourth-grade history standards as their new students arrive at the start of the school year.

Janet and Olivia want to know if their fourth-grade students acquired map development and interpretation skills in the third grade. These skills are prerequisites of new skills they will acquire in their study of California history. In this vignette, we eavesdrop on these two teachers as they begin their first collaborative planning session in late August 2006.

"Janet," said Olivia, "I'm concerned about the number of activities students must perform that call for their application of map and globe skills as seen in the History-Social Science Framework for California Public Schools, in particular, this specific expectation that I found on page 75, 'Students use map and globe skills to determine the absolute locations of places. . . .'[1] As I looked through the framework's description of the fourth-grade standards, I noticed a number of standards that rely on these skills," she concluded.

"I couldn't agree more," answered Janet. "Standard 4.1 expects our students to identify the locations of various California places by latitude and longitude. Looking further at other standards, I noted that students are expected to identify the locations of various regions in California where certain topographical features are located. I also noted that they are to determine the location of certain towns and cities that are significant in California history."

"I think we should go to the California State Department of Education website and download released test items from prior years," added Olivia. "We should see if Standard 4.1 has been assessed recently, and more important, we can examine the test items for this standard to identify the nature of the skills students have been expected to demonstrate. We should also look for the key vocabulary they are likely to encounter in test items," she concluded.

Janet added, "I wonder if our incoming fourth graders learned how to interpret maps last year. I imagine they all know something about maps, but are they prepared to apply the skills identified in the frameworks to the achievement of the standards we will be working on early in the year? I hope they have some familiarity with maps, because longitude and latitude are difficult concepts to acquire and use."

Olivia, having examined suggested activities in the framework, proposed an activity that would help students recall skills and knowledge related to Standard 4.1 from third-grade curriculum. "Perhaps we can plan a warm-up task that will serve two purposes," she said. "We can refresh their memory about locating places on a map or a globe, and we can identify students who have not yet developed place locating skills. We could look at the frameworks to identify skills that were to be acquired in the third grade and develop an exercise from one or two of the standards they worked on last year."

"I looked over the third-grade standards this morning," Janet declared. "In third grade, students should be able to identify topographic features using symbols and features on a map, but they are not expected to use longitude and latitude or understand relative position of two locations on the earth's surface until they get to our grade level."

"Well, let's start by providing students with maps of the local area and see if they can recognize major topographic features," said Olivia. "We could think of some questions for them to answer that would call for the application of map interpretation skills. We could include some items that are similar to test questions about this standard that have appeared on the state standards exam in prior years. I hope they can identify major geographic features, including mountain ranges, lakes, rivers, and valleys," she said, building on the ideas mentioned by Janet.

"I agree that we should have some questions about relative position of certain features," said Olivia. "I believe the third-grade teachers followed the recommendations of the framework by taking their students on a field trip that called for them to recognize major topographical features in our area and to determine the relative position of those features using a compass. Perhaps many of them will still be able to tell the relative position of major features in terms of north, south, east, or west. Of course, they may have learned to determine relative position of real objects outdoors, and not on maps in the classroom, but I guess we can find out about that if we include appropriate questions," Olivia concluded.

"Well, maybe we can just pick up where the third-grade teachers left off by conducting our own field trip," suggested Janet. "We can take our students outside with an exercise that requires them to identify physical features near the school and their relative positions. Then we can have them attempt map drawing when they go back inside to see if they can represent what they saw on the field trip with symbols in proper locations."

Olivia agreed. "That's a great idea. Let's work on some questions together that will allow our students to express what they currently know as they work together to make maps of what they see outside. Then we will really know the right way to introduce map reading skills based on the skills that they currently have." After some further thought she added, "I think we better take a look at the specific standards that are developed for our first benchmark test this year and also at released test items for the fifth-grade state standards test in social studies. If I recall correctly, we need to develop our students' ability to identify lines of longitude and latitude for a variety of assessment tasks. I think they are expected to identify a point on a map that corresponds with a longitude and a latitude before the second benchmark test in December," she concluded.

Formative Assessment Has Changed through the Years

The distinctions between the assessment activities in Mrs. Whang's class as it was conducted in the 1990s and the activities planned by Janet Carlson and Olivia Guardino in a standards-based school are evident in their interaction and the issues they consider. First, the two teachers in this vignette collaborate in the development of their assessment activities. We can observe through their interactions that they build on each other's ideas to develop a common formative assessment activity intended to measure the achievement of skills and information of specific standards taught in the third grade. Further, they are developing a common assignment with a focus on the same district-selected content standards. It is clear that these two teachers have synchronized their teaching.

It is important to note the specific reference to a **benchmark assessment** by Olivia Guardino in the closing statements of the vignette. The benchmark assessment in California history is administered to all fourth-grade classes in the school district. Benchmark assessments are another form of formative assessment that guides teachers toward student success with state standards exams. When the benchmark assessment is administered and scored, the results will show teachers what progress their students are making in the achievement of state standards included in the school district's standards pacing guide (Herman & Baker, 2005). The school district's use of benchmark assessments for all students in a given grade level or subject area also serves as an accountability tool to ensure that all teachers are covering the same state curriculum standards within the same time period. This convergence of the curriculum on state standards achievement means that teachers will convey the same skills and knowledge within the same time period throughout the year. With these conditions in place, it makes sense for teachers to help each other as they work on the same challenges at the same time. Furthermore, they are using the same curriculum and state standards resources for the achievement of shared learning goals, and these commonalities provide incentives to guide their collaborative planning.

The use of state standards resources by Olivia and Janet is another difference between the two vignettes. We note throughout the second vignette that Olivia and Janet make reference to the History–Social Science Framework for California Public Schools, specific history standards that are included within the framework, released test items provided by the California State Department of Education, and the school district's curriculum pacing guide that determines the specific standards to be achieved and the sequence and pace with which they should be developed through the school year. The two teachers do not make much reference to the textbook or other curriculum materials that they may be using to convey the content of the standards. As the standards reform movement progresses, teachers are becoming less textbook dependent and more reliant on the skills and knowledge described in frameworks and standards to design the lessons they teach (O'Shea, 2005)

Despite these two substantial differences between the vignettes, they do have much in common. In both vignettes, the teachers are planning activities that will evoke student production of academic language, desired behaviors that display knowledge about subject matter, and production of student work that provides evidence of student retention of previously learned information. In both vignettes, reference is made to the use of a recording instrument, perhaps a checklist or form that helps the teacher record data about student performances as they are observed. What we do not observe in the vignettes is the essential follow-up with the data obtained through structured classroom observations. Hopefully, the teachers analyzed their results to identify patterns of student performance. If underperforming students are few in number, then additional assistance in the form of tutorial sessions, small-group activities, and assignments to be completed at home may be sufficient to help a few underperforming students meet selected standards. If, on the other hand, several students or the entire class have not met expectations, then reteaching skills and concepts with alternative approaches may be needed.

An additional feature we would expect to see in modern classroom-based assessment is the involvement of students in the assessment process. When students understand the reasons for the activity, the nature of the skills and knowledge that are being evaluated, and their performance regarding expectations, they are able to focus their efforts on improving their academic performance.

FORMATIVE ASSESSMENT THROUGHOUT THE YEAR: METHODS AND PROCEDURES

In the two vignettes, teachers planned activities intended to evoke specific student behaviors or performances. The behaviors were observed during instruction and recorded on a checklist or other type of form. Student work samples that result from the activity are analyzed after instruction to identify areas of relative strength and underperformance.

Structured activities are but one of several methods of formative assessment that are appropriate for classroom use. In this section, we will examine other methods that can be used at the beginning of the school year, as new units or material are introduced, or at any other time during lessons to measure student progress in acquiring skills and knowledge.

Informal Observation of Student Efforts

Informal approaches to student observation are another formative assessment technique. Teachers can observe student behavior at any time during the course of a lesson, and they do not have to design specific activities for this purpose. Opportunities to observe student understanding of subject matter can arise when teachers are presenting new information, often through direct instruction. As former and continuing students, we are familiar with direct instruction as the dominant modality for teaching in upper grades, secondary schools, and higher education. During direct instruction, the teacher is involved in activity intended to communicate information to students. While the teacher is presenting information, students are paying attention to the teacher's behavior (hopefully), perhaps taking notes, or responding to directions that guide students to important understandings as the lesson proceeds.

As new information or skills are presented, effective teachers include practice sessions to facilitate knowledge acquisition and skill development. The value of this kind of activity is grounded in principles of learning that support the effectiveness of guided practice in helping students learn properly.

WHAT RESEARCH CAN TELL US...

• About Practice

Learning psychologists have extolled the virtues of two kinds of practice in helping students retain skills learned in the classroom, but does this admonition play out in other walks of life? Moreover, which kind of practice leads to longer-term retention—mass practice or distributed practice? In mass practice, a newly learned skill is repeated over and over until it is fully habituated into almost automatic action. In distributed practice, the learner practices the skill with less intensity, but repeated trials are spread over days or weeks. Researchers Teresa Dail and Robert Christina (2004) reported in *Research Quarterly for Exercise and Sport* that golfers learning to putt proficiently found that distributed practice was far more effective in improving their golf putting accuracy than massed practice, an outcome that the student golfers predicted in the first place.

When students are acquiring new information and their understanding is only partially developed, one of two possible outcomes may result if the teacher does not check for understanding. Either the student continues to develop and organize understanding in an appropriate way, or the student may form misconceptions or misunderstanding that may last for an indefinite period of time. Incorrect procedures or misconceptions can be difficult to dislodge. By interspersing tasks for students to perform throughout the presentation of new information, the teacher is provided with an opportunity to guide their early efforts, make corrections, and not reinforce patterns of difficulty. This is usually done by directing students to work problems similar to an example just provided or apply a principle or analyze a situation similar to one just conveyed. As students begin work, the teacher moves among students, providing assistance as needed and looking for patterns of misconception or incorrect understanding. Typically, these episodes are brief if the teacher is in the process of developing student knowledge and skills. If extensive time were taken to observe each student carefully, the flow of the lesson would be disrupted, and it might not be completed.

Episodes of student observation can be reduced to a brief period of time by reviewing a representative sample of student work, perhaps just the work of four or five students. On these occasions, it is important to observe the efforts of a representative sample of students that includes struggling students as well as more successful performers. If the teacher finds that all students are making mistakes or are unable to grasp ideas just presented, then reteaching the material through the use of alternative explanations or examples may be necessary. If, on the other hand, only one or two struggling students are having difficulty, then it may be appropriate to continue the lesson as planned for the majority of students who are keeping up and understanding the new material as it is presented. The few students who are having difficulty may be helped during a longer practice session planned for the end of the lesson.

Informal observations of student efforts need not involve the use of checklists or forms. Nor do they involve an analysis of student work at the end of the lesson. Informal observations are conducted quickly and adroitly to sustain the flow of the lesson. They do need to be planned, and the results of the assessment need to be recorded in some form of notation that will come to the teacher's attention prior to teaching the same material again.

As a teacher plans instruction and encounters difficult skills and concepts students may struggle to understand, attention is given to providing clear explanations or providing opportunities to practice or apply the difficult material. It is during these early practice sessions, when student skills are partially developed, that informal observation should be included as a planned activity in the lesson. As new teachers become experienced, they will begin to recognize the most difficult concepts and skills for students to grasp. During lessons, they arrange for opportunities to make note of specific topics or skills that cause students difficulty and the nature of student difficulties that they observe. These notes can be made on lesson plans when students are doing seat work or after the lesson. If the notes are consulted prior to teaching the same or a similar lesson on a subsequent occasion, they will prompt the teacher to check for understanding and adjust the presentation to help students learn the difficult material. Just a few words written in the margin of a lesson plan as students are continuing their individual work or at the end of a lesson will serve as a reminder to adjust instruction next time and to include an informal observation of student efforts to check for understanding.

Informal observation of student practice of new material serves as a powerful guide to student learning if the teacher makes adjustments in response to student efforts and students receive immediate feedback regarding the accuracy of their efforts. As a teacher moves about the room observing a few students practicing or applying new material, individual assistance is provided, but the teacher remains mindful of patterns of student difficulty with the task. As the teacher becomes aware that several students are struggling with a common aspect of the lesson, the teacher may cease moving from student to student and return to the front of the classroom to inform all students of common errors observed, without indicating particular students who are challenged. Note that this opportunity to clarify misunderstanding arises only if the teacher is mindful of patterns of misunderstanding as they emerge.

As improper understanding or inaccurate performances surface during informal observation of student efforts, it is important that the teacher provides corrective feedback to the class. Corrective feedback should emphasize the attributes and procedures of a correct performance. It is usually not effective to discuss or explain incorrect procedures or discuss misunderstandings seen during observations of student efforts (Anderson, Reder, & Simon, 1996). Explications of incorrect information may be identified by students as information to be learned, leading to confusion rather than understanding. As new material is introduced, some students may become confused and not understand which of two different procedures is to be learned.

When observing a pattern of student difficulty in performing a task, it is better to say, "In activity three, be sure to follow these steps in proper order," and to proceed with an explication of the proper method, rather than to say, "I'm seeing people carry out the process in this manner," followed by an explanation of what some observed students are doing incorrectly. This creates a high likelihood that other students with only tentative understanding will learn the improper procedure that the teacher focused on.

Occasionally a teacher encounters feedback about student learning efforts that suggest teaching methods were not effective. Perhaps the teacher's presentation was poorly matched to the students' ability to understand or the presentation depended on presumptive understandings that students do not have. In these circumstances, where the majority of students are confused or simply not understanding information presented, focus on small details or particular corrections is not likely to be effective. The teacher needs to consider a new approach to the material and begin again. But what is to be done if most students are confused at the beginning of a lesson? In these instances, it is important for the teacher to prepare other approaches, which will only happen if the teacher has considered the likelihood that an initial strategy may fail. Early informal assessment, conducted before the lesson has progressed too far, can preclude instructional failure for many students. In addition, the foresight to plan alternative approaches should the first approach fail can save the lesson from becoming a disaster.

Eliciting Student Feedback to Adjust Instruction

By far the most common method for obtaining feedback about student understanding of new material is to ask questions. Effective teachers master this instructional technique in many dimensions. They use questions frequently, while maintaining coherence in their presentation. They arrange opportunities to move from direct instruction to student-focused engagement with new material and use these opportunities to probe understanding by particular students. They know how to distribute questions equitably and strategically when indicated. Most important, they use questioning to both guide and deepen the learning process.

A number of means can be used by new teachers to ask good questions, to use them formatively in assessing student understanding, and to distribute the questions among students or to strategically focus on learners of concern. Good questions are rarely thought of extemporaneously, particularly by beginning teachers who have not developed habits of questioning. Therefore, good questions should be developed during the lesson planning process and used at appropriate times in the lesson. Fortunately, resources are available to guide the preparation of good questions that disclose student understanding of subject matter.

Asking Good Questions   Experienced teachers are familiar with the taxonomy of educational objectives in the cognitive domain that was developed by Benjamin Bloom (1956) and characterizes various levels of sophistication in student cognitive skills. The means for eliciting the various levels of student reasoning through questioning are well described on a number of Internet websites.[2] A review of a number of these Internet locations will reveal appropriate prompts and the use of action verbs to guide teachers in developing questions that probe student understanding above the knowledge recall level and into such taxonomic categories as comprehension, analysis, and synthesis.

Over time, teachers can develop the mental habit of asking good questions extemporaneously during the course of a lesson. Until these habits and skills are firmly developed, it is useful for teachers to introduce prepared questions at appropriate points in their lesson plan and to have at hand, during the questioning process, a chart or table of question stems that reflect the various levels of Bloom's taxonomy.

As lesson planning takes place and the teacher considers salient features of new material, questions regarding the important features or understanding can be written on note cards and saved for use during class time. Alternatively, a list of questions can be constructed. The quality of questions can only be improved while planning the lesson. In the classroom, questions should not be posed that have a simple "yes" or "no" answer, yet these kinds of questions are typically the ones we ask of others in our daily noninstructional lives. Hence, we are generally in the habit of asking such questions with this simple recall format. As teachers, we find it difficult to break the habit of asking factual recall questions or questions with one-word answers. Good questions call for prior consideration before they are asked and can be written down for use during the lesson.

Distributing Questions across the Classroom

The distribution of questions to learners is another dimension of questioning skill. Many teachers tend to ask more questions of some students than others (Wimer, Ridenour, Thomas, & Place, 2001). This is an unacceptable situation because ignored students do not have their understanding of new material assessed, and they can become distracted or disengaged as they see they are not held accountable for the learning experienced by others. There are many reasons why questions are not evenly distributed in the classroom:

▶ The teacher may be only familiar with a few names of students at the beginning of the year and only calls on those students the teacher knows by name.

▶ Assertive students who raise their hands are more often called on than shy students, who are only passively attending to the lesson.

▶ Students who have the correct answer are more likely to be called on again compared to students who regularly provide wrong answers.

▶ Students closest to the teacher or in the front of the room are more likely to receive and respond to questions.

The effective distribution of questions is best achieved through supportive strategies and prompts used in the classroom during instruction. Typically, teachers will use their class enrollment list to identify students for questioning. Another method of distributing questions is to use a seating chart and to note checkmarks next to student names each time a question is asked in class. A seating chart helps the teacher remain mindful of the distribution of questions across the classroom space. As checkmarks accumulate next to names on the seating chart during the lesson, an alert teacher will note areas in the classroom that have not received a question. One or two questions directed to an area of the class that has been relatively ignored will pique student interest in the lesson and increase attentiveness at that location. More important, it will serve to provide a more accurate sample of students to assess student understanding prior to moving on with the lesson.

It is valuable to review the checkmarks on the seating chart at the end of a lesson. The pattern of questioning may provide clues to inequitable questioning by gender, ethnicity, or the distribution of students through the classroom. Reflective teachers are mindful of their questioning behavior and make corrections if they see unintended bias or disproportionate allocation of questions to particular groups of students.

Note cards with student names can be effective tools for both equitable and focused questioning. At the beginning of the school year, when students' names may not be fully known, the teacher can overtly select names randomly from a deck of note cards. When students see the teacher using the cards, they become attentive because they know their name may come up at any time. The note cards will help the teacher learn student names as questions are asked and faces of students are associated with the names on the cards and the responses given. After student names are learned, the deck of note cards can be used at any time of the year to achieve equitable allocation of questions to all students.

A deck of note cards with student names can also be used to ensure that some students, perhaps those who tend to be less attentive, are more likely to receive questions than others. In addition, the cards can be used to ask questions more frequently of certain students and to check the understanding of new material by students who are struggling as learners. To achieve these ends, the teacher uses a "loaded" deck of note cards. The names of particular students are placed on two or three cards and are randomly dispersed through the deck. When the teacher uses a "loaded" deck with student names, students with two or three cards in the deck will be called on with greater frequency than students in general. The deck can be used at any time during the school year as a mechanism to sustain either the equitable or focused allocation of questions. By returning to the use of the deck of student names, the teacher will avoid falling into the habit of calling on a favored few.

Managing Student Responses to Questions

Yet another dimension of questioning is the process of guiding student responses in a manner acceptable to the teacher. One immediate indicator of a poorly managed class is unguided calling out of answers by several students at the same time (Kounin, 1970). When students respond in this fashion, the teacher cannot make sense of what individual students are saying. Students will generally respond in this manner if they are not directed to respond in a more organized, meaningful way.

Effective teachers know that good questioning includes both the interrogative statement intended to measure student understanding and a directive statement that informs students of the manner by which they should respond. This example question includes these two elements: "I'd like to see a raised hand from someone who can state a rule or principle that includes all these examples we have been talking about." In this example, it is clear that the teacher will recognize only one student from among those who have raised their hands. By contrast, some questions are incomplete because they lack a guiding statement that describes the proper student response, for example, when a teacher merely states, "Who can recall for me the critical attributes of a rhombus?" Following such a statement, students may respond by raising their hand if properly habituated to doing so, or several students may call out answers that become unintelligible noise the teacher cannot interpret. This unacceptable situation provides the teacher with no information about student understanding in the course of instruction.

A more effective approach to asking questions includes the provision of an explicit direction intended to inform students of the protocol to be followed in responding to the question. Quite commonly, teachers will ask students to raise their hands if they believe they have the correct answer prior to being called on to respond. "May I see a hand from someone who can recall the evidence that suggests the Rocky Mountains are younger than the Appalachians?" is an example of an explicit direction for responding that precedes an interrogative about comparative ages of mountain ranges. Although this method of questioning is quite common, and it does lead to an orderly environment where only one student will provide an answer that can than be understood by the teacher, it does not lead the teacher to evaluate understanding of students who for some reason choose not to raise their hands.

 WHAT RESEARCH CAN TELL US...

• About Teachers' Questioning

In 1984, Meredith Gall published a survey of the research on questioning. Prior to its publication, several studies had been conducted across the United States in an effort to identify specific teacher behaviors that led to improved student achievement, typically measured by standardized test score results. The methods used by these studies were similar in design and referred to as "process-product" research. We might as easily refer to this work as "cause-and-effect" research. Gall's findings regarding numerous studies of this nature concerned with questioning revealed that approximately 60% of all questions asked by teachers were knowledge recall oriented, 20% were merely procedural, and 20% were higher-order reasoning prompts. Gall concluded that the value in the question–answer relationship depends largely on student ability to seek clarification of questions and to probe more deeply into the teachers' expectations. Ultimately, she suggests that students will benefit more from effective questioning if they are taught how to respond more effectively.

Another approach is for the teacher to ask a question and then identify a student to respond, having taken note of the distribution of questions in the lesson so far. If students are eager to respond to questions that do not include a direction for responding, the teacher can establish the manner of recognizing students before the question is asked, as in this example, "I need everyone to think about this question, and then I will call on someone for an answer, How would you explain 'manifest destiny' in your own words? (After some wait time for student thinking) Juanita, how about you?" In this example, all students in the class see themselves as accountable for the task of defining manifest destiny until Juanita is specifically asked to respond. This method of questioning is superior to simply calling on students who have raised their hands for two reasons. All students in the class are included in the group of possible responders, not just students who may choose to raise their hand, which lets the teacher assess the understanding of all students in the classroom. Second, by withholding the identification of the student until after the question is asked, the teacher prompts all students to listen to the question. If the teacher calls for a raised hand, or identifies students by name before the question is asked, other students in the classroom will know that they need not pay attention to the question because they did not raise their hand or their name was not called before the question was asked.

Eliciting Choral Responses

All across the United States, teachers go about the business of presenting information, followed by asking questions of students, one at a time. This method of questioning is referred to as **recitation** (Mroz, Smith, & Hardman, 2000). It is not an efficient means of assessing student understanding in the course of instruction because only one student responds at a time. If the teacher stops to ask questions of three students in the middle of instruction during a challenging presentation to a class of 28 students, no information will be obtained from the other 25 students. One way of overcoming this difficulty is to call for the entire class to respond to a question at the same time.

If some manner of student response can be devised other than having all students call out an answer at the same time, sometimes referred to as **choral responding**, then asking questions in the course of instruction can be both an effective and efficient means of obtaining information about student understanding. In most instances, teachers who use choral responding to assess understanding of all students simultaneously use visual cues or prompts to elicit a physical response that the teacher can see. After specific directions about the appropriate manner of responding are given, the teacher scans the classroom visually, noting the proportion of students responding correctly. If several students make an incorrect response, corrective action can be taken by using more conventional, but focused, questions of the students who did not provide the proper response, or remediation can be provided during a quick practice activity that will engage correct responders with additional learning while incorrect responders are helped individually.

Many teachers of mathematics have obtained small, student-sized dry erase whiteboards that they provide to each student in the classroom during a math lesson.[3] After a method of problem solving or a mathematical procedure is taught, students are asked to work an example on their whiteboards. At the conclusion of their efforts, the teacher asks all students to hold up their whiteboards and to reveal their written procedure or problem answer to the teacher at the same time. A glance around the classroom provides the teacher with evidence of each student's understanding as the lesson proceeds.

A number of electronic companies are producing student handheld responding devices that are used for student responses after the teacher proposes questions in selected response format (e.g., true-false or multiple choice). When each student responds, the teacher can observe a display that shows the number of students selecting each possible answer. A number of companies are providing this technology for K-12 classrooms.[4]

Another method for obtaining choral responses is to request a visual clue in the form of a gesture in response to the teacher's prompt. This method can be augmented with follow-up questioning, as in this example, "I would like everyone to look at each of the five foods items I have described on the board. Please raise your hand if you can identify which of the items is a good source of protein." After asking the question, the teacher scans the class to see how many students are responding with a raised hand to gauge the entire group's understanding of the question. Next, the teacher identifies one student to respond: "Susanna, which food item do you think is a good source of protein?" In this example, the teacher is using raised hands to measure the understanding of the entire class. This method is less effective than student use of small whiteboards, as described earlier, because it can only reveal misunderstandings by the one student who is eventually called on to answer.

Other choral responses include asking students to respond to a question or prompt on a piece of paper, followed by the teacher making quick rounds to examine papers, looking for salient clues in the student work that provides information about student understanding. If too many incorrect responses are evident, the teacher can go over the material just taught using an alternative approach. If only a few students do not understand, a practice session or after-class experience can be used to guide these few students to understand what others seem to have grasped.

Another approach to assessing student understanding through questioning is a compromise between individual responding and choral responding. Mathematics teachers will often call on several students in the class to write their solution to a problem on the whiteboard for other seated students to see. This procedure reveals understanding of the group of students that have worked problems on the board, but others remaining at their seats will not have their content assessed unless they are called on to comment about the work placed on the board by their peers. Teachers can address this shortcoming by assigning problems to students who remain seated while others are placing their solutions on display.

Small-group presentations are another example of a blend between individual and choral responding. This approach is particularly effective in assessing student application of understanding of a multistep task or problem. Bakari Holmes, a physics teacher in California, relies on this method to assess student understanding of principles of physics after they have been taught to the class as a whole. Following a presentation of new information to students, small groups of three or four students are asked to observe a phenomenon, analyze recorded data, find solutions to problems using the data, and prepare a brief presentation to the class. During the presentations, Mr. Holmes asks questions of students in the presenting group and in the rest of the class to assess understanding and promote attentiveness. Within a half hour, each group has made a presentation, revealing the understanding of the group as a whole and the understandings of particular individuals through the follow-up questioning process conducted by Mr. Holmes.

Asking questions and directing students to apply skills and knowledge as they are conveyed during a lesson are foundational elements of good formative assessment. Teachers want to know that their instruction is effective as it proceeds. If too much time lapses before student understanding is assessed, then students can become lost without the teacher knowing where understanding ended and confusion began. The following questions can be used as guidelines in using classroom-based questioning to improve instruction.

Are Questions Used to Inform Students about Their Progress in Learning?

Although it is important for the teacher to know that students understand the lesson as it proceeds, it is equally important for students to know that they understand the new material and that they are making progress toward the achievement of important instructional objectives. The quality of the feedback to students about their learning efforts is crucial in this regard. It should include very clear, explicit information about the attributes of a correct performance or correct answer when an incorrect response is provided. Further, the correct response should be related back to essential concepts and ideas that are being developed in the lesson or unit, so that students see the correct performance and its important features as a part of overarching principles or ideas that are under development. Finally, additional follow-up questioning should follow explanations to determine if students have gained correct understanding before moving on.

Are Student Responses to Questions Used to Modify Instruction?

If a pattern of student responses begins to emerge that suggests many students do not understand skills or content as it is presented, then the teacher needs to consider the approaches used in teaching or the nature of the curriculum that may be leading to confusion or misunderstanding. Taken individually, incorrect answers may lead a teacher to be concerned about student abilities or prior learning experiences. At some point, a preponderance of student incorrect responses or patterns of misunderstanding reveals that teaching practices or curriculum are not meeting students' needs. Changes to instruction informed by student difficulties are best achieved during moments of thoughtful reflection, which are not generally available during a lesson. Therefore, if student learning problems become evident during class time, it is important to take notes about the problems observed while their nature is clearly understood. These notes will guide the reflective process, helping the teacher to decide which of a variety of approaches (e.g., reteaching, tutorials, or additional practice sessions) will be successful in helping students with their difficulties.

Do Student Responses Suggest That Instructional Objectives Are Being Achieved?

If questions are tangential, or unrelated to content for which students will be held accountable, then students can become confused about what they are to learn and the material they will be held accountable for on future learning assessments. In our current reform environment, schools are held accountable for student achievement of state curriculum standards. Questions asked of students and tasks they are expected to perform should tell the teacher whether students are achieving curriculum standards. Important tests are usually administered to students after completing a unit or a set of related topics. Questions posed to students or exercises they are asked to perform as the unit and topics are in development should inform the teacher of likely student success on these important assessments used for grading purposes.

In the event that tangential, off-the-topic questions are included in the instructional process, it is important to clarify for students that the material under discussion is not a part of the instructional objectives to be achieved. Teachers can become annoyed when students ask the question, "Will this be on the test?" If teachers clearly indicate the relationship of content taught to larger purposes, and the form and content of assessments are used to evaluate attainment of those purposes, then this question is unlikely to be asked frequently. Students deserve to know before the fact how the material they learn will ultimately be assessed, why it is important to their lives, and what they are expected to know or be able to do that is measured by the assessment system.

PROGRESS CHECKING

Informal observation may include other activities that evoke both affective and cognitive feedback from students as the lesson proceeds. Cognitive responses inform the teacher about student success in understanding and interpreting new information. **Affective responses** inform the teacher about student emotional reaction to material that is being presented.

Students may react emotionally to the presentation of new information in ways that affect understanding. Within the same classroom are students who may be confused, frustrated, or even fearful of failure as new material is presented. Other students in the classroom may be fully confident and display a casual ease about the same lesson that leads less-able students to higher levels of concern and anxiety (Volet, 1997). Assessing affect goes a long way toward reducing anxiety simply because the anxious student perceives the teacher as sensitive to student responses and caring about students who are struggling with new material. As prior students, we have all experienced the anxiety that accompanied the sensation of being lost and falling further behind as a teacher turned repeatedly to only a few very able students to gauge student understanding. Less-confident, and often less-assertive, students are reluctant to inform the teacher that they are confused and anxious when they see other students, perhaps a small minority of the class, confidently displaying understanding through quick, accurate responses. In these circumstances, the teacher's questioning behavior and exclusive interaction with the more able students is reinforcing the teacher's perception that all students understand and that the lesson is moving forward successfully.

Responses to questions and observation of students as they perform tasks can suggest the need to make midcourse corrections during a lesson or unit. Other strategies of **progress checking**, used less often than daily practice, inform the teacher about student and class progress toward successful performance on tests and major assignments. These activities, conducted occasionally but typically not daily, guide the teacher's decision making about lessons to be taught, materials to be used, and instructional methods to be applied. These strategies include quizzes that check student achievement of instructional objectives conducted weekly or perhaps more frequently.

Quizzes are particularly useful because they provide students with feedback about their progress in learning material prior to taking a high-stakes test. They are also helpful to the teacher because they serve to identify problematic areas of instruction in time to provide correction before a major exam. They are typically brief and easy to administer. If a few quizzes are administered intermittently within a unit of instruction, the teacher will have a good idea of relative areas of strength and weakness for the entire class, which can guide a successful review process before a test. The following suggestions may be helpful in using quizzes successfully from upper elementary grades through the high school years.

▶ Plan to administer two or more quizzes within a unit or other coherent body of knowledge, leaving time after the last quiz to clarify student misunderstandings prior to administering an important test. If a hypothetical unit takes 3 weeks to teach, then quizzes administered at the ends of the first and second weeks will leave time to review missed material and provide additional content prior to the exam. Ideally, quizzes will cover a substantial portion of the content that will appear on a major exam.

▶ The format and item types used on quizzes should be representative of the format and item types to be used on major exams. If students have experience with the tasks they are to perform on a test in a context that actually resembles the formal test session, they are likely to experience success with the test itself. This suggestion is particularly important in our standards-based world, where students take high-stakes standards-based exams in the spring of each year. If teachers examine released test items of their state standards tests and the content of the standards and frameworks intended to guide their instruction, they can include test items on quizzes that prepare students for these exams.

▶ If students encounter items on quizzes in conditions that resemble the high-stakes tests, then they will be prepared for success in the spring. Released test items and other guiding state standards documents demonstrate the test item format, test item difficulty, and content to be covered on the exams. If quizzes include items that are similar in format, content, and difficulty to exam questions that were administered in the past, they are likely to be comfortable with similar test items they encounter on the state standards exams.

Another approach to progress checking is regular assignment and evaluation of homework and class work. These traditional forms of student work, if of sufficient quality, can lead to inferences about student understanding of content before major exams. If skills, abilities, and knowledge important for student learning are developed through classroom presentations and exercises, then student class work and homework should be complementary to these efforts.

When teachers examine their state curriculum frameworks, state curriculum content standards, and released test items that undergird their subject matter, they will find descriptions of student work expected in a standards-based classroom along with test items and tasks students will be expected to perform that demonstrate achievement of state standards. Class work and homework should be developed from these state-level expectations and other teacher-developed expectations .

Throughout the United States, students spend far too much time completing worksheets that bear no relationship to state standards test items, authentic tasks related to the subject matter they are learning, or the use of information and skills as it would be applied in daily life or in the workplace. These time-consuming activities include the identification of vocabulary words in a matrix of letters called word searches, matching exercises where students draw lines between words in one list and corresponding words in another list, crossword puzzles that use the vocabulary of the lesson, and sentence completion exercises.

In truth, word searches and related puzzle format worksheets are used to entertain students with simple knowledge and fact recall tasks, and they are not in keeping with the goals of standards-based instruction or any instruction that reflects academic rigor and student intellectual engagement (Radford, 1998). These tasks, which are often referred to as **"sponge activities,"** lend themselves to effective classroom management by replacing rigorous, valid learning experiences with "edutainment."

Class work and seat work should be congruent in rigor and format with recommended tasks, skills, and abilities that are described in state standards documents and national curriculum standards. Ultimately, they should lead students to higher levels in reasoning described in Bloom's taxonomy. If we provide students with simple knowledge and fact recall tasks unrelated to expectations on major assessments, we are not preparing them for the accountability measures they will encounter at the end of instructional units, terms, or the academic year.

Student class work and homework activities should assess instruction covered in the day and should include opportunities to practice skills and apply knowledge through the completion of tasks that are congruent with anticipated assessments and authentic performances. State standards documents, including curriculum frameworks, descriptions of content and skills in the standards, and state-released test items provide teachers with guidance in the preparation of high-quality student class work and homework. Often, textbooks and other curriculum resources provide activities for students to perform, but these should be evaluated in relation to the learning expectations and task proficiencies described in standards documents before they are used.

Ultimately, well-written instructional objectives will guide the teacher to the development or selection of high-quality student work assignments. If the instructional objectives of the lesson reflect the learning expectations of the district curriculum and state standards, they will serve as a good guide in selecting or developing class work and homework. In addition, class work and homework tasks should be congruent with tasks that will appear on important assessments, and they should help students prepare for successful performances on high-stakes tests.

Students need to receive useful feedback regarding their efforts to achieve instructional objectives. Some teachers choose to grade homework and class work and include these grades in the determination of final marks. Other teachers merely make note that student work was completed. Regardless of the role that student work plays in determining grades and marks, it is important that students receive written feedback on their efforts as they attempt to achieve instructional objectives. Feedback about student work should include demonstrations of the proper performance expected, not just identification of errors.

One effective approach to guiding students to improved performance is the completion and distribution of a teacher-completed, correct assignment. These model assignments can be the basis for conducting a whole-class review of completed work. If time only permits the review of sample items before moving on to the next lesson, students will have a copy of the correct performance prepared by the teacher to compare to their own efforts at a later time. Teacher-completed homework and class work can be a valuable resource for students as they prepare for assessments.

Student self-appraisal and student interviews are two other strategies teachers can use to formatively assess student learning. As a unit of instruction is under development, the teacher can distribute a checklist of topics and skills already addressed in class sessions. The checklist should be prepared in outline form, reflecting the topics and skills of the unit. Students can be asked to place an appropriate symbol in a space next to each outline item already covered in class. These symbols will constitute a self-assessment of their need for additional development and practice with various areas of the unit. For instance, a "C" might convey, "I feel confident that I have fully acquired this skill or knowledge element," an "N" may mean, "I am not confident that I fully understand this skill or knowledge element," and an "S" might mean that the student has some ability to perform tasks related to the matching skill or knowledge element. When the teacher collects these self-appraisal outlines, a quick review can identify patterns of student concern for the content and skills that have been covered. If some items have scores of "N" or "S," then it behooves the teacher to address these topics in a subsequent class and to address misunderstandings before students are held accountable for the material on major assessments.

Student interviews can be very useful in probing student misunderstandings and difficulties with lessons. Typically, interviews are conducted with students who are not performing well with respect to the class as a whole. Interviews of this nature can be counterproductive and alienate the underperforming student unless measures are taken to ensure their success, such as the following.

▶ **Notify Parents and Other Stakeholders of the Intent to Interview a Student** Before the interview is undertaken, the parents or guardians of the student should be called to inform them of the reason for the interview and the specific concerns to be addressed.

▶ **Understand the Student's Perspective** Students are generally nervous and afraid when called to meet with the teacher about concerns with their progress in class. Every effort should be made to clarify the intentions and purposes of the interview before it is conducted. Students should know that you will be helping them with difficulties that are specifically identified. Admonitions about effort or attitude stated in general terms are not generally helpful.

▶ **Limit the Interview to a Small Number of Concerns** Students will feel overwhelmed and powerless to improve if the teacher identifies a large number of concern areas to address during an interview. If several concerns are apparent to the teacher, then the most salient or foundational can be discussed at a first session, and other topics or concerns can be addressed later.

▶ **Spend More Time Listening Than Talking** Prepare probing questions that focus directly on skill or performance areas of concern. Ask questions of a general nature about problematic content, then focus on specific concerns you have observed in that area. Provide plenty of opportunity to observe student efforts. Ideally, the student will be doing most of the talking.

▶ **End the Interview with a Plan for Performance Improvement** The student should leave the interview with confidence that follow-up activities will lead to performance improvement. These follow-up activities may include tutorial help, attending after-class help sessions, or scheduling additional follow-up interviews.

ASSESSING AFFECTIVE RESPONSES TO INSTRUCTION

Student anxiety and confusion are strong barriers to learning. Some confident students will ask questions and seek assistance when they feel lost or confused in class. Too many students will assume a passive role and avoid being identified as they fall further and further behind. If student confusion and misunderstanding are identified as they begin to emerge, the teacher can address these problems before they turn into despair and a sense of hopelessness. Student emotional responses can be assessed along with cognitive responses, and students will appreciate the teacher's concern for their emotional well-being.

Several formative activities are available that a teacher can undertake to identify anxious or fearful students. One of these is immediate, anonymous written feedback from students regarding their emotional response to the lesson under way. As a concept with

FIGURE 5.2 A Teacher's Student Affect Feedback Slip

Right now I feel.......
_____ Confident that I am understanding today's lesson.
_____ A little confused and in need of some clarification.
_____ Really confused . . . I may need some extra help.
Please write down one thing that is confusing or a problem right now:

complex or difficult information is presented, the teacher can pass out preprinted small squares of paper that can be filled out during a practice activity. Students are more likely to provide an honest, revealing response if they can place their paper sheets upside down and not put their name on the paper. As the students conduct their practice activity, the teacher can review the feedback provided while the students continue with their practice exercise.

Alternatively, students can provide affective responses to an entire lesson, and the teacher can pick up their response slips at the end of the class. Prepared response sheets can be distributed to each member of the class prior to the close of the lesson. An example of such a prepared reflection sheet is shown in Figure 5.2.

It is important to keep in mind that students generally do not want to convey to each other that they are confused, anxious, or falling behind in class. The means by which students are able to reveal their feelings about their learning efforts should reflect their desire to express this information to the teacher confidentially. Keep in mind that many students would like to describe their anxiety and concerns, but are hesitant to do so unless the teacher displays compassion for student learning efforts, a desire to listen to student concerns, and a willingness to support their efforts.

Summary

Formative assessment is the teacher's tool for ensuring student progress in daily achievement of instructional goals. Through formative assessment, teachers learn about students' understanding of subject matter for the purposes of improving instruction and helping students learn. When embedded in instruction, assessment practices provide teachers and students alike with feedback regarding the effectiveness of teaching efforts and student learning efforts.

A variety of tools can be used for formative assessment purposes. These include structured activities that elicit specific student responses, informal observations of student efforts during practice sessions, and questioning strategies that elicit both individual and choral responses. Teachers can check student progress with learning through effective use of quizzes, reviews of student work, and student self-appraisals of their own learning progress. Some indicators of quality to be found in formative assessments include the following:

- They are planned to guide students to the achievement of instructional objectives.

- In contemporary classrooms, they indicate progress in meeting curriculum standards.

- They evaluate student understanding of prerequisite skills.

- They prepare students for success with high-stakes assessments.

Student emotional responses to learning experiences can impede or encourage progress toward the achievement of instructional goals. Student can provide confidential feedback to teachers regarding their possible anxiety or frustrations with learning experiences through the use of specific instruments designed for this purpose.

In the standards-based classroom of this reform era, formative assessment assures the teacher that student are achieving the content and skills that will ultimately be assessed through high-stakes testing programs.

Exercises

1. Formative assessment is intended to be beneficial to both the student and the teacher. On a piece of paper, make two columns labeled "Teacher" and "Student." Under each column, list the benefits of formative assessment to the person in the classroom. Distinguish these benefits from the summative assessment used to establish grades and feedback to students after instruction of a body of knowledge is completed.

2. Review the vignettes about Ann Whang, Janet Carlson, and Olivia Guardino, which displayed formative assessment in the recent past and in contemporary classrooms. Devise a structured activity guided by their examples. Describe the activity, the student responses the activity should elicit, and the knowledge or skill understandings the responses would convey to you as the teacher.

3. Make two lists with the headings, "Conventional formative assessment" and "Contemporary formative assessment." After reviewing the vignettes described in exercise 2, list the features of both contemporary and conventional formative assessment that you are able to recall. After examining both lists, identify the new features that appear in contemporary formative assessment practices.

4. Refer to your state standards and frameworks and other curriculum resources at your state department of education website intended to guide teachers to state standards achievement. Describe a product or performance that a student could generate that would demonstrate achievement of the selected standard. Then describe an activity or prompt that would elicit the performance or product you have described.

5. Examine Bloom's taxonomy and the related questions that are available at numerous websites.[2] Devise two questions at each of the following levels of cognitive challenge to be asked in the classroom: knowledge, comprehension, application, and analysis. Select two or three of the questions and use them in the course of instruction, making note of student responses. Analyze the student responses after teaching and reflect on your success in using the questions you selected.

6. After reading the section on choral responding, devise a procedure to use in class that will elicit choral responses you can evaluate. All students should respond simultaneously and in a manner that conveys information to you about each student's understanding. Use the procedure in class and determine its effectiveness for conveying knowledge about student understanding of content.

7. Describe the testing and student assessment program in your district at the classroom, school, and district levels. Does the system represent a coherent layering of assessments that complement each other and lead students to perform well on high-stakes state standards assessments? Where do you see coherence? Where do you see inconsistencies that need to be addressed?

Resources and Suggested Readings

Richard Stiggins (1997, 2001) is a prolific writer and researcher on classroom-based assessment. Much of his work has focused on the learner's involvement in the assessment process. Dr. Stiggins describes student roles in the design of assessments and use of assessment instruments to understand their own accomplishments and learning needs. Throughout this book, note an emphasis on the relationship of classroom-based assessment to the achievement of state standards. As No Child Left Behind (NCLB) continues to develop and adequate yearly progress targets continue to rise toward 100% student proficiency with state standards, formative assessment is likely to focus on assessing student prior learning of standards for lower grades and student success in achieving standards for the current school year. In *Student-Involved Classroom Assessment*, Stiggins (2001) suggested a number of strategies for involving students in assessing their progress in learning, and these strategies can be adapted to the assessment of student learning outcomes linked to state curriculum standards.

One popular approach to link formative assessment to support state standards achievement is the use of benchmark tests administered by the school district following several weeks of instruction dedicated to the achievement of district-selected standards. Presumably, the benchmark test results can be used by teachers to adjust their teaching before students take state standards tests in the spring. It can be reasonably argued, however, that benchmark tests do not help adjust student learning as it is happening, which is an issue of concern to Dr. Stiggins. If school districts can provide teachers with immediate feedback following the administration of benchmark tests, then they can have some value in helping modify instruction so that students learn effectively and perform at high levels on high-stakes state standards tests.

References

Anderson, J. R., Reder, L. M., & Simon, H. A. (1996). Situated learning and education. *Educational Researcher, 25*(4), 5–11.

Bloom, B. (1956). *Taxonomy of educational objectives: The classification of educational goals. Handbook I: Cognitive domain.* New York: Longmans.

Butler, S. M., & McMunn, N. D. (2006). *A teacher's guide to classroom assessment.* San Francisco: Jossey-Bass.

Chinn, C. A., & Malhotra, B. A. (2002). Epistemologically authentic inquiry in schools: A theoretical framework for evaluating inquiry tasks. *Science Education, 86*(2), 175–218.

Dail, T. K., & Christina, R. W. (2004). Distribution of practice and metacognition in learning and long-term retention of a discrete motor task. *Research Quarterly for Exercsie and Sport, 75*(2), 148–155.

Gable, R. A., & Manning, M. L. (1997). The role of teacher collaboration in school reform. *Childhood Education, 73*(4), 219–227.

Gall, M. (1984). Synthesis of research on teachers' questioning. *Educational Leadership, 42*(3), 40–47.

Herman, J. L., & Baker, E. L. (2005). Making benchmark testing work. *Educational Leadership, 63*(3), 48 –54.

Kounin, J. S. (1970). *Discipline and group management in classrooms.* New York: Holt, Rinehart and Winston.

Mroz, M., Smith, F., & Hardman, F. (2000). The discourse of the literacy hour. *Cambridge Journal of Education, 30*(3), 379–390.

O'Shea, M. (2005). *From standards to success: A guide for school leaders.* Arlington, VA: Association for Supervision and Curriculum Development.

Radford, D. L. (1998). Transferring theory into practice: A model for professional development for science education reform. *Journal of Research in Science Teaching, 35*(1), 73–88.

Sadler, D. R. (1989). Formative assessment and the design of instructional systems. *Instructional Science, 18*(2), 119–144.

Stiggins, R. J. (2001). *Student-involved classroom assessment* (3rd ed.). Upper Saddle River, NJ: Merrill/Prentice Hall.

Valenia, S. W. (1997). Authentic classroom assessment of early reading: Alternatives to standardized tests. *Preventing School Failure, 41*(2), 63–70.

Volet, S. E. (1997). Cognitive and affective variables in academic learning: The significance of direction and effort in students' goals. *Learning and Instruction, 7*(3), 235–254.

Wimer, J. W., Ridenour, C. S., Thomas, K., & Place, A. W. (2001). Higher order teacher questioning of boys and girls in elementary mathematics classrooms. *Journal of Educational Research, 95*(2), 84–92.

Endnotes

1. Reprinted, by permission, California Department of Education.
2. Many different websites show Bloom's taxonomy with related prompts, including: www.teachers.ash.org.au/researchskills/dalton.htm and www.coe.uga.edu/epltt/bloom.htm.
3. Student dry erase boards for choral responding are available from The Markerboard People, 1611 N. Grand River Ave, P.O. Box 80560, Lansing, MI 48906.
4. Smartroom Learning Solutions Inc. and Turning Technologies provide products that allow electronic choral responding.

Chapter 6

Summative Assessment: Measuring Student Learning

LEARNER OBJECTIVES

At the conclusion of this chapter, learners will be able to

► Distinguish between summative assessment and other forms of assessment.

► List essential purposes of summative assessment.

► Describe the new role of summative assessment in today's reform environment.

► Describe characteristics of a reliable and valid summative assessment.

▶ Identify effective means for using summative assessment to improve instruction.

▶ Use summative assessment to improve student academic performance.

GRAPHIC ORGANIZER

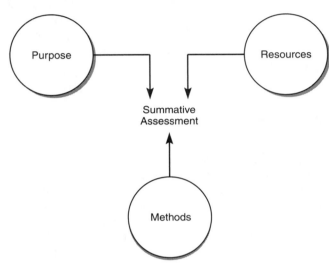

Then:
- Grading and progress reporting
- Teacher determined resources
- Multiple measures
- Reasoning skills

Now:
- Grading, feedback and instructional improvements
- Standards achievement
- Collaborative effort
- Preparation for state standards tests

ASSESSMENT VOCABULARY

Distractors: Wrong answers that are included along with the correct choice on multiple-choice exams. When well written, they can increase the reliability of the test and help the teacher assess student understanding of subject matter.

Evaluative criteria: The characteristics or properties of a student assignment or assessment exercise that will be used to evaluate the quality of student work.

Rubric:	When used in assessment, a scoring guide that matches evaluative criteria in relation to performance ratings. Rubrics contain descriptions of student performances that help the teacher rate the quality of student work in relation to each evaluative criterion.
Test item stem:	The question, or prompt, that precedes four or more alternative choices in a multiple-choice exam question.
Test-wiseness:	The skills and knowledge that students acquire from testing experiences that lead them to score high on tests in comparison to the performance of other students, who have equivalent knowledge of the subject matter but lack experience or skills in test taking.

INTRODUCTION

When teachers reflect on their experiences as learners through the years, they can typically recall summative assessment activities that caused them either great joy or great stress. These were activities that resulted in an important grade that may have affected marks they received in certain elementary grades or course grades they received in high school or college. Summative assessments are primarily used to evaluate student learning, and they usually include grades used to determine final course marks. These are the assessments that affect student attitudes toward school, teachers, and themselves as learners. They are also the assessments that society supports as a means to identify individuals who are qualified to pursue certain career opportunities or obtain licenses and authority to work in a trade or profession.

Although many of the quality features found in good formative assessments are also important in constructing summative assessments, they take on greater importance due to the consequences that can befall students because of poor performance when taking an exam, completing a major assignment, or performing a structured activity that is evaluated for a grade. These quality features include validity, reliability, and fairness. As former and continuing students, we can recall instances of unfair or inappropriate testing. Clearly, we want to prevent these circumstances when we use assessments to evaluate the performance of our students.

As students, we were probably quite unaware that our teachers used summative assessments for purposes other than assigning grades and raising our anxiety on big test days. In this chapter, we will identify the ways summative assessment can be used for improving instruction, improving the curriculum, and guiding student learning. We will also learn about new forms of summative assessment that are applied to the teaching and learning process in our new standards-based reform environment. State standards resources, expectations related to student achievement of state curriculum standards, and reporting requirements of federal and state governments have changed summative assessment dramatically in the last 15 years. These changes will be described in some detail to ensure that new teachers can succeed in schools that are at the forefront of the reform process.

PURPOSES OF SUMMATIVE ASSESSMENT

The most evident purpose of summative assessment is the evaluation of student work. Ultimately, the value placed on student work is communicated to others. First among those to receive the message about academic performance on a test or project is the student (Stiggins, 2001). If it is important for students to receive graded work, than it must have some relationship to other purposes than merely informing students about their progress. We expect some response from the student who receives a grade for completed work. The obvious response is increased or maintained motivation and effort to perform at the same level or a higher level than on the graded test or project. Therefore, summative assessment shares a purpose with formative assessment: to inform students about their progress in learning.

But students need more than motivation to improve their performance. They need to understand how they have performed in relation to some clear expectation, how they may improve on their performance in subsequent assessment exercises, and specific information about incorrect or unsatisfactory aspects of their performance that guides the student to improved performance in the future. When students receive specific feedback about their performance on an exam, with incorrect features explained, then the teacher is using summative assessment to guide student learning (Leahy, Lyon, Thompson, & William, 2005).

Historically, summative assessment has focused on comparing one student's academic performance with the performances of peers. If the student performed above average, a good grade such as "A" or "B" was assigned to the product submitted. If, on the other hand, the student did not perform at levels reached by peers in the class or grade, a lower grade such as "D" or "F" was assigned. In recent years, due to reforms brought about by the standards movement, grading by comparing student performances in relation to performances of others has lost favor (Shepard, 2000). By contrast, descriptions of student satisfactory performance in content knowledge and skill development, known as curriculum standards, are now used as the basis for evaluating student work (Guskey, 2004).

In a standards-based classroom, student performances are compared with those described in curriculum standards (O'Shea, 2005). Student work may be seen as "proficient" or "advanced" through these evaluations. Other students who do not reach the performance levels described in standards may have their work evaluated as "basic" or "below basic." In our current reform environment, students are informed through grades and marks about their performance in relation to a description of expected performances found in state standards. They are not merely compared with each other and graded solely on the basis of their standing in relation to others in their grade or class. Hence, a new purpose of summative assessment is to inform students about their academic performance in relation to expectations held for all students (Stiggins, 2001).

Important grades on student work and course or grade-level marks are intended to convey messages to other individuals besides students. Primary among these stakeholders are the parents who affect learning conditions in the home and motivate the learners to succeed. Schools have an obligation to keep parents informed of their children's progress in school. Therefore, parents need to understand what grades and marks communicate. If a parent attended school when academic performance was measured in comparison to the performance of other students, than the changes brought about through the current reform movement need to be communicated in clear and unambiguous ways.

In addition, teachers want parents to know exactly how their children can benefit from assigned grades and marks. Next, steps toward improved academic performance should be conveyed along with grades that evaluate current levels of performance. When parents see student grades and marks, they should be able to act on this information by partnering with the teacher to benefit the student (Fan & Chen, 2001).

Other stakeholders of student academic performance are teachers who will work with students in subsequent years. Teachers in the next grade will want to know how students have performed in prior instruction. Ultimately, important grades influence final course marks, and a variety of agencies and individuals may be interested in this information, including college admissions officers, employers, and any other organization to which a person may apply at the conclusion of public education.

The teacher, as well as the student and other stakeholders, should be interested in summative assessment outcomes for reasons beyond idle interest in how students are performing. Student performances on major assignments can be used to improve instruction. Student tests and final projects can be analyzed to find patterns of error that may suggest alternative ways of teaching important concepts and skills that, for some reason, were not well expressed by students on the exam.

Finally, summative assessments can be used to plan upcoming instruction. Teachers who simply move on to the next unit or series of topics following the administration of a major exam will have missed an opportunity to help students improve on subsequent testing. Tests and other important assessments can reveal patterns of student reasoning, relative abilities to perform well with certain kinds of test items, and even the ability to interpret questions that include academic language. When teachers analyze student tests to identify either reasons for underperformance or foundational understandings that may impede future efforts to learn, they can find information that will help them teach more effectively (Crooks, 1988). Teachers can use summative assessments to modify instruction in upcoming topics or units of instruction that may lead to improved student performance on later exams.

SUMMATIVE ASSESSMENT: THEN AND NOW

In the next section, we will examine conventional uses of summative assessment as they might have been practiced in a secondary school classroom in Colorado in the mid-1990s. We will eavesdrop on Mr. Carlos as he plans a unit exam for his U.S. history class taken by most juniors at Centralia High School. Then we will contrast his conventional planning and test construction practices with those of a teacher in the same state working in today's standards-based environment.

A vignette of conventional approaches to summative assessment:

It is late December 1997, as we find ourselves with Mr. Ruben Carlos during a planning period between classes. He is in the process of writing a final exam for the end of the first semester of a U.S. history course. The exam will be administered to his students before they are dismissed for a holiday break. This cumulative exam will cover the pre-Colonial era through the early years of the 19th century. Mr. Carlos is drawing on a number of curriculum materials on his desk to identify the content and skills he expects to include in his exam. These include the assigned textbook students have been reading since the start of the term and the school district's curriculum guide. Mr. Carlos has also gathered copies of the unit tests he administered earlier in the term, his lecture notes, outlines of material covered in class, and an old, dog-eared copy of Bloom's taxonomy that he received in his teacher credential program several years ago.

Mr. Carlos also brings his considerable experience and insights on teaching and learning to his test preparation efforts. During his preservice years, and during some professional development programs, he learned about test construction principles that include choosing among test item types, writing test items, and organizing the final test document to ensure student ease of understanding the test directions. Mr. Carlos understands the essential differences between, and relative advantages of, different test items, including multiple choice, short answer, matching, true-false, and essay.

He likes to use a blend of item types when he writes a test. He recalls his own struggles with testing as a student, which leads him to think about the tests he writes from the students' perspective. These concerns are seen in his selection of item types and the order in which students will encounter them as they proceed through the exam.

Mr. Carlos sets to work by planning the layout of his test. He decides to begin with a true-false section, largely because students prefer this type of test item. Mr. Carlos believes that students are likely to find relief from some of their pretest anxiety if the first items they encounter are true-false. He knows that true-false items only serve to assess student factual knowledge, and that students have a 50% chance of getting each item correct, so he allocates only 10 of 100 points to this portion of the test.

Mr. Carlos decides to follow the true-false items with a sentence completion section, followed in turn by a multiple-choice section. He reasons that these first three formats for test items will lead students from relatively easy, low-stress, true-false questions to the more challenging multiple-choice items. Finally, Mr. Carlos will close the test with three essay questions. From his perspective, he reasons that the first two formats of his exam will require students to demonstrate reasoning at the first two levels of Bloom's taxonomy: knowledge recall and comprehension. By the time the students encounter the multiple-choice and essay questions, they will be exercising application and analysis reasoning skills.

He also recognizes the need to have the test follow the same developmental sequence of knowledge structures as the lessons that were used to convey them. At the start of the semester, Mr. Carlos presented a unit on the Native Americans who inhabited North America. The unit included Native American origins, locations, and cultural features. He looked over his notes and the unit test that covered this material. Next, he wrote down ten statements for students to evaluate and respond to by selecting "true" or "false." For example, the first statement is, "The Algonquian tribe lived in huts made of cedar boughs in the Pacific Northwest." He then moved on to the sentence completion section of the test. He decided that this section would be a little longer, perhaps 15 items, for a total of 30 points within his 100-point end-of-semester exam. He composed each sentence as a factual statement that includes an underlined space where the student must place a key academic term. If done correctly, the student will form a sentence that is factually correct.

Mr. Carlos remains consistent with his intent to follow a chronological order of events as he moves from the true-false section about Native Americans to the next time period in the course, the discovery of America and its exploration by Spanish, French, Dutch, and English explorers. He begins his sentence completion section with the statement, "The first European to sail around the African continent toward India was _____." He continues with this format, leaving space at the end of each statement until he composes his 15th and last item, which he borrows from the unit exam on early discoveries and exploration in the Americas: "Soon after the pilgrims arrived in New England, they signed a document establishing the laws of the colony called the _____."

After completion of this second section of the test, Mr. Carlos selects several multiple-choice items from prior tests he used to measure student understanding of the Colonial era in America, leading through the Revolutionary War. He decides to include 15 multiple-choice items for a total of 30 exam points for this section.

Mr. Carlos knows that multiple-choice questions can lead students to thoughtful engagement with subject matter and the application of higher levels of reasoning when the questions are well designed. To this end, he decides that two of his questions will call for the interpretation of graphs, two questions will require interpretation of a map, and two more questions will require the analysis of historical documents: The Declaration of Independence and the Constitution.

He begins the section by having students compare and contrast the early colonies. His first question, intended to ease students into this section of the exam, requires only knowledge recall from his students: "This colony began under Dutch control, but thereafter fell into British hands: a) Rhode Island, b) Virginia, c) New York, or d) Massachusetts. From this relatively easy question, Mr. Carlos moved into his graph interpretation questions. The first graph for student interpretation is a line graph, showing the growth in population of four Colonial cities between the years 1680 and 1760. Lines showing relative rates of population growth for Philadelphia, Boston, New York, and Williamsburg, Virginia, appear on the graph. Mr. Carlos wrote the **test item stem**, or question posed within the multiple-choice item: "Which city demonstrated the most rapid population growth between the years 1720 and 1750? a) New York, b) Williamsburg, c) Boston, or d) Philadelphia." Mr. Carlos was pleased with this question because students would be required to compare portions of four graphs over the same time interval to identify different rates of population growth.

For the last question in the multiple-choice section, he wrote an item calling for students to identify one statement among four statements excerpted from the Constitution that reflects the concept of a balance of powers among the governmental branches. For this item, he wrote three wrong answer choices, often called **distractors**. The first choice was a statement from the preamble to the Constitution, the second statement was an excerpt describing the role of the Senate in ratifying treaties (the correct answer), the third statement described how new states would be brought into the union, and the last statement was an excerpt from Second Amendment about the right to bear arms.

Mr. Carlos was pleased with his progress, because he had 10 points of his exam finished with the true-false items, 30 points assigned to the sentence completion section, and 30 additional points for the multiple-choice section. That left three essay questions to write for 10 points each, which would account for all 100 points of the exam.

One concern came to his attention as he was completing this last section of the exam. Would the students have sufficient time to answer three essay questions after they completed the previous sections? He did some quick paper-and-pencil figuring: three true-false items should be answered in 1 minute for a total of 4 minutes to cover the first exam section, 15 sentence completion items at one-half minute for each item would be another 8 minutes to finish the sentence completion section. That would be 12 minutes in the 50-minute period, with 38 minutes left. He reasoned students would start the multiple-choice section no later than 12 minutes into the exam, and they would need 1 minute to answer each multiple-choice item, for a total of 15 minutes for that section. That would leave approximately 15 minutes to answer all three essay items. Mr. Carlos reached the conclusion that 5 minutes per essay item was insufficient time to answer extended questions. He would need to keep the essay question prompts tightly focused so that students would be able to answer each of the three questions within a 5-minute period.

His first essay question was intended to be quickly answered, and he wrote these words with that intention in mind: "Identify three regulations imposed on the colonists by the British government that led to the Revolutionary War. Select the one regulation you believed to be the most offensive to the colonists, and defend your choice by comparing it with the other regulations you identified." As he finished writing that statement, he was satisfied that it had sufficient focus to require no more than 3 or 4 minutes to complete. He was pleased that this was the case because he wanted to close his exam with this last essay question: "Defend or refute the following statement through a carefully written persuasive statement: 'Our Constitution allows Americans to participate in an ideal democracy.'"

As he finished this last question for the exam, Mr. Carlos looked over all the items with some satisfaction as Miss Sandra Graziela, a new teacher in the history department, announced her presence.

"Hi, Ruben," she said. "What have you been working on all this time?"

Mr. Carlos described the task that he was completing, "I've just finished writing my final exam for this semester. Now there is nothing more to do than to administer the exam and see how well they do."

"What units will you be emphasizing on your exam?" asked Miss Graziela, with an interest in knowing if her exam would be similar to that of Mr. Carlos.

"I do a little bit of everything," he responded, "from Native American life before the discovery of the New World right up to Jackson's administration and the Trail of Tears."

Miss Graziela, expressing a little concern for decisions already made, answered a bit defensively, "I haven't started on my exam yet, but I don't think I'll have any items on the early explorers. I put a lot of emphasis on the Colonial era leading up to the Revolutionary War," she concluded. She had reasoned to herself that students learned about Native American tribes and cultures during the seventh grade, and that she could forego that unit and spend more time developing student understanding of the Colonial era.

Before departing, Miss Graziela asked one more question of Mr. Carlos. "Will you be giving your students the entire period for your exam? And what kind of test items will you be using?" she asked, with some interest in understanding how much Mr. Carlos emphasized the semester final in his overall assessment approach for the semester.

"Oh, I'll use the whole period," he responded. "My exam is 30% of their final grade, so I want to give them sufficient time to respond to all items. I'm using a little bit of everything, from true-false items to essay questions."

"Well, good luck with your test, Ruben, I have to decide just what I'm going to do, because I've already given a lot of emphasis to a major project on the Constitutional Convention that I think will only leave time for a shorter exam," she said. As she left Mr. Carlos to finish his preparations, she gave thought to administering a 30-minute test to her class with all multiple-choice items.

In this vignette of a teacher preparing a major exam for his U.S. history students, we see a number of practices evident in test preparation prior to the installation of state curriculum standards. Mr. Carlos considers a number of important issues in his deliberations, and he calls on information that he has gleaned through years of experience, including some information on testing and educational measurement that he learned in his preservice program. His considerations and his practices, though conventional in nature, focus on the interests of his students and his desire to develop a fair assessment experience. We will explore a number of these issues next.

Constructing the Assessment from the Student's Perspective

It is evident through his deliberations that Mr. Carlos considers the test-taking experience his students will encounter as they sit for his exam. We see early in the vignette that he is concerned about student anxiety and emotional response to a high-stakes test as they first encounter the exam. He begins the test with a set of 10 true-false items to put his students at ease, even though he recognizes the poor reliability that these items bring to the assessment experience. Mr. Carlos believes that student anxiety will be diminished as they encounter alternative, constructed responses that leave them a 50% chance of getting each item correct. Indeed, a student who knows nothing about the content assessed by the true-false section can select 7 of the 10 correct answers by chance, usually considered a passing performance, with approximately a 30% chance. Perhaps Mr. Carlos, knowing his students and their concerns about major tests, is willing to trade some assessment reliability for the prospect of ensuring a good test performance by setting his students at ease.

Relating the Assessment Experience to the Instruction It Evaluates

Mr. Carlos chose to develop all his test items in the same chronological dimension as he presented the content of his U.S. history course over the first semester. He began the course with a unit on Native American history and culture before the age of exploration, and he begins his test with the same material. As they move from one test section to the next, students will encounter questions and other challenges about content and skills in the order that the content and skills were developed during the semester. This similarity in form between the organization of the content and the organization of the test that it evaluates will help students recall information that they presumably retained in the same chronological orientation as it was presented. Again, Mr. Carlos is attempting to provide each student with the opportunity to attain the best possible test outcome by facilitating his or her recall of information. He continues to view the test from his students' perspective as he develops its structure

Variety in Form and Challenge of Assessment Tasks

Mr. Carlos includes a variety of item types in his test, and he develops them in an ascending order of challenge. He reasons that students will start out anxious, and then they will develop confidence as they encounter relatively easy items. As the test progresses, he will change assessment types to ensure more reliable methods, where the chance of getting a right answer becomes limited, and students are obliged to generate more information. He begins with true-false, then quickly moves to a short-answer items that require students to exercise knowledge recall or comprehension to provide correct responses. By the time students encounter multiple-choice items, the chance of getting any one item correct has been reduced to 25%. More important, the wording of the stem, or the body of the multiple-choice question, and the selection of alternative choices can be manipulated to adjust the cognitive challenge of each multiple-choice item. Hence, a multiple-choice question can be a mere knowledge recall exercise, where one of four alternatives matches a definition provided in the stem, or it can call for application, analysis, or synthesis levels of reasoning by posing a challenging question in the stem that calls for several reasoning processes to identify a possible answer.

At the end of the exam, students will encounter essay questions that require them to compose original, written statements. Typically, this kind of exercise is the most challenging for students, because a satisfactory outcome calls for organizational and written expression skills in addition to responding to the prompt with correct information or skill application.

HAT RESEARCH CAN TELL US...

- **About Test Items and Test Bias**

  Test bias and the influence of student background is an area in need of more research. As our classrooms become more diverse, we are concerned about fairness in assessment for English language learners and students with special needs. A study titled "The Impact of Language Characteristics in Mathematics Test Items on the Performance of English Language Learners and Students with Special Needs" suggests that elementary school teachers have reasons to be concerned. The researchers (Shaftel, Belton-Kocher, Glasnapp, & Poggio, 2006) correlated item difficulty with linguistic challenge of test items in mathematics and found that elementary-aged students were challenged by language characteristics of mathematics test items to a greater extent than their secondary school counterparts. Mathematics vocabulary was consistently difficult across the grades, but older students were able to understand ambiguous words or words with double meanings that posed challenges for younger students.

Careful Consideration of Pacing and Item Completion Rates

As Mr. Carlos continues through his exam preparations, he makes estimates of the amount of time students will need to respond to each item type, then he considers how long it will take to complete each item set by multiplying the time to complete each item by the number of items in the set. He uses these calculations to determine how much time students will have to complete each of the essay questions at the end of his test. Mr. Carlos is attempting to develop a test that will allow students to complete the exam with sufficient time to minimize guessing and anxiety as factors, yet have a sufficient number of items and variety of assessment types to contribute to a reasonably valid and reliable measure of his students' knowledge and skills.

Careful Consideration of Knowledge Domains to Be Assessed

It is apparent that Mr. Carlos has considered a number of curriculum issues, and he has used a number of resources to construct his test. As he wrote test items, he looked over the student textbook, questions used on previous tests, and his own notes about presentations and activities conducted in class. These materials serve to remind Mr. Carlos of the skills and knowledge taught during the semester that should be assessed by the test he is writing. It is evident that he is examining all the learning resources students were accountable to use as they learned the content and skills of U.S. history.

Further, Mr. Carlos paid attention to the need to help students develop certain skills that they will need to perform well on future high-stakes assessments or apply later in life. These skills and abilities are important to students' growing knowledge of the social studies, but they are also skills expected of well-educated secondary school graduates by prospective employers and institutions of higher education. Mr. Carlos intentionally included graph interpretation and analyses of historical documents in his end-of-semester exam to assess the skills and abilities of his students with respect to these additional expectations of the school and society.

PROBLEMS WITH CONVENTIONAL TESTING PRACTICES

As a teacher planning a test for his students in the closing years of the 1990s Mr. Carlos is performing his responsibilities in a thoughtful and professional manner. Unfortunately, the conversation that transpires between Mr. Carlos and Miss Graziela discloses some issues that led in large part to the emergence of regulations and policies associated with No Child Left Behind (NCLB), particularly having to do with state curriculum standards and assessment practices.

As their conversation evolves, we soon learn that Miss Graziela will not be assessing the same information on her U.S. history test as appears on Mr. Carlos's test. Apparently, Miss Graziela places far less emphasis on the study of Native Americans than does Mr. Carlos. We learn later in her discussion that Miss Graziela had her students produce major projects having to do with Colonial-era developments leading to the Revolutionary War. Perhaps this is an area in which Miss Graziela provides quite a bit more information or deeper analysis of issues than does Mr. Carlos. As she leaves his classroom following their brief conversation, Miss Graziela decides that her students will have a shorter exam, with a different allocation of test items, and with different content than the exam prepared by Mr. Carlos.

When two teachers of the same course teach quite different content and assess their students differently, there is evident incoherence in the school district's curriculum practices. Typically, local school boards of education approve course curricula and adopt curriculum resources with the intention of providing students in the same course with similar experiences and expectations. It is evident that students who found themselves in Miss Graziela's course have not learned the same information as Mr. Carlos's class with respect to at least two units of the curriculum, Native Americans before the age of exploration and developments in the Colonial era preceding the Revolutionary War.

Absent clear procedures and policies, teachers in years past would diverge in their teaching and curriculum coverage practices in large part due to the isolation in their daily teaching lives (Schlichte, Yssel, & Merbler, 2005). One can infer from the conversation between Mr. Carlos and Miss Graziela that takes place in December that the two teachers had not previously determined the content of the course that all U.S history students should experience and the specific instructional outcomes or achievement that all students should demonstrate at the end of the semester.

Students enrolled in the same U.S. history course should be expected to achieve similar learning outcomes, demonstrate achievement of essential knowledge and skills, and have access to the same curriculum as other students taking the same course. In this instance, students in Miss Graziela's course are not achieving the same learning expectations as students who study with Mr. Carlos.

ALTERNATIVE FORMS OF CLASSROOM-BASED SUMMATIVE ASSESSMENT

In our vignette of past practices involving summative assessment, we observed a teacher planning a major test. Although testing is the predominant method of summative assessment, it is by no means the only method of measuring student knowledge and skills, nor should testing be exclusively used to measure student learning. The limitations to reliance on paper-and-pencil tests are widely known and often discussed by those who have experienced many years of public education, but a number of these limitations remain a concern as large-scale assessments are used with increasing frequency.

Although conventional paper-and-pencil tests are efficient means for assessing breadth of knowledge in a limited period of time, they do not represent an ideal demonstration of student knowledge and skills as they would be applied to more practical purposes (Airasian, 2000; Wiggins, 1999). Although higher education institutions will require students to complete exams, the world of employment and daily life consists of applications of knowledge that are quite different from examination questions. As adults, we apply our knowledge in discussions, persuasive arguments, report writing, making judgments about alternative solutions to complex situations, and evaluating the moral and legal aspects of events or consequences of actions. Carefully crafted exams prepared by professionals with expert knowledge in assessment and plenty of time to write thoughtful items can mimic these daily life circumstances, but teachers who are obliged to find fleeting minutes to put together an exam do not have the resources to produce paper-and-pencil exams with these qualities (Worthen, 1993).

Further, we know that some students develop special abilities, sometimes known as **"test-wiseness"** (Airasian, 2000). Those who are test-wise have a set of skills or insights that lead to higher test scores than other students. Unfortunately, these are not the skills and knowledge that the curriculum is intended to convey. Test-wiseness diminishes the validity of paper-and-pencil tests as tools for assessing the intended curriculum, and the advantage to the test-wise student is enhanced with each additional paper-and-pencil test that a course requires. Given our concern that all students be able to express their skills and knowledge of the intended curriculum to the best of their abilities, it is incumbent on us as teachers to provide them with opportunities to express their understanding in a variety of ways that mirror the applications of knowledge that students will experience in later life.

Projects and reports can serve as valid and reliable summative assessment tools (Falk, Wichterle Ort, & Moirs, 2007). They can be authentic and valid means for demonstrating knowledge or skills of a particular subject area. In skill development courses such as the visual arts, performing arts, or graphic design courses, it is appropriate to measure a student outcome that synthesizes a number of skills in a final product or performance. However, we need to be mindful that student products are not always prepared under controlled conditions.

Science educators have viewed science fair projects skeptically for many years (Syers & Shore, 2001). When a student works with a parent or sibling to create a model of a volcano made from papier-mâché, questions arise about the project as a vehicle for expressing student knowledge about volcanoes, their origins, the nature of eruptions, and their relationship to geological and ecological phenomena. If, on the other hand, a student designs an experiment in school that demonstrates a variety of scientific skills, including observation, description, identifying variables, controlling variables, measurement, recording data, and interpreting data, then the project may represent a valid means of demonstrating the student's scientific knowledge and skills. The following guidelines can be helpful in using student projects and reports to assess student skills and abilities.

Be Sure the Product Demonstrates the Skills and Abilities of the Student

In the science fair project described earlier, a parent or sibling might take over much of the creative work to ensure a good evaluation outcome. If projects are developed at home doubt must be cast on the amount of work the student actually put into the project independent of the contributions of friends or family members. Concerns regarding the proper performance of major projects or reports can be managed through careful description of the project and placing limitations on the manner and place where the project is developed. Most important, expectations for the performance of tasks by the student should be clearly stated with appropriate controls that preclude other individuals from contributing improperly. Clearly, projects that involve parents or siblings should not be used as assessments of student knowledge and skills.

Projects Should Require the Application of Knowledge, Skills, and Abilities Included in Course Outcomes

Projects and reports are time-consuming exercises that carry an opportunity cost in their performance. Projects typically take a great deal of time to plan, organize, construct or develop, and explain. This time could probably be used to undertake a number of other less time consuming activities. Therefore, completed projects should demonstrate a variety of skills and abilities in ways not easily demonstrated by conventional tests and quizzes. These activities could include appropriate library or field research activities, construction or development of intermediate products that are separately evaluated, analysis of results, and reflections on improvements or changes that could have been made to improve the outcome.

Projects Should Reflect the Application of Academic Skills to Situations That Can Occur in Daily Life or the Workplace

Authentic assessments require students to apply academic, organizational, and information-processing skills to academic knowledge to find solutions to problems and develop products that constitute original responses. Such is the nature of real problem solving in daily life. Often, a teacher will pose a problem derived from circumstances that are found in public or daily life situations that calls for resolution through the development of a plan, the acquisition of resources, and the use of skills to modify resources into desired outcomes or products (Barron et al., 1998; Solomon, 2003)

Projects Should Be Evaluated through a Systematic Application of Evaluative Criteria

Evaluative criteria are descriptions of properties of a student product that are used to assess its qualities. The properties can take on values that are either quantitative or qualitative in nature. Most important, the criteria should measure desired student outcomes that map to course goals and learning targets (Black & William, 1998). For example, a student work product might include a persuasive paragraph that begins with a topic sentence stating a position or thesis. Sentences that follow within the paragraph are expected to support the position stated in the topic sentence. The desired attributes of the paragraph, the topic sentence, and the sentences that form the body of the paragraph are the criteria to be evaluated. In Figure 6.1, an assignment is written for the student that explicitly states the evaluative criteria to be used in the assessment of a persuasive paragraph.

FIGURE  6.1 An Assignment that Includes Evaluative Criteria

Write a paragraph in support of, or in disagreement with, new municipal regulations that place a limit on carbon-emitting industries in your city or town. Your paragraph should begin with a topic sentence that clearly states your position and three or more reasons that support your position. The sentences that follow should develop each of the reasons that you list. Conclude your paragraph with a summarizing sentence. Your paragraph will be evaluated with respect to the quality of the topic sentence, each of the supporting sentences, spelling, punctuation, and grammar.

FIGURE 6.2 Sample Rows of a Rubric Used to Evaluate Student Paragraphs

	Excellent	Good	Acceptable	Poor
Topic sentence	Clear position, each argument introduced	Clear position, some arguments provided	Topic sentence does not state thesis	No distinguishable topic sentence
Paragraph body	All theses arguments supported	Some points supported	Body only loosely connected to topic sentence	No coherent support for or presence of thesis

In conventional settings, the following quality ratings may result from the application of the evaluative criteria: excellent, good, acceptable, or poor.

Due to the fact that four quality ratings have been identified for the various criteria (topic sentence states a position or thesis, supporting sentences develop the argument, spelling and punctuation, etc.), a scoring guide or **rubric** can be created that describes performances corresponding to each quality rating for each criterion.

Rubrics have become popular measurement tools for making subjective evaluations of student work. The descriptions of properties found in each cell of the rubric are used to find matching elements in student work samples. When the student work matches a description of a cell in the rubric, the evaluative criterion for that cell is given the rating value of the corresponding column. Each row of the rubric is used to evaluate a different criterion, and ratings for all the criteria are used to evaluate the student product as a whole. A portion of the rubric for evaluating the persuasive paragraph is seen in Figure 6.2.

Projects and reports are authentic means to assess student knowledge and skills because projects and reports are the stuff of daily work lives of so many of us. Their use in assessing student achievement of intended instructional outcomes depends on coherence between elements in the assignment, the selection of evaluative criteria shared with students at the time the assignment is given, conditions that describe the parameters that circumscribe the work to be done, and the use of an assessment tool, such as a rubric or checklist, that applies the evaluative criteria. The next section focuses on summative assessment as it is practiced in the standards-based reform environment of today's schools. We will develop these concepts of authentic assessment in greater detail as we relate them to principles and practices of standards-based teaching and learning.

SUMMATIVE ASSESSMENT IN TODAY'S CLASSROOMS

One aspect of teachers' daily lives that has been more substantially affected by the current reform environment and NCLB than any other is assessment (Kornhaber, 2004). The national mandate for adequate yearly progress in student achievement of state content standards is driving curriculum and assessment planning in all states. New and experienced teachers alike are struggling to adapt to these circumstances. In our next vignette, we will observe an experienced teacher and a new teacher in the mathematics department of a western middle school as they struggle to plan assessments incorporating their school district's response to NCLB.

A vignette of summative assessment in a standards-based school:

Gwendolyn George, now in her 11th year at James Farmer Middle School, has just welcomed Julie Nelson to a test planning session for their prealgebra course. Julie is in her second year, having completed an internship program operated by the local state university in partnership with the school district. Julie and Gwendolyn will be planning the second unit test of the school year together. They will administer it to all students enrolled in prealgebra within the next 2 weeks.

For some time now, the school has administered common exams for all core subjects, including math, science, social studies, and English. Initially there had been some resistance to the idea that all teachers of the same subject would plan and administer the same exam together. There was also resistance to the idea that all exams would be graded in relation to proficiency targets set for all students, regardless of teacher. But the district administration and many lead teachers accepted the idea that common assessments were the natural outcome of the standards reform movement.

For Julie and Gwendolyn, the common exams for prealgebra include the unit tests they typically administer at the end of a 2- or 3-week unit, benchmark tests administered by the school district three times a year at 10-week intervals, and the state standards exam for all seventh-grade math students required by the State of Colorado in compliance with NCLB regulations. All these exams relate to each other through the state's model curriculum standards.

The unit exams are the only major tests prepared exclusively by teachers, but like the other exams, they are designed to prepare students for success on high-stakes state standards tests. Most of the test items on unit tests are derived from the state standards and assessment guides in anticipation of content that will be covered on the spring standards exam. Although the content of unit exams is completely up to the teachers to develop, Julie and Gwendolyn understand that the unit exams are stepping-stones to student achievement of proficiency on the benchmark tests that are compiled by the school district.

The benchmark tests are designed to assess student mastery of standards developed and assessed through the first 10 weeks of school. Benchmark exams mirror the content and format of items expected to appear on the state standards exam in mathematics for seventh-grade students. Although unit exams may include some items that assess student mastery of the curriculum that falls outside the domain of the state's model curriculum standards, most of the items are intended to assess seventh-grade math students' progress toward successful acquisition of the content and skills of the standards. The benchmark exams cover approximately 25% of the standards that students will need to master as measured by the state exam.

The first benchmark exams of the year will be administered at James Farmer Middle School before the end of October. All students in all grades will take benchmark exams in the core curriculum that is assessed by state standards exams. They are used to assess student progress in the achievement of selected state standards, and they are also used to identify students in need of intervention if their test scores fall at the "below proficient" level. If students fail to meet a specific percentage of correct items on the first benchmark test, they will be scheduled for additional instruction in mathematics included in the school's master schedule for underperforming students.

It is in this environment of shared accountability for student success on unit, benchmark, and state standards exams that Julie and Gwendolyn collaborate on the design of unit tests. As they sit down together to begin the design of a test that will be reviewed by all prealgebra teachers for approval, they make sure that they have all the resources they need to perform their work quickly and efficiently.

"I brought along the prealgebra curriculum guide with the pacing calendar," Julie reported, while placing several items on the table where the two teachers would be working. "I also have my copy of the teacher's edition of our text."

"That's good because I printed out the most recent test items that appeared on the state standards exam for seventh-grade mathematics available from the Colorado Department of Education website, and I have the test matrix. We need to consider several sources of information related to the Colorado Student Assessment Program (CASP) if we are going to get the best possible results on the spring test," responded Gwendolyn.

"Well, let's just set these related items out on the table," said Julie, in an effort to keep organized. She sensed a need to set all text materials in one place and all state assessment information in a second place to facilitate the process of selecting and writing unit test items. "Do you have any other information pertaining to the test students will take in the spring?" she asked.

"I do have these other items," Gwendolyn responded. "Along with the released items from prior years of CASP administration, I printed out the fact sheet with general information about the number of items and item formats that will appear on the test, and I also have the Framework/Blueprint, which is really helpful. This last item provides insights about the particular Colorado Model Content Standards that are likely to be assessed, with descriptions of the content and skills students will need to demonstrate on the exam. As you know, there is a great deal of emphasis on number sense, area, and perimeter at our grade level," she stated in closing.

"Well, our text materials, including supplemental assessment resources from the publisher, should be helpful," Julie added. "The text includes an assessment matrix that maps certain test pages and units to our Colorado standards, and a variety of end-of-chapter assessments and other assessments are available on a compact disc provided by the publisher. The CD may include items similar in content and format to items that may appear on the test. We can compare the publisher's items with the released items from the Colorado Department of Education website and select or modify items from the teacher's edition and the publisher's CD that will prepare students for the CASP," she concluded.

"I guess we can get started with two additional planning resources I brought with me, and that's the pacing guide for our school and the lesson plans we developed together during common planning time," said Gwendolyn. "I suggest that we refer to the pacing guide to find the specific objectives of the math standards we are teaching at this time of the year, then look at released test items and matching publisher's items for that objective and all the others we have been working on in class. We also expended a great deal of time and effort preparing lesson objectives from our standards that described student skills and knowledge they were to acquire. We don't want to forget that we have an obligation to test what we taught."

"Okay," said Julie. "Why don't we list the objectives we were to achieve in the order that we were to convey them, then we can search for appropriate items and line them up in the order that we taught them."

"Sounds fine by me," said Gwendolyn. "Here's an objective we should address, though I'm not so sure I would like to begin the exam at this level of difficulty: 'Construct a coordinate graph and plot ordered integer pairs in all four quadrants.' I think we should start by assessing some of the elements of this objective first, such as recognition of ordered integer pairs. I think that should come before plotting the ordered pairs," she said with some authority and confidence.

"I certainly agree," said Julie. "I developed my student understanding of coordinate graphs as you just described."

This vignette involving the test preparation activities of Julie Nelson and Gwendolyn George at James Farmer Middle School is markedly different than the vignette involving Ruben Carlos, which took place before standards had affected curriculum and teaching deeply. To begin with, Mr. Carlos developed his test alone without considering the input of other teachers covering the same subject. He did not sense a need to plan a common test to be administered by all teachers in the same assignment. When Miss Graziela joined him in conversation long after a number of test writing decisions had been made, the differences between their tests in format, duration, and content to be covered emerged quickly. These differences did not cause either of the teachers any concern. If each of them was teaching quite different content, as was revealed in their conversation, then there was no need for their tests to be similar.

By contrast, Julie and Gwendolyn in our second vignette were totally absorbed in the shared responsibility of writing an exam that they would commonly administer to their students. They worked together toward the identification of content and skills to be conveyed.

An additional distinction was their use of quite different resources. Mr. Carlos used his notes, his textbook, the district curriculum guide, and an old copy of Bloom's taxonomy, but none of these resources was seen as an authoritative resource for selecting content and skills to be assessed on the exam. Julie and Gwendolyn, on the other hand, were focused intently on assessing the standards and objectives identified in their school district's pacing guide. Other resources included the textbook, the state assessment/frameworks, and released test items, but the pacing guide determined the standards and objectives to be addressed by the unit test, and these were deemed the most critical elements to be included.

Julie and Gwendolyn concerned themselves with test item formats, but their source of possible test items was greatly affected by the format and variety of test items that students encounter on high-stakes standards-based tests, including the upcoming benchmark exams and the spring administration of the CASP in math. Mr. Carlos drew on his formal preparation in testing and assessment to develop a mix of test items that reflected general principles of assessment and test construction, but he was not influenced by the format of other tests students might encounter. Julie and Gwendolyn referred to Colorado Department of Education information about test item formats and the content likely to be assessed to select or write items they planned to use on their test. It is evident that they wanted their test structure to anticipate other higher-stakes tests they know their students will encounter.

The summative assessment practices of Gwendolyn George and Julie Wilson are collaborative in nature. They work as partners in gathering necessary resources, using the resources in the planning process, and identifying the content and format of test items. They are greatly influenced by testing their students will experience that is largely beyond their control. Regularly scheduled benchmark tests administered by the school district and the CASP exam administered by the Colorado Department of Education in response to NCLB regulations heavily influence their selection and development of item types and the content of test items.

In response to these exams, Julie and Gwendolyn bring new resources to the test planning process that did not exist when Ruben Carlos developed his test in the 1990s. These include the fact sheets published by the Colorado Department of Education that describe the characteristics and purposes of the CASP math exam, the item maps and assessment/frameworks that reveal the complete list of test objectives from which the state administers test items, and released test items, including student work samples and student answers to questions not appearing in multiple-choice format.

Mr. Carlos considered student interest and possible test anxiety as he chose to use a variety of assessment types not typically seen on standards-based tests, including true-false items, sentence completion items, and essay questions. He also used Bloom's taxonomy to instill higher-order reasoning skills in his tests, rather than a centralized source of learning objectives, such as state curriculum standards. Evidently, testing is changing substantially in both purpose and process as a result of emphasis placed on student achievement of state curriculum standards required by NCLB regulations. In our next section, we will look closely at a variety of summative assessment tools now commonly used in classrooms and schools to measure student achievement and guide instructional and curriculum improvement.

CONTEMPORARY SUMMATIVE ASSESSMENT PRACTICES

In today's reform environment, summative assessment of student academic achievement is taking place at several levels, leading to a tiered system of assessment, with each level greatly influencing the practices at a lower, more localized level. At the lowest level, we see classroom-based assessment that has conventionally used tests, quizzes, and student projects to evaluate student achievement of learning goals. These conventional forms of assessment are affected by evolving school district–level assessment practices, including the development of benchmark testing programs, to gauge student progress in achieving district-selected state curriculum standards (Linn, 2000).

At the school district level, central office administrators and assessment coordinators use software to determine relative success in the achievement of standards by particular groups of students identified by gender, race, ability, and student native language (Goertz & Duffy, 2004). NCLB regulations impose these assessment practices on district administrators. States are required to prepare reports of academic progress by various student subgroups and to demonstrate that these groups are showing adequate yearly progress. School district assessment coordinators inform principals of their school's progress in achieving state standards at each grade level, in particular subjects, and by particular student groups. Teachers are expected to use this information to adjust teaching and assessment practices so that subsequent testing reveals progress made by previously underperforming groups (Spillane, Halverson, & Diamond, 2001).

Federally mandated use of annual testing to evaluate student achievement of state content standards in core subjects is driving the change in assessment practices (Sunderman, Kim, & Orfield, 2006). The standards tests are typically administered in spring, and school districts respond by monitoring student achievement of standards likely to be tested each year through the use of benchmark testing programs. These exams are typically administered quarterly and include test items that are similar in format and content to those that may appear on the state standards tests. In many districts, a pacing guide or pacing calendar informs teachers of the particular standards that will be assessed on each benchmark exam. When the district releases benchmark exam results to teachers, they know how their students are progressing toward a successful outcome on the state exams.

In our vignette of the test planning activities of Gwendolyn George and Julie Nelson, we could see the influence of the state testing program, the local school district standards pacing guide, and public information about the state standards tests on their test preparation activities. We will examine each of these levels of assessment, beginning with state assessment of curriculum standards, and move progressively down to the classroom level, where conventional practices that we observed in the test preparation activities of Mr. Carlos are undergoing substantial modification, as reflected in the activities of Mrs. George and Miss Nelson.

State Assessment of Curriculum Standards

The passage of NCLB in 2001 required all states to prepare annual assessments of state standards achievement. The law requires annual assessment in math and English/language arts from Grades 3 through 8, and assessments in science have since been added. In California, science is assessed in Grades 5, 8, and 10 in compliance with NCLB requirements that science be tested once in the elementary grades, once in the middle grades, and a third time in the high school years. Each state may propose the particular grades when science will be tested in compliance with federal law.

The format of the tests, the standards likely to be tested, the frequency with which any one standard will be tested, and the test item types students will encounter may be found at websites of state departments of education. These websites also report the progress of specific schools and districts in making adequate yearly progress toward state standards achievement. Adequate yearly progress is measured against a progressive proficiency target that includes more students each year. Federal law mandates that all students perform at a proficient level by the year 2014, and that no child will be left behind.

NCLB provides substantial sanctions for schools that fail to demonstrate adequate yearly progress (Goertz, 2003). As a result, schools and districts have organized to ensure student success on the state standards exams. These exams may be developed expressly for the purpose of measuring state standards achievement on criterion-referenced exams. State authorities determine the percentage of items that must be scored correct to meet the criterion of "proficient." Other percentage-based scores may be provided for rankings of "advanced," "basic," or "below basic."

Typically, large states with substantial resources are able to contract with testing companies to produce these criterion-referenced exams, which are derived from state standards. In some states, the specific standards to be tested and related test objectives for the standards can be found on the state assessment website. Other states will not disclose specific standards likely to be tested, so a statewide guessing game ensues. Gwendolyn George and Julie Nelson have the good fortune to teach in Colorado, a state that reveals assessment objectives for standards that will be tested. In California, by contrast, the state board of education insists that all standards are important and that any one of them may be tested. There are so many standards that only a few may be tested in any one year, so school districts must estimate the likelihood that any one standard will be tested. This guessing process is applied to local selection of state standards. It is also applied to the selection of standards that will be assessed in the district benchmark testing program.

Some states do not have sufficient wealth to administer a custom-made test for their state standards. In these states, an existing test that a company has already produced, typically a norm-referenced test that compares an examinee's results with the performance of other students, is used to assess the state's standards. Items on the test that align with specific state standards are identified, and these are used in a new scoring formula to assess the state standards. Often, additional items are added to the existing test to ensure certain other standards are assessed, leading to a norm-referenced, "off-the-shelf" test with augmentations and adjustments that repurpose the test for measuring state standards.

Teachers can help their students score high on state standards tests by looking for specific information on their state department of education website that reveals information about the tests that will be administered to students. They can use this information to prepare their students for the test by focusing on the content and skills to be tested, the item types and test format that students will encounter, and the testing conditions, including amount of time students will have to answer questions. If teachers use these strategies, their students are likely to benefit and perform well on the state test.

Appendix 1 includes the fact sheet for mathematics tests provided by the State of Colorado. It describes the test items and test conditions that students will encounter when they take the state tests. A teacher who looks over this fact sheet will see that students will encounter multiple-choice items and "constructed response items," which may be short, medium, or extended. In constructed response items, students write their computations or reasoning on paper, perform written mathematical procedures, and write down their answers. In multiple-choice items, students read possible answers, select one, and merely fill in a small circle or make a pencil mark indicating which of the possible choices is correct. When reading a multiple-choice item, the correct answer is provided, and must only be identified among other incorrect alternatives. In constructed response questions, the student must provide the correct responses, not merely select them.

If a teacher in Colorado wants to know more about constructed response test questions, further reading in the Colorado State Department of Education website will reveal released test items that display correct responses students provided on recently administered exams. This information is invaluable in understanding what skills students will need to perform well on the test. Other states provide similar information of enormous value to teachers. This information has implications for planning summative assessments, as we shall explore further when we consider the implications of the state testing program information with respect to planning classroom-based summative assessments.

School District Assessment of Curriculum Standards

Across the country, school districts have responded to the NCLB mandates through curriculum modifications and the installation of centralized assessment practices. In years past, an assistant superintendent for curriculum and instruction would be expected to include standardized testing and results reporting as one among many responsibilities. With the advent of the new accountability movement led by NCLB, larger school districts are establishing new staff positions to oversee districtwide assessment and evaluation. Centralized assessment activities have expanded to include expectations for schools to report progress toward successful outcomes on state standards tests through the year.

School districts, working with principals and teachers, are identifying state curriculum standards that are most likely to be tested, and they are requiring teachers to convey the content and skills of these selected standards according to pacing guides or pacing calendars (Bay, Reys, & Reys, 1999). In curriculum pacing, teachers are informed of the sequence and pace with which selected standards are to be achieved. For instance, the first 8 of 32 identified fifth-grade social studies standards may appear on a pacing calendar as content to be conveyed between the start of the academic year and the end of October. The district curriculum guide may direct teachers to allocate a certain number of hours or days of instruction to the development of specific standards in a prescribed sequence before the end of October.

After school districts identify critical standards and develop pacing guides that list the sequence and pace with which standards are to be conveyed, they prepare benchmark tests that measure the extent to which students have achieved the sequenced standards within a given time period. For example, teachers will administer a district-composed benchmark test at the end of October to assess student achievement of the standards conveyed since the start of the school year.

In some instances, these tests are used only as a guide for teachers and administrators regarding progress students are making in achieving standards. In other instances, teachers may use these tests as major summative exams that are graded to determine course or subject marks. In some settings, students may be reorganized into different learning groups based on benchmark test results, with underperforming students provided with supplemental instruction or other interventions that include tutoring or small-group work.

Benchmark exams are intended to predict student performance on state standards exams (McGehee & Griffith, 2001). Therefore, they function best when they are similar in format, item type, content assessed, and exam conditions to the state standards tests. A committee of teachers and administrators may be asked to review the state-provided information about state standards tests included on a fact sheet, a directory of test speci-fications, lists of test objectives, prior state exams, or released test items. Using this infor-mation, they prepare a benchmark test to assess the standards conveyed over several weeks (Burstein et al., 1995). State-released test items are often used in modified form as test items on district-developed benchmark tests. When benchmark tests demonstrate a similarity to state standards tests, they prepare students for success on the state tests by providing them with assessment experiences quite similar to those they will encounter when they take the state test.

When benchmark test reports are provided to teachers, they can be used to identify standards that were well achieved and other standards that were challenging for many students. At the classroom level, teachers can make decisions about students who should receive supplemental instruction in areas of underperformance. At the district level, stu-dents who perform "below basic" on several items of a benchmark test may be scheduled for supplementary instructional experiences, including specially designed classes in-tended to address their needs. Alternatively, some students may be provided tutorial serv-ices to improve subsequent testing results (Elkins, 2002).

Although some teachers may serve on a committee to plan benchmark test items, most teachers do not have a role in constructing the test, as is the case for the state exam. In many districts, school district administrators in charge of the district's large-scale assessment programs select the items on benchmark tests. These administrators will use results of state tests, often reported by the end of summer or early autumn, to select benchmark test items that are similar to those on the state standards exams.

Teachers use formative and summative tests in addition to standards-based instruction to prepare students for success with benchmark tests. State standards tests and district benchmark testing programs have affected classroom-based assessment, as we noted in our vignette of the test preparation experiences of Gwendolyn George and Julie Nelson.

Classroom-Based Summative Assessment for Standards Achievement

Teachers must consider many issues and resources as they undertake the complex process of classroom-based summative assessment. In our first vignette, we visited Mr. Ruben Carlos as he prepared a unit test for a course in U.S. history. His test preparation activities were guided by his textbook, class notes, quizzes and related summative as-sessment items that he used in the course of teaching the material to be covered on his unit exam, and an old copy of Bloom's taxonomy. He also brought considerable experi-ence to the test development process, including the relative merits of certain test item types, including true-false, matching, sentence completion, multiple-choice, short answer, and essay questions. Mr. Carlos also brought another dimension to test preparation that led him to construct fair and reasonable tests: He plans his tests with the student per-spective of the test experience in mind.

Miss Julie Nelson and Mrs. Gwendolyn George consider additional factors in the test development process because they are teachers in a school district that is responding to federal and state assessment mandates of NCLB. Most important among these is the desire to use classroom-based summative assessments to prepare students for success on school district benchmark tests and state standards tests. These concerns bring new resources to the test planning exercise, including state standards, state standards-based curriculum frameworks, released test items, and other information from their state department of education website, including descriptions of the state test and the items used during the assessment. They also refer to the instructional objectives of the lessons that make up the unit to be tested.

We should recall from Chapter 3 that instructional goal setting and the preparation of instructional objectives have been dramatically altered by state curriculum standards. When teachers use state standards and frameworks to plan lessons effectively, they describe the specific student behaviors and products that will result from their lessons. The behaviors and products show the teacher that students have mastered the skills and content applications described in their state standards documents.

Gwendolyn George and Julie Nelson consider the student products and performances that result from their standards-based lessons as they prepare or select test items. If one of their lesson objectives, derived from a state standard, expects students to read and write decimal place values from tenths to ten thousandths, then assessment items that appear on the unit test should assess this skill. Moreover, the teachers may choose to modify a released test item from a prior state standards exam used to assess this particular skill. Through this use of state released test items, the teachers will be preparing students for success on the high-stakes standards test by acquainting them with the format of item types that they are likely to encounter.

It is important to note that Miss Nelson and Mrs. George tend to give less attention to certain item types that were used by Mr. Carlos, including true-false, matching, and sentence completion items. There is good reason for this neglect. These item types are rarely seen on state standards tests or benchmark tests because their tendency to introduce chance into the assessment process diminishes their reliability. In addition, they are useful for assessing knowledge recall and low levels of comprehension, rather than higher-order thinking skills such as application, analysis, and synthesis. Multiple-choice items can serve the purposes met by true-false, matching, and sentence completion items while maintaining higher levels of reliability. Moreover, multiple-choice items lend themselves to analyses of group performance on tests, which we will explore in Chapter 7.

Summary

As former students, we are familiar with summative assessment. Normally consisting of tests, quizzes, reports, and projects required by the teacher, students see these exercises as the means by which teachers assign grades and ultimately report on student progress to parents and other officials. As teachers, we learn that summative assessment serves other purposes beyond reporting achievement scores to students and parents.

Summative assessments prepare students for challenges they will encounter later in schooling and in all walks of life. In today's standards-based reform movement, summative assessments evaluate the extent to which students demonstrate the knowledge and skills of their state's K–12 curriculum standards. They do this by aligning test and project items with the tasks that are described in state standards and frameworks. They also prepare students for strong performances on state standards tests in core curricular areas.

As teachers plan their lessons and assessments to include the learning expectations of their state's standards and to exceed these with other aspects of the local curriculum, they are preparing students for life's expectations. Summative exams also help teachers improve their own instruction. When thought of this way, summative exercises for students are the formative assessment tools for teachers who seek to improve their own instruction. When teachers examine the results of their students' assessments, they can identify areas of student misunderstanding and improve instruction and performance on future assessments.

The two vignettes in this chapter revealed how summative assessment has changed in response to the current reform environment in public education. Unit tests, projects, and reports now prepare students for exams prepared outside the classroom, including school district benchmark tests and state standards tests. Today's teacher uses many resources to guide summative assessment development, including state standards, curriculum frameworks, state-released test items, and instructional objectives derived from state standards. Test item types reflect the formats of large-scale assessments and district benchmark tests, which rarely use true-false, matching, or sentence completion item formats.

Our vignettes continued to emphasize how the reform movement of today is pulling teachers out of their historical isolation and into collaborative planning and assessment practices. Teachers are planning instructional objectives together and working on the development of commonly administered assessments. Grade-level teams of teachers in elementary schools and teachers with common subject assignments in secondary schools are administering the same unit exams to all their students with increasing frequency.

Student projects and reports are useful products for assessing student knowledge and skills, and analytic assessment tools, including rubrics, are now used to score student work in relation to learning expectations of standards.

Finally, we noted that new approaches to summative assessment, administered by various levels of authority, have resulted in a hierarchy of student evaluation tools that include classroom-based assessment, district-developed benchmark assessments, and state-administered standards-based tests. These three different layers of student performance evaluation are related to the extent that they focus on student achievement of learning expectations found in state curriculum standards.

Exercises

1. Summative assessment has purposes that extend beyond the assignment of student grades. On a sheet of paper, jot down your recollection of as many purposes as you can recall that lead to improvements in student learning.

2. Examine a copy of a teacher-made test or quiz. Examine the format, student directions, distribution of item types, and vocabulary used in the exam. Evaluate the quality of the exam in relation to principles of effective summative assessment described in this chapter. Does the exam maximize student performance in any way? Is there evidence of bias? Will the exam elicit the best possible performance from students?

3. Teachers frequently use commercially produced tests and quizzes that accompany a textbook or curriculum program. What issues might a teacher consider before using a commercially produced exam as a summative assessment? Provide a written response to this question, and include consideration of content validity as it was presented earlier in this text.

4. It is Wednesday, and you have almost finished teaching a unit. Tomorrow you will have time to review the unit with students and give them information about the unit test they will take on Friday. Prepare some notes that will inform them about the test with the intention of maximizing their performance without compromising the integrity of the exam.

5. Go to your state's website and obtain information about your state standards test in an area in which you teach. Read information about the state tests, including test item types, released state test items, or any other descriptive information about the test that may be available. Now consider how you might modify a unit test to prepare students for success on your state's standards test based on the information you found on the website. List some augmentations to your unit test that would prepare students for success on high-stakes tests.

6. Examine your summative assessment practices across the year. Within one semester, how many unit exams or quizzes do you administer? Which of these are formative, and which are summative? What additional student work is collected that constitutes summative assessment? Comment on the extent to which students have an opportunity to demonstrate the skills, knowledge, and disposition of the subject you teach through a variety of experiences that respect variation in student expressive skills. If you detect a need to add variety to your assessment methods, suggest some approaches you might add in addition to variety of item types on tests and quizzes.

Resources and Suggested Readings

Summative assessment is the centerpiece activity in efforts to evaluate instruction and improve student learning. Students have submitted tests, quizzes, oral reports, and papers to teachers as evidence of their learning ever since pens, ink, and paper have been available to record student thoughts. The advent of new technologies have contributed to an acceleration in classroom-based assessment cycles, making more frequent assessment possible, much to the chagrin of teachers, who believe today's student is overly tested.

NCLB has also changed summative assessment, resulting in more frequent alignment of teachers' assessment practices with the measurement of student achievement of state curriculum standards. In this chapter, the writings of two researchers have contributed to our understanding of changes in assessment practices and their alignments with standards-based instruction. Margaret Goertz (Goertz & Duffy, 2004) and James Spillane (Spillane, Halverson, & Diamond, 2001) have contributed a substantial body of research in educational policy and practice in the context of our current reform movement in public education. Both of these researchers have been contributing members of the Consortium for Policy Research in Education (CPRE). CPRE provides a number of policy briefs and research reports at its website. Nationally recognized thinkers who provide useful direction and understanding amid the confusion that can arise in reform efforts are members of the consortium, and readers may find helpful insights to guide teaching and assessment practices at www.cpre.org.

References

Airasian, P. W. (2000). *Assessment in the classroom: A concise approach* (2nd ed.). New York: McGraw-Hill.

Barron, B. J. S., Schwartz, D. L., Vye, N. J., Moore, A., Petrosino, A., Zech, L., & Bransford, J. D. (1998). Doing with understanding: Lessons from research on problem- and project-based learning. *Journal of the Learning Sciences, 7*(3/4), 271–312.

Bay, J. M., Reys, B. J., & Reys, R. E. (1999). The top 10 elements that must be in place to implement standards-based mathematics curricula. *Phi Delta Kappan, 80*(7), 503–506.

Black, P., & William, D. (1998). Assessment and classroom learning. *Assessment in Education, 5*(1), 7–74.

Burstein, L., McDonnell, L. M., Van Winkley, J., Ormseth, T. H., Mirocha, J., & Guiton, G. (1995). Validating national curriculum indicators. *Rand Publications MR All Series, 658*.

Crooks, T. J. (1988). The impact of classroom evaluation practices on students. *Review of Educational Research, 58*(4), 438–481.

Elkins, J. (2002). Learning difficulties/disabilities in literacy. *Australian Journal of Language and Literacy, 25*(3), 11–18.

Falk, B., Wichterle Ort, S., Moirs, K. (2007). Keeping the focus on the child: Supporting and reporting on teaching and learning with a classroom-based performance assessment system. *Educational Assessment, 12*(1), 47–75.

Fan, X., & Chen, M. (2001). Parental involvement and students' academic achievement: A meta-analysis. *Educational Psychology Review, 13*(1), 1–22.

Goertz, M. E. (2003, April). *Implementing the No Child Left Behind act: The potential for a "perfect storm."* Paper presented at the annual meeting of the American Educational Research Association, Chicago, IL.

Goertz, M. E., & Duffy, M. (2004). Mapping the landscape of high-stakes testing and accountability programs. *Theory into Practice, 42*(1), 4–11.

Guskey, T. (2004). The communication challenge of standards-based reporting. *Phi Delta Kappan, 86*(4), 326–329.

Kornhaber, M. L. (2004). Appropriate and inappropriate forms of testing, assessment, and accountability. *Educational Accountability, 18*(1), 45–70.

Leahy, S., Lyon, C., Thompson, M., & William, D. (2005). Classroom assessment: Minute by minute, day by day. *Educational Leadership, 63*(3), 18–24.

Linn, M. C. (2000). Designing the knowledge integration environment. *International Journal of Science Education, 22*(8), 781–796.

McGehee, J. J., & Griffith, L. K. (2001). Large-scale assessment combined with curriculum alignment: Agents of change. *Theory into Practice, 40*(2), 137–144.

O'Shea, M. (2005). *From standards to success: A guide for school leaders*. Arlington VA: Association for Supervision and Curriculum Development.

Schlichte, J., Yssel, J., & Merbler, J. (2005). Pathways to burnout: Case studies in teacher isolation and alienation. *Preventing School Failure, 50*(1), 35–40.

Shaftel, J., Belton-Kocher, E., Glasnapp, D., & Poggio, J. (2006). The impact of language characteristics in mathematics test items on the performance of English language learners and students with special needs. *Educational Assessment, 11*(2), 105–126.

Shepard, L. (2000). The role of assessment in a learning culture. *Educational Researcher, 29*(7), 4–14.

Solomon, G. (2003). Project-based learning: A primer. *Technology and Learning, 23*(6), 1–20.

Spillane, J. P., Halverson, R., & Diamond, J. B. (2001). Investigating school leadership practices: A distributed perspective. *Educational Researcher, 30*(3), 23–28.

Stiggins, R. J. (2001). *Student-involved classroom assessment* (3rd ed.). Upper Saddle River, NJ: Merrill/Prentice Hall.

Sunderman, G., Kim, J. S., & Orfield, G. (2006). NCLB meets school realities: Lessons from the field. *Harvard Educational Review, 76*(1), 123–124.

Syers, C., & Shore, B. (2001). Science fairs: What are the sources of help for students and how prevalent is cheating? *School Science and Mathematics, 101*(4), 206.

Wiggins, G. P. (1999). *Assessing student performance: Exploring the purpose and limits of testing.* San Francisco: Jossey-Bass.

Worthen, B. R. (1993). Critical issues that will determine the future of alternative assessment. *Phi Delta Kappan, 74* (6), 44.

Chapter 7

Constructing and Using Assessments

LEARNER OBJECTIVES

At the conclusion of this chapter, the learner will be able to

▶ Apply test construction methods that improve reliability and validity.

▶ Design tests that reflect important test construction principles.

▶ Identify item types used in construction of tests and quizzes.

▶ Recognize strengths and weaknesses in test item types.

GRAPHIC ORGANIZER

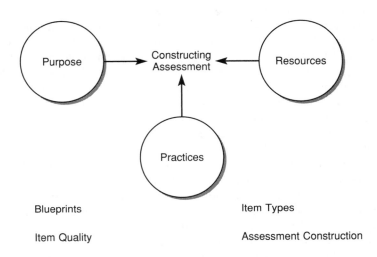

| Blueprints | Item Types |
| Item Quality | Assessment Construction |

ASSESSMENT VOCABULARY

Advance organizer: An outline or graphic depiction of the conceptual and organizational structure of a body of knowledge presented before instruction as a means for linking content of a lesson with prior knowledge of the learner.

Constructed response items: Test items that require the examinee to provide an answer as a word, symbol, or written statement. A correct answer is not provided for selection.

National Assessment of Educational Progress: A nationally normed examination administered across the country that is used to assess the relative academic rigor of state standards tests.

Propositional statements: A declaration of fact that is either completely true or false. Propositional statements form the stem of true-false questions.

Selected response item: A category of test item types including true-false, matching, and multiple-choice questions. Examinees select a correct choice from among several provided and do not need to generate their own words or symbols.

Test blueprint: Often referred to as a table of test specifications, this guiding document identifies the process skills or levels of cognitive challenge that will be applied to specific domains of content. The cells of the resulting matrix describe tasks that can form the basis of a curriculum and an assessment of the curriculum.

INTRODUCTION

In previous chapters, we explored assessment purposes, principles of assessment practice, and changes in assessment through the years as the standards-based reform movement has progressed. In particular, we examined preinstructional assessment conducted before the school year begins, formative assessment as work with students gets underway, and summative assessment to evaluate student learning at the end of instructional units. At all times we have emphasized assessment as an integral part of instruction and learning. We used vignettes of assessment practice as seen prior to the current reform movement and in the present day to underscore changes in assessment driven by K–12 curriculum standards and the high-stakes testing brought about by No Child Left Behind.

In this chapter we will examine the development, administration, and evaluation of assessments in greater detail, as we look into planning the design of an assessment, including the distribution and kinds of assessment items, writing various types of assessment items, and the construction and administration of tests to improve their reliability and validity. We will learn quick and efficient methods for using assessment instruments to improve instruction and student learning.

Our repertoire of assessment methods will expand to include the use of projects, reports, and performances to understand broader dimensions of student growth and development. Fortunately, state and national curriculum standards can guide our development and use of these less conventional forms of assessment. We will see that projects, reports, and performances invite students to express their depth of understanding, perspectives, creativity, and dispositions in ways that reflect the expression of these personal attributes in daily life.

We begin this chapter by examining the planning and construction of conventional forms of assessment with which teachers are most familiar. These include tests and quizzes with such popular items as true-false, multiple-choice, and essay questions. We will see how planning tools and resources, including test blueprints and standards-based documents, can be used to increase the validity of teacher-made tests during design. Then we will look closely at conventional test item types, their construction, and their purposes. Suggestions will be provided to increase the reliability of teacher-made tests through the improvement of each item type. Suggestions for test administration will be provided along with ideas and methods for scoring item types, with an emphasis on scoring **constructed response items**, including short-answer and essay questions.

As we progress through this chapter, we will note how conventional practices are adjusted to accommodate the assessment of state curriculum standards. Test construction and administration can be adjusted to enhance the likelihood that students will achieve standards both in the assessments we develop for the classroom and in district- and state-administered standards-based exams. At the end of this chapter, we will look at the use of assessment results for the improvement of instruction and student learning. Assessments are ultimately intended to provide students and teachers with information about student achievement. How teachers and students respond to this information is greatly affected by the interpretation of test results and analysis of student performance at both individual and group levels (Wiggins, 1999).

LINKING INSTRUCTION TO ASSESSMENT

Recall from Chapter 2 that we want our classroom assessments to be valid and reliable. That is, we want them to evaluate a body of knowledge and skills conveyed to students and to do so in a manner that treats all students fairly, equitably, and accurately. Validity of the assessment experience is addressed as we consider the scope of content and the nature of tasks students will encounter during an assessment. Reliability of the assessment is addressed as we plan the structure and organization of the test or quiz. The distribution and frequency of use of item types, an issue that usually follows after the format and structure of the test have been planned, can substantially affect the reliability of an assessment. Both validity and reliability can be improved by applying certain principles as we write and edit test items.

Two vignettes were provided in Chapter 6 that gave us insights into the thoughts of teachers as they planned conventional assessments. Mr. Ruben Carlos considered the perspective of the student as his dominant frame of reference in organizing his test and selecting item types. Mrs. Gwendolyn George and Miss Julie Nelson, working in the current reform environment, looked at test construction from a frame of reference that sees unit tests as part of a larger system focused on student achievement of K–12 curriculum standards. How can these different perspectives be combined to maximize the effectiveness of teacher-made tests as evaluation tools and to guide improvements in teaching and learning?

Several resources and concepts are available to help teachers plan and construct tests and quizzes. When used thoughtfully, these resources will help the teacher measure the content and skills taught within a given time period. Assessment planning resources, when used effectively, can also lead us to good decisions about the emphasis placed on various topics and skills during instruction and the appropriate depth of understanding and skill application we want to see from our students (Linn & Gronlund, 2005).

BLUEPRINTS ARE TOOLS FOR INSTRUCTION AND ASSESSMENT

The **test blueprint**, sometimes referred to as a table or directory of test specifications, is a tool typically used by professional assessment experts, but it can also guide teachers in planning and organizing instruction, conventional tests, and quizzes (Thorndike, 2005). A test blueprint is a matrix or table that matches the sequence of topics and skills to be assessed with cognitive or performance skills to be demonstrated by students. As the blueprint is prepared, the teacher describes desired expressions of student performance in the cells of the matrix. These cell descriptions are the interface between processes, seen as headings for each row and content domains that are seen as headings for each column (Wilson & Sloane, 2000). The blueprint can serve as an instructional guide, identifying various manifestations of student behavior or products that would be desirable outcomes of instruction over the course of a unit.

Ideally, teachers in the same common assignment can prepare a blueprint as they plan a unit. As each cell is completed, they have a sense of the cognitive and applied skills they would like to develop with their students and the content areas within which those skills are applied (Notar, Zuelke, Wilson, & Yunker, 2004). As the teachers envision manifestations of skills applied to content and write these descriptions in the cells, they are taking the first steps toward writing instructional outcomes to be achieved during the unit of instruction.

The value of a blueprint as an instructional planning tool may be seen in many applications. It can guide teachers in the development of a coherent sequence of lesson plans that achieve important outcomes. The cognitive and process skills of the unit, described in the first column of the matrix, will ensure that students achieve higher-order learning outcomes as they work on the topical areas of the unit (Downing & Haladyna, 1997).

The topic heading of blueprints, typically describing major categories or themes to be studied during the unit, serves to link disparate facts and ideas into larger concepts and principles of significant learning.

Students Can Use Blueprints as Instructional Guides

Blueprints can be distributed to students when a unit of instruction is introduced. As students review the blueprint, the teacher can explain the skills they will apply to the content to be learned. The blueprint will also describe in general terms the kinds of products that students will develop or new abilities they will demonstrate as they progress through the unit. If the blueprint includes a description of the lessons that will convey the knowledge described within the blueprint, students will understand the relationship of each lesson to unit concepts and themes. Used in this manner, the blueprint becomes an **advance organizer**, an instructional tool that research has demonstrated to be an effective means of helping students acquire and retain new knowledge (Marzano, 2001).

An advance organizer can be a graphic representation of the knowledge and skills a learner will acquire, as seen before the introduction to each chapter in this book. When an advance organizer is presented to students along with a description of the activities and experiences that will convey the knowledge and skills, it becomes a powerful tool that assists students with their learning.

Finally, a blueprint can be shared with students before a test to show them the domains of knowledge and skill for which they will be held accountable. When used as an assessment tool, the blueprint typically includes notes about the percentage of items to be attributed to each of the processes and content area, resulting in cell intersections that reveal the estimated emphasis on each area within the test itself. The teacher may also reveal the nature of item types that will be used to assess the processes and knowledge found in each cell of the blueprint matrix. Teachers who present this detailed information about an assessment before it is administered believe that students should be given every opportunity to understand the nature of the testing experience they are going to encounter. When students know what to expect, they will be less anxious. Student general anxiety and emotional response to assessment uncertainty reduces the reliability and validity of an assessment experience (Hancock, 2001).

Although blueprints can serve many useful purposes as instructional tools in general and as advanced organizers in particular, their predominant use is for the preparation of tests, quizzes, and other forms of assessment. When the cells of the blueprint matrix are completed, they can be used to guide the selection of test items and the overall format of the test itself. At this juncture, it is helpful to see one or two blueprints, how they are developed, and how they can be used in planning a test.

WHAT RESEARCH CAN TELL US ...

• About Advance Organizers

In 1963, psychologist David Ausubel published a groundbreaking study on student expository learning facilitated by the introduction of new material through a graphic or written introductory communication intended to link the new material to prior student learning. He named this introductory information a graphic organizer. Since 1963, many studies (Hawk, 1986; Horton, Lovitt, & Bergerud, 1990) have supported Ausubel's original contention that student learning and retention are improved when instruction begins with the introduction of a graphic organizer. Now that learning is extending into the electronic age with an emphasis on distance learning media and visual content, researchers are exploring the feasibility of graphic organizers for facilitation of unconventional instruction. Researcher Carol Story conducted a review of the research in 1998 and reached some preliminary conclusions about the application of advance organizers to visual learning. She concluded that both retention and initial understanding of content presented through a video presentation was facilitated by use of an introductory advance organizer. In particular, she noted that advance organizers may be of particular use in distance learning where explanations and descriptions of content are required for student understanding. This finding should encourage further research on the application of advance organizers in distance learning experiences.

BLUEPRINTS: THEN AND NOW

Our first blueprint will be developed using general principles of test construction that were applied by Mr. Ruben Carlos in the first vignette of Chapter 6. At the time Mr. Carlos was introduced, state curriculum standards were not dominating public school instruction at they are today. You may recall that Mr. Carlos used his textbook, district curriculum guide, general principles of test construction he learned in his teacher education program, and the *Taxonomy of Educational Objectives: Cognitive Domain* developed by Benjamin Bloom to develop his test and sequence item types (Usova, 1997). Our first blueprint (Figure 7.1) will reflect this emphasis on test development, which will be evident because a modified version of Bloom's taxonomy will appear as the set of process and cognitive skills found in the first column of the blueprint.

Our second blueprint (Figure 7.3) will be suitable for instructional and assessment planning as it was encountered by Mrs. Gwendolyn George and Miss Julie Nelson during their assessment planning in today's standards-based reform environment. However, both blueprints pertain to the same unit of U.S. history as taught by Mr. Carlos, so that comparisons and contrasts will be apparent.

In developing the second blueprint, which reflects the current emphasis on state standards achievement, we will use the California History-Social Studies Framework that includes the California History–Social Studies standards as a resource. For this matrix, the process skills of Bloom's taxonomy will be replaced by the Historical and Social Sciences Analysis Skills (California Department of Education, 2005).

FIGURE 7.1   A Conventional Blueprint That Applies Bloom's Taxonomy

Cognitive or Process Skill Objectives	Content Area: Colonial History—the South	Content Area: Colonial History—the North	Content Area: Colonial Government
Recognizes essential terms and definitions	Jamestown John Smith James River	Plymouth Colony John Winthrop William Penn	Williamsburg
Recalls ideas and important facts			Essential ideas in the Mayflower Compact
Applies facts to novel situations	Design a plantation based on knowledge of crop varieties		
Analyzes situations using principles			Site selection of a colony based on identified concerns
Prepares original positions, opinions using principles	Prepares argument against importation of slaves		
Evaluates a statement using criteria			Rights of men implied in the Mayflower Compact

Reprinted, by permission, California Department of Education.

Figure 7.1 shows the first of the two blueprints. It reflects the traditional approach that might have been used by Mr. Carlos and includes modifications in the *Taxonomy of Educational Objectives: Cognitive Domain* developed by Benjamin Bloom as process and cognitive skills. Note that the content of instruction, pre-Colonial U.S. history, has been aggregated into three major themes to be assessed on the unit test. These are Colonial History of the American South, Colonial History of the American North, and Colonial Government.

The cells that result at the intersections of each of the major themes and the skill objectives include different kinds of descriptive information about intended student learning, depending on the skill level of the matrix row. When the skill levels include name recognition or recall of ideas and facts, names, locations, or ideas to be recognized or understood by students, they are indicated in the related matrix cells. When the rows of the blueprint are headed by higher-level cognitive skills, including applications, analyses, or principles, the matrix cells describe a task or a product that will manifest the skill or ability as it is applied to the relevant theme.

You may note that Figure 7.1 shows a blueprint that has many cells without entries. This may arise because some themes or topical areas may not have a relevant counterpart process or cognitive skill application in the planned unit of instruction.

Note that the cell entries result from a teacher's exercise of creativity and professional judgment. As the blueprint is completed, the teacher proposes appropriate expressions of skill or knowledge that relate the process skill of a given row to the theme or topical area of the related column. For instance, the intersection of the row headed by "Analyzes situations using principles" and the column headed by "Colonial Government" displays an application of the analysis skill to the topic area resulting in the entry "Site selection of a colony based on stipulated concerns."

Given the limited information in the matrix, we can only infer the broader dimensions of this expectation the teacher holds for students in this course on U.S. history. Perhaps the teacher will present information about factors colonists considered in selecting sites for their first settlements, possibly to include safety, transportation, food production, food gathering, and potential for resource exploitation. Students may be asked to identify a location on the map of a hypothetical land grant where they would install their colony. They would defend their site selection based on certain geographical, political, and environmental factors. The student project intended to manifest the understanding for this cell might include the completed map, commentary about features found on the map, and an essay justifying the selected site.

As the teacher recalls the instruction that students experienced in producing work related to this particular blueprint cell, the recollection informs the writing or selection of test items that would best measure student understanding and retention of skills and knowledge used to produce the site location exercise. After descriptions of student performance are provided for several cells, the number of test items that might be used to elicit the performances is included in the blueprint. A blueprint serves as a guideline for the construction of a test or quiz when it includes the process objectives, the content domains to be considered, and the number and type of items to elicit desired responses (McDonald, 2002). Figure 7.2 shows our first blueprint seen in Figure 1.1 with the addition of teacher notes regarding the possible item types and the percentage of assessment items and assessment time to be allocated to measuring the skills and content in each cell of the matrix.

FIGURE **7.2** **Conventional Blueprint That Applies Bloom's Taxonomy**

Percentage of test items to be allocated to each thematic area:

		30%	30%	40%
	Cognitive or Process Skill Objectives	**Content Area: Colonial History— the South**	**Content Area: Colonial History— the North**	**Content Area: Colonial Government**
10%	Recognizes essential terms and definitions	Jamestown John Smith James River	Plymouth Colony John Winthrop William Penn	Williamsburg
15%	Recalls ideas and important facts			Essential ideas in Mayflower Compact
25%	Applies facts to novel situations	Design a plantation based on knowledge of crop varieties		
15%	Analyzes situations using principles (5% of test)			Site selection of a colony based on identified concerns
20%	Prepares original positions, opinions using principles	Prepares argument against importation of slaves		
15%	Evaluates a statement using criteria			Rights of men implied in the Mayflower Compact

FIGURE  **7.3   A Blueprint That Uses Process Objectives Taken from Skills and Abilities of California's History-Social Studies Standards**

Skills and Abilities from California History-Social Studies Frameworks	Content Area: Colonial History— the South	Content Area: Colonial History— the North	Content Area: Colonial Government
Place events in chronological sequence	Time line for establishment of first colony holdings	Time line for establishment of southern colonie	
Compare and contrast events in two time periods	Agriculture then and now	Relative population growth of cities: graph interpretation	Tax law development then and now
Determine absolute and relative locations with maps		Latitudes and longitudes of northern colonies	Latitude and longitude and relative growth: Williamsburg and Philadelphia
Contrast fact with fiction; historical documents and interpretive narrative	Washington as fact and fiction: Washington as great general		

We will now examine our second blueprint, which reflects the emphasis on student achievement of K–12 curriculum standards brought to test construction by contemporary teachers, including Mrs. George and Miss Nelson of our second vignette in Chapter 6. Note that the process objectives arranged along the vertical axis of the first column of the blueprint in Figure 7.3 include skills and abilities taken from page 75 of the History-Social Studies Framework for California Public Schools. The content, related to pre-Colonial U.S. history, has been modified to include major content standards of pre-Colonial U.S. history also found in the frameworks.

Blueprints Facilitate Alignment of Instruction and Assessment with Standards

The standards-based blueprint, containing process skills and content themes of the disciplines extracted from state standards or frameworks, is used to plan student performances that manifest achievement of the standards (Rothman, 2002). Teachers developing a standards-based blueprint for teaching or assessment purposes can use their state standards resources for completing the rubric cell descriptions. State standards resources, including state assessment guidelines and released test items, provide descriptions of expected student applications of process skills to major themes found in the standards or frameworks. Moreover, the use of these resources to complete cell descriptions of expected student work ensures alignment between instruction, the expectations of the standards, and particular abilities or knowledge likely to be tested by state standards tests.

When a test blueprint is used to plan a test or quiz, the percentage values attributed to topics or themes are multiplied by the percentage value identified for process skills seen at the beginning of each row. This results in the percentage of the assessment that will be attributed to the content of the cell (Downing & Haladyna, 1997). In Figure 7.2, where these values have been placed, 30% of the content domain to be assessed will be related to Colonial history of the South. Additionally, a corresponding 25% of the assessment will be attributed to the process skill of row 3, "Applies facts to novel situation." The performance expectation of the cell "Design a plantation based on knowledge of crop varieties" is at the intersection of these two percentage allocations, and their product is 7.5%. If the principle of allocating item types on the test to each cell were carried out with fidelity, 7.5 points of a 100-point test, or 7.5% of the time of the assessment, would be attributed to assessing student abilities and skills related to plantations, the crops they produced, and the planning of a feasible plantation, including crops to be cultivated based on agricultural and economic conditions of the Colonial South.

After the task of multiplying row and column percentages results in cell percentages, the amount of time or percentage of test items allocated to the measurement of each cell's content can be estimated. Note that adjustments need to be made because empty cells will not be assessed, so cells containing performance descriptions will end up having an adjusted percentage based on the total percentage or point value attained in the entire blueprint. Hence, if 70% of the cells have content descriptions, one particular cell with content may represent 8% of the test through the multiplication process. Based on a 100-point test, 8% divided by 70% will result in the cell item having an actual percentage value of approximately 11%. Therefore, 11% of the test will assess this item. Please note that this mechanism serves as an indictor to the test writer of the relative amounts of time and effort students should apply to each area of the test to achieve optimal content validity achievable through the use of allocated time (Downing & Haladyna, 1997). It is a useful guideline and not a rule.

After time or percentage of item allocations have been determined, the next step is to identify the appropriate item types that are effective for measuring the content and skills of each cell, which then suggests a possible layout or organization of the test. As certain areas are deemed to be evaluated by a selected response item, perhaps a matching or multiple-choice item, and other cells are deemed to be best measured by constructed response items, such as a short-answer sections or an essay, a vision of the test begins to emerge.

In a conventional blueprint that includes process statements at the beginning of each row, the top rows of the blueprint will be lower cognitive skill questions that may lend themselves to selected response format questions, including multiple-choice items. The rows toward the bottom of the blueprint will lead to cells derived from process skills that are high-order reasoning tasks, which are likely to be best evaluated through constructed response items such as short-answer and essay questions (Downing & Haladyna, 1997). Multiple-choice items have the power to assess these skills as well.

If the usefulness of a test blueprint is extended to the development of the format of the test and the selection or writing of test item types, a first effort at constructing a test design from the conventional blueprint seen in Figure 7.2 might call for

▶ A 12-item matching exercise asking students to associate particular events with particular colonies and colonial cities.

▶ Fifteen multiple-choice items related to the selection of sites for the establishment of colonies.

▶ Several short-answer items and a brief essay dealing with plantation economics, agriculture, and society, in contrast to the developing mercantile economies of the Northern colonies.

▶ A final essay question or two involving the emergence of enlightenment thinking in the political evolution of the colonies in contrast to the persistence of slavery.

Assigning Values to Test Items

As the test begins to take shape, with sections organized sequentially by item type, the issue of score value to each item in a section will surface. These values should derive from the blueprint used to produce the test. If, for instance, the true-false section has been used to assess 10% of the test attributable to one process skill, then each item in the 10-item section should have a value of one point on a 100-point test. After this general plan is reached, the final step is the writing and selection of items that complete the plan's design and measure the content and skill expressions seen in the blueprint cells.

Unfortunately, the development of a text matrix for test planning and test item writing is a substantial effort that takes a great deal of time and thoughtful effort (Doolittle, 2002). As a result, few teachers ever use actual blueprints to design their tests. Nevertheless, a "virtual" test blueprint can be used as a guiding mental construct that a teacher can call on in test design. Better tests can be made by simply noting the process skills and content themes that will interface to form the content of a unit and the corresponding content of an assessment. Ideally, teachers with collaborative planning time will be able to plan units together where a blueprint can lead to coherence between the content that is taught and the content that is tested. In our current reform environment based on state standards achievement, a standards-based blueprint can guide the alignment between the curriculum that is taught, the content that is assessed in class, and the standards that are to be achieved in class and on state standards examinations (Porter, 2002).

AN OVERVIEW OF TEST ITEM TYPES

As teachers, we have all encountered teacher-made tests that used a variety of item types. Teachers may consider several factors in selecting item types, including ease of construction, motivating student performance during testing, conformity of the item type with skills developed in the curriculum, and the power of certain item types to evoke higher-level reasoning from students. Now that we have explored the use of state standards documents, cognitive reasoning constructs such as Bloom's, taxonomy and test blueprints for the purpose of planning instruction and assessment, it is time to review several item types and comment on their relative merits and usefulness in the assessment process. After we have determined the structure and duration of a test or quiz and know the layout in terms of the number and order in which students will encounter assessment types as they proceed through the test, it is time to write the item types and map them back to the skills and knowledge that were taught in class.

Test Items Sort into One of Two Categories

Test item types fall into two categories identified by assessment professionals, and this overview will describe the commonly used item types in these categories. They are selected response items and constructed response items (Popham, 1995). The distinctions between these categories are seen in terms of the behavior expected of the student when a test item is encountered. If the student is directed to select a symbol representing a written statement or other form of a possible answer, the item falls within the selected response category. Perhaps the student is asked to circle or underline one of a few alternative statements or figures. Alternatively, a student may connect items by drawing lines between them. In each of these possibilities, the student is merely selecting from possible answers or choices that have been provided by the test writer. In selected response items, students choose from a limited set of possibilities that are provided by the test author.

If, on the other hand, the student is expected to write words or symbols and provide statements or calculations, then the student is constructing a response to a prompt provided by the test writer or assessment administrator. Items that call for the student to generate words, figures, or other manifestations or knowledge or skill fall within the constructed response category of test items.

Selected Response Items

Many selected response items call for students to recognize the meaning of a term, associate a word with an idea, or know the definition of a word. These mental tasks are considered relatively easy and of minimal challenge to students in comparison to the challenge of responding to constructed response items. As a result, teachers often use selected response items to overcome student fear or resistance to testing. They can be good motivators for students during test administration. When a student's mind is put at ease during a testing experience, anxiety or fear is minimized as factors affecting students' choices. Students respond to fear and anxiety differently, which results in diminished reliability of the assessment experience (Hancock, 2001). Selected response items can be strategically placed in exams to set students at ease. We saw in Chapter 6 that Mr. Carlos considered student responses to testing, and he planned to start his test with true-false items. Although true-false items can reduce anxiety, they have another property that minimizes their effective use on any test. That factor is the introduction of the element of chance.

True-False Items

True-false questions can take on many forms (Gronlund, 1998). Essentially, they are relatively simple exercises that call for students to choose between one of two alternative answers. In most true-false items, the student has a 50% chance of getting a correct answer on each question in the exercise. Conventional true-false questions include a listing of declarative statements followed by the letters "T" and "F." Students select the "T" if they believe the declarative statement to be true, and they select the "F" if they believe the statement is false. Typically, these sections contain 10 to 20 items. Alternatively, a teacher can use different categories of responses as long as only two alternatives are available. These might include "Yes" and "No," "Right" and "Wrong," or "Correct" and "Incorrect." The important factor to consider is that there can be no shades of gray regarding the possible

FIGURE 7.4   A Sample Set of True-False Questions

The capital of Virginia is Richmond.	T	F
Dredd Scott led the raid on Harper's Ferry.	T	F
Fort Sumter is located off the Georgia coast.	T	F
Some states seceded before Lincoln was president.	T	F
The first land battle of the war was at Antietam.	T	F

answer in these kinds of items. The proposed alternative answers must include only one that is at all times correct (Linn & Miller, 2005).

Figure 7.4 includes a set of true-false questions that might appear on a unit test about events that led to start of the Civil War. A teacher might develop the items from a blueprint that included knowledge recall and factual comprehension process skills.

Although seemingly simple to construct, true-false items can lead the teacher into murky waters if they are not prepared with care. Most important, true-false questions must be unequivocally true or false in all cases and circumstances. If the test included the item "West Virginia fought in the Civil War" as an intended false statement because the state did not exist until after the war, a student who chose "true" might challenge that assertion by stating, "I thought that meant that the region of western Virginia was in the conflict, like the Shenandoah Valley," or another student might say, "I knew that the state had not been legally formed, but people in that area did fight in the war." If objections like these are raised after the test is scored, graded, and returned for discussion, the validation of the test comes into question for both the students and the teacher.

Examples of declarative statements that are not suitable include statements that are subject to interpretation or represent an opinion or a point of view (Airasian, 2000). It is not acceptable for the declarative statement to be true or correct in some circumstances or in certain situations. Figure 7.5 includes examples of true and false items that are poorly written because they lack definitive choices.

The first question about George Washington is an opinion statement. Experts might choose other presidents as greater. The statement regarding the preparedness of the Union Army is a matter of conjecture or opinion as well. Minnesota may normally be colder than New York, but there are places in New York where the average January temperature is lower than the average January temperature in some locations of Minnesota. Finally, it would be reasonable for a student to argue that Emerson was a writer, not a philosopher.

FIGURE 7.5   Examples of Poorly Crafted True-False Items

George Washington was our greatest president.	T	F
The Union Army was not prepared for the Civil War.	T	F
Minnesota is colder in winter than New York.	T	F
Ralph Waldo Emerson was a philosopher.	T	F

Guidelines for Using True-False Items

True-false items are an appropriate type of assessment item when they serve specific purposes not well suited to generally more reliable forms of assessment, including multiple-choice items. True-false items, when written as brief declarative statements, may be quickly read and answered. A student can answer 10 true-false items more quickly than most other item types, including multiple choice. In 5 or 10 minutes of test time, a large number of true-false questions can be answered that assess a relatively wide scope of factual knowledge (Haldyna, Downing, & Rodriguez, 2002).

Additionally, true-false questions can assess student factual knowledge while demanding only modest levels of student reading ability. English language learners and struggling readers may find true-false items easier to understand and respond to because they do not have to interpret complex statements including such forms as compound sentences with conjunctions, independent clauses, and dependent clauses. When test items consist of simple declarative statements, the student is assessed for fact and knowledge recall rather than the ability to interpret complex written language. Students who struggle with reading or with English will be able to answer questions correctly and be evaluated for their understanding of a specific content area, not their ability to read English effectively (Lacelle-Peterson & Rivera, 1994).

As previously stated, true-false items tend to set students at ease and allow them to settle into a testing experience with confidence that they will perform well. True-false items, and other formats that are relatively readable and easy to interpret, are well placed when they appear at the beginning of a test (Hedge, 2000). Once all students are at ease about the test, they are more likely to respond correctly to questions. True-false items can help coax the best performance from students on an assessment, which is clearly a fundamental purpose in testing. After all, we want to measure what our students know, and this can only happen when we see their best work.

True-false items are not only easily written by teachers and easily read by students, but they are also easy to score, either by direct observation, using a scoring template consisting of a sheet of papers where the correct answers are punched and missing correct scores are easily recognized and scored, or by machine scoring that involves the use of purchased response sheets. In machine scoring, a test key is prepared that includes marked correct answers, which is passed through the grading machine to "program" it for reading correct answers. When student response sheets are subsequently passed through the machine, they are quickly and automatically graded. The relative ease of scoring true-false items saves the teacher time and adds to the ease of assessing student knowledge (McDonald, 1999).

The less-desirable feature of true-false items should lead the reader use this item type sparingly in classroom tests and quizzes. Although it is tempting to use many true-false items on a test because they are easy to read, write, and score, this temptation needs to be resisted because such items tend to make teacher-made tests insufficiently demanding of student reasoning skills (Barootchi & Keshavarz, 2002). A review of assessment recommendations by organizations that have written state and national standards and frameworks will reveal that these curriculum experts hold true-false items in low regard. As we progress through life, we do not frequently encounter problems and challenges posed as simple dichotomies (Gaberson, 1996). If the completion and filing of federal tax forms consisted of answering a series of simple true-false questions, taxpayers would be quite pleased. Unfortunately, life does not present many clear-cut alternatives to problems as simple declarative statements.

We should keep in mind the intentions that led to the use of test blueprints in constructing assessments. We want students to exercise different kinds of reasoning as they encounter content and process skills. The exercise of higher-order reasoning skills identified in Bloom's taxonomy, including application, analysis, synthesis, and evaluation skills, cannot be conducted through mere knowledge recognition and recall exercises that include true-false questions. Our use of a test blueprint will typically lead to the attribution of no more than 30% of test items in the knowledge recall and comprehension stages of reasoning. True-false items would be included in this limitation.

Improving True-False Items

Most suggestions for improving true-false items are intended to remove ambiguity from the declarative statements that must lead to one of two possible choices as the correct answer (Clark & Watson, 1995). Other suggestions are intended to reduce the role of chance in obtaining correct scores on the true-false section of a test. If these concern areas are addressed effectively, the reliability of the test as a measuring tool and the validity of the assessment experience are both increased. The following suggestions are intended to make use of true-false items and test sections the most effective application of this particular item type.

Use 15 or More Items in the True-False Section

When 10 or fewer items are available in a section, the opportunity of obtaining a high absolute score on the section due to chance is substantially increased (Kubiszyn & Borich, 2000). Given that one positive attribute of true-false test sections is students' ability to answer many questions in a brief period of time, you have an opportunity to assess student comprehension and factual recall of a broad range of knowledge if several related items appear in the true-false section.

Place the true-false section or other item type section that is useful for factual recall of facts and ideas at the beginning of the test. Simply stated item types that only demand factual recall have the salutary affect of setting an anxious student's mind at ease. Additionally, students who are English language learners or struggling readers are more likely to be anxious about tests that may have complex written expressions to interpret. These students may understand the content and skills they have been taught but are unable to communicate them effectively because of limited ability in written expression or reading interpretation. If they are aware of these limitations, then they are more likely to be fearful of complex and wordy items types. A well-placed section of true-false items at the beginning of the test will set the minds of many English language learners and special-needs students at ease (Young, 1991).

▶ Try to write all the declarative statements of approximately equal length. Students may infer that particularly long sentences are true and that particularly short items are false. This invites guessing and strategic application of test-wiseness, which reduces the reliability of the overall assessment (Airasian, 2000).

▶ Make the declarative statements simple **propositional statements**. James McMillan (2004) stated specifically that propositions make a claim about content or relationships among ideas that may be judged as either true or false, right or wrong, correct or incorrect. If all the declarative statements in a true-false section are similar in structure and length, typically consisting of state-of-being verbs (to be), then this common structure will help students move rapidly through a section that should not take up too much test time due to its limitations in evoking student reasoning skills. Further, the common sentence structure will preclude students from using this characteristic of item types to guess answers.

▶ Avoid the use of qualifying words and phrases, including "mostly," "some of the time," or "usually." When these terms are included in a propositional statement, they are likely to render the statement as not always true or false in all circumstances. Further, they invite guessing, with students tending to guess that such statements are likely to be true (Thorndike, 2005).

▶ Remove inappropriate interpretive expectations from simple knowledge recall items that increase the likelihood you are using your test or quiz as an invalid measure of factual recall or comprehension. Avoid the use of negatives, especially double negatives, including "never," "none," or "no" as in: "None of the generals were from Wisconsin." When students are expected to reason their way through statements that call for excluding all possibilities rather than including one specific correct or true fact or idea taught in class, the validity of the test item for measuring content of the curriculum is reduced, and guessing is invited (Thorndike, 2005).

The declarative sentences in the completed true-false section should have uniform appearance. None should visually stand out or be distinctive. If each statement used the verb "to be" in a simple propositional statement, you will have a relatively more reliable true-false section. Be sure to provide clear directions in the section introduction that describe the reasoning task to be conducted and the performance expectation to make a correct response. Keep the directions brief and simply stated in keeping with the principle that true-false questions can elicit understanding and comprehension from students who struggle with reading. An example might be, "Read each statement and decide if it is true or false. If you believe the statement is true, circle 'T' on your answer sheet next to the test item number. Circle 'F' if you believe the statement is false." You can then illustrate the expected performance with an example, showing the format of a typical question on the left side of the example and the format of the corresponding response section on the answer sheet on the right side of the example. Remind students to be sure that the number of the test question corresponds to the number of the response item on the answer sheet. Students often score poorly on tests by placing their answers to prompts in the wrong location on the response sheet (Levine & Rubin, 1979).

Modified True-False Items

Some teachers choose to reduce the effects of guessing and/or clarify the nature of the proposition in the declarative statement by modifying the structure of true-false items. Some of these modifications, particularly those that reduce the affects of guessing, tend to increase the amount of time it takes students to complete the true-false question section, which tends to remove quite a bit of the value of this item type.

One technique for clarifying the nature of the proposition is to instruct students to determine if the underlined word or phrase in a statement is specifically true or false:

The first successful airplane developed by the Wright brother <u>had two wings</u> T F

In the example, we want the student to be clear that the question is about the nature of the airplane, not the names of the inventors of the plane.

Another technique used to limit guessing is to have students write correct answers when they select "false" as the answer (Linn & Miller, 2005). Typically, this approach is called modified true-false. When students choose "false" as their answer by mere guessing, they will not know the word or phrase that would make the declarative statement true. If the teacher requires that the phrase or word making the statement true be provided in instances where false is selected, student understanding of the item will be revealed. In the following example, the student who guesses false must insert the correct organelle name and display that specific knowledge.

Cellular respiration takes place in the ribosome T⑤ Mitochondrion.

A student who does not know the function of various organelles could select "F" and have the correct answer. If the student must select "F" and write in the correct organelle, "Mitochondrion," in the space provided to get credit for a correct answer, then guessing is reduced. Of course, student response time is expanded as well.

One approach to the use of the true-false item format does allow for higher reasoning to be evaluated, and this approach calls for students to respond to several statements that declare aspects of some figure such as a graph to be either true or false. When students read the statement, they must examine the figure to determine if the statement is true or false as it relates to the specific figure. This approach has value because it can be used to evaluate student map or graph interpretation skills very quickly, but the effects of guessing can be substantial because only a few items typically follow the figure to be analyzed.

In the example in Figures 7.6 and 7.7, students encounter a set of true-false items that follow a pie graph that displays a state budget. Several sections of the budget appear for

FIGURE 7.6   Patio State Budget

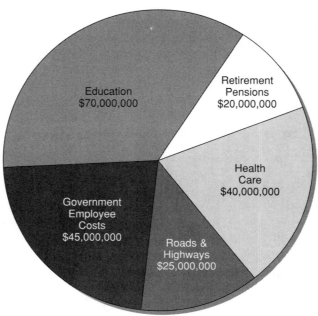

FIGURE 7.7 **True-False Questions about a Graph**

All transportation expenses exceed the cost of health care.	T	F
The largest expense category is public employee expenses.	T	F
Less than one-third of the budget is allocated to education.	T	F
Retirement expenses are more than 50% of the budget.	T	F
Roads and highways expenses are less than government costs.	T	F

student analysis, including education, roads and highways, other transportation, public employee expenses, administrative expenses of the government, state health-care benefits to the elderly, and aid to families with dependent children. By restricting the set of true-false questions to the analysis of the pie graph, the instructor is able to write declarative statements with confidence that comparisons suggested are true in all instances, because the choices pertain to the particular graph, not general financial situations for all states.

It is important to note the role that chance can play with the small number of items on this true-false section. Only five items are provided, giving students a substantial opportunity to get more than half of the items correct just by chance. The assessment task would be more effective if the graphs of similar budget categories for two states were presented and compared with the use of 10 or more true-false items.

True-false items have their place in assessments, but teachers in today's classroom should use them sparingly. The high-stakes state standards examinations and high school graduation tests emerging across the country as part of the current accountability movement tend to use multiple-choice items and constructed response items. Because of the limitations of true-false items discussed earlier, they rarely appear on large-scale assessments used by states and public schools. Students can be lulled into a false sense of confidence in their test-taking abilities and be ill-prepared for high-stakes testing if their teacher relies on true-false and similar selected response items in most classroom assessments (Mislevy, Steinberg, & Almond, 1999).

Matching Items

One of the most common **selected response items** is the matching exercise. These items are similar to true-false questions because they assess factual knowledge and comprehension quickly. They have the additional benefit of being somewhat more reliable than small sets of true-false items. Matching items include two lists of words or phrases placed side by side. Students are expected to associate one expression in a list with its counterpart in the other list. Association may be done by writing the letter or number of one item in a list in an available space in another list of items. An example of a matching question is provided in Figure 7.8.

In this example, students are expected to associate the lettered responses with the listed cell organelles. Note that the topic, "cell organelles," lends itself to matching item assessment because the number of cell organelles included in the assessment falls between 7 and 10 items. If there were less than 7 items, the likelihood of guessing correct associations by chance would be substantial, particularly if half of the correct answers are

FIGURE 7.8   A Matching Exercise from Biology

Write the letter before each cell organelle description in front of the proper organelle name.

___Nucleus	A. Site of protein synthesis
___Cell membrane	B. Form before cell division
___Mitochondrion	C. A fluid throughout the cell
___Golgi	D. Contains other cell organelles
___Endoplasmic reticulum	E. Transportation structures
___Cytoplasm	F. Source of energy for the cell
___Ribosomes	G. Associated with packaging and shipping
___Chromosomes	H. In plant cells only

known. If, on the other hand, there were 12 or more organelles listed for which matching responses were to be found, than the process of searching and finding would constitute an important skill related to a successful outcome, which would contribute to low validity in the assessment process (finding and searching in lists is not a valid measure of knowledge of cell structures).

When a student begins the task of making associations between responses and the list of prompting terms, they must find one correct answer from the entire list. As the student proceeds from one prompt to the next, the list of unused response items on the right diminishes. When the student arrives at the last few items, the process of eliminating responses leads to increased opportunity to guess correctly, or to simply find the correct answer by elimination. If the number of response items is equal to the number of prompting terms on the left-hand list, then the final answer is provided though the process of elimination. This inherent deficiency in sets of matching items can be addressed rather simply by including more possible responses than prompts. Alternatively, students can be informed that prompts may have more than one correct choice in the list of responses.

Matching items are appropriate when all the prompts in the matching item section of the test are thematically related yet distinguishable (Airasian, 2000). In the example provided, all the prompts fall into the category of cell organelles. Each organelle provided in the list has a unique term in the response list with which it can be associated. It is important for the teacher to determine that each prompt has only one correct response provided. As stated earlier however, it is permissible to have response items associate correctly with more than one prompt.

Matching items are an ideal means for quickly assessing student ability to associate functions, appearances, definitions, or other critical attributes with particular prompts in a list of thematically related terms that form all the prompts in the exercise. They also have some of the other positive qualities of true-false items (Taylor & Nolen, 2008).

Matching items call for student vocabulary mastery but not high-level reading skills. They measure student fact recall and comprehension skills while eliminating reading ability as an unintended factor in the assessment process. Matching items can be even easier for struggling readers and English language learners to understand than true-false items, which require understanding of complete sentences that form a proposition to be evaluated as true or false (Carrasquillo & Rodriguez, 2002). They are generally easy to construct, particularly if a list of related but clearly distinct terms can be constructed that includes sufficient items to measure a body of knowledge and eliminate guessing as a dominant factor in selecting items.

Improving Matching Items. Suggestions for improving matching items tend to focus on reducing the role of chance, particularly as students work their way through the list of prompting terms on the left side of that section (Nitko & Brookhart, 2008; Thorndike, 2005). They also relate to the benefits of matching items that are similar to those of true-false items. Finally, methods for improving matching items can focus on limiting the role of searching and finding as factors of successful performance.

Provide for a Recognizable Pattern in the List of Responses So That Finding Associated Expressions for Each Prompt Is Easy. This will diminish searching as a factor in performing the exercise well. For instance, if the list of responses is historical events, than the first item on the list could be the most recent event and the last could be the earliest. On a biology exam, anatomical features in the response list could be listed from head to foot, and in an astronomy test, responses could form a list of objects from those that are near the earth to those that are quite distant.

Provide Directions to Students That Will Help Them Perform Well. Some students will already know that if they put a line across used responses, they will see unused responses readily. If this is a factor that will improve student performance, then instruct all students to do so. If crossing out used choices will not help due to planned redundancy in having some responses associate with more than one prompt, then inform students that this is the case beforehand. The essential principle in giving directions to students on matching items is to eliminate advantages or disadvantages some students may have as a result of prior assessment experience.

Have Students Place a Letter or Number Appearing in Sequential Order before All the Responses with an Appropriate Space Placed before the Prompt. Teachers will sometimes have students draw lines from responses to prompts. This method of responding is prone to error in scoring, particularly when more than eight items appear in the matching section.

Matching Sections Work Well If Prompts Are Single Words and the List of Responses Includes Short Phrases or Words of Similar Length. This will reduce the likelihood that students are making associations on the basis of response structure, rather than response meaning (Linn & Miller, 2005).

Be Mindful of Grammatical Clues That Can Lead Students to Form a Correct Association. Plural and singular noun forms, articles, and verb tenses can lead students to eliminate choices in the response list.

The List of Responses Needs to Be Close to the List of Prompts. Ideally, the lists will appear side by side on the same sheet of paper so that students can see the associations quickly and easily. They should not have to turn a page to compare lists.

Matching sections are good motivators at the beginning of the test. They have the same positive attribute as true-false items of eliminating reading skill as an important factor in obtaining a good score (Arvey, Strickland, Drauden, & Clessen, 1990). Teachers with English language learners, struggling readers, and students with reading disabilities should consider beginning their tests with this kind of activity. It is important to note, however, that matching activities are rarely found on large-scale assessments, including state standards tests and high school graduation tests. Overreliance on matching exercises and true-false items will not prepare students for either the format or higher reasoning expectations they will encounter on important large-scale exams.

Multiple-Choice Items

Perhaps the most recognizable and most frequently encountered of item types, multiple-choice items are the darlings of professional test writers and the bane of many test takers (Birenbaum & Feldman, 1998). These items usually consist of a question or an incomplete statement, referred to as the stem, followed by three to five alternative response words or statements from which students are to select the correct answer. The other alternatives that constitute an incorrect response are referred to as distractors (Thorndike, 2005). Typically, students encounter in sequential order a series of stems with related alternatives in a multiple-choice section.

Occasionally, a series of multiple-choice items will be related to a more substantial prompt, which could be an excerpt from a poem or other literary piece, a section of a primary source historical document, a set of data from a science experiment, a graph, or a chart. The stems of the related multiple-choice items consist of incomplete statements or questions pertaining to the prompt. Students are likely to encounter these kinds of complex multiple-choice item sets on large-scale assessments, including standardized achievement tests and state standards tests. These complex sets of items lend themselves to the evaluation of higher-order reasoning skills, including application, analysis, and evaluation (Thorndike, 2005). In fact, multiple-choice items are admired by test writers because of their power to address all forms of reasoning in Bloom's taxonomy, with the exception of synthesis, which is best evaluated through constructed response items, particularly essay questions (Airasian, 2000). Figure 7.9 is an example of a multiple-choice item that might appear on an exam about the Civil War.

FIGURE 7.9   U.S. History Civil War Multiple-Choice Question

President Lincoln decided to replace George McClellan as the general in charge of the Union forces because McClellan:

   a. lost a series of crucial battles.
   b. was hated by his subordinate officers.
   c. did not lead his men into battle.
   d. refused a direct order from Lincoln.

The stem consists of the statement describing Lincoln's dismissal of George McClellan, and the alternatives consist of four numbered statements for students to choose from. Choice number three is the correct answer, or correct alternative, and the other alternatives are the distractors.

Multiple-choice items have a number of both benefits and disadvantages. In addition to their ability to assess a wide range of reasoning tasks, multiple-choice items can be written so that guessing is substantially reduced as a factor (Burton, 2001). It would appear that students have one chance in four of getting an answer correct, but that is only the case if students have no knowledge of any of the items in the section, which is unlikely to be the case. Typically, students have some knowledge about the stem of at least some questions. The teachers can use partial knowledge to craft attractive distractors that will lead unprepared students to select the wrong answer. In the example provided, the distractor, "lost a series of crucial battles," is made attractive by the use of the adjective "crucial," and the general idea that loss of battles is the leading reason why some generals are viewed as failures. Historians generally accept that Lincoln was far more concerned that his generals engaged the enemy, believing that in the long run the overwhelming resource advantage of the Union would lead to victory (Hattaway & Jones, 1983).

Multiple-choice items should be considered for frequent use on teacher-made tests for classroom-based assessment because students will become familiar with this item type before encountering them on high-stakes tests. When teachers use multiple-choice items, they are preparing their students for success on exams prepared by professional test writers.

Multiple-choice items can be easily scored, and the likelihood of scoring error can be reduced by using an electronic scoring machine. The machine is far less likely to make a scoring error than a human who may be tired after a long day of teaching.

Although it is a challenge to write good multiple-choice items, it is possible to find such items in public domain to match the topics students have been taught (Ross & Nilsen, 2000). Items from the Internet or the teachers' edition textbook can be modified for a particular unit test. Most important, multiple-choice items can be written that are similar in format and content to items students will encounter on high-stakes tests. The use of released test items from professional sources of multiple-choice items, including the **National Assessment of Educational Progress** (NAEP),[1] can guide teachers to the use of questions that are at the same level of challenge that students will encounter on state standards exams and standardized achievement tests used for college admissions and other important purposes.

In this reform era, there seem to be two opposing opinions about multiple-choice items, one held by a group of professionals that includes testing and evaluation experts, and the other held by educators concerned for the comprehensive purposes of public education. Assessment experts admire multiple-choice items for their high reliability when used effectively in test writing, administration, evaluation of student knowledge and skills, and data analysis (Haladyna, 1999) As we shall see in Chapter 8, multiple-choice items lend themselves to a performance analysis that reveals information about student understanding well beyond what can be learned only by looking at the questions students either missed or selected correctly. Many educators are troubled because they perceive an overreliance on high-stakes multiple-choice tests to measure student knowledge and skills. The frequently heard admonishment, "Life does not consist of a series of multiple-choice tests," speaks to questions of validity that arise when multiple-choice items are used almost exclusively to measure student knowledge or ability.

Many experienced educators are calling for authentic assessments that better represent anticipated student performance in life or the workplace (Darling-Hammond, Ancess, & Falk, 1995). Portfolios, projects, and various types of reports are similar to the kinds of work many adults perform in our knowledge-based society. Society, on the other hand, has relied on standardized tests and other kinds of large-scale assessments that rely on multiple-choice items to assess the quality of public schools (Berliner & Biddle, 1995). Clearly, this conflict of opinions is likely to persist into the foreseeable future.

Improving Multiple-Choice Items. A multiple-choice section that consists of well-written items that measure student learning of the curriculum and is similar to external measures of student performance that rely on multiple-choice questions is fulfilling two important purposes. Often a multiple-choice section will follow a matching or true-false section. Although good multiple-choice items may take students from 30 seconds to 2 minutes each to answer, the general quality of these item types as measurement tools justifies their predominance in major tests that consist of a variety of item types (Thorndike, 2005). The following suggestions may help strengthen multiple-choice sections in teacher-made tests.

Leave Knowledge and Factual Recall Tasks to Matching, True-False, and Completion Exercises. Multiple-choice items consume far too much reading time to be wasted on mere factual recall assessment. Students should apply application, analysis, and evaluation reasoning in selecting answers to multiple-choice items. The example item concerning President Lincoln and General McClellan calls for a minimal amount of student interpretation and represents a low-level reasoning task When stems end with probing questions that include, "Which answer best reflects...," or "We can infer the relationship to be...," and related prompts that call for the exercise of judgment or application of procedures, we can be confident that we are using the power of multiple choice to assess the midrange of student reasoning in Bloom's taxonomy.

Although Stems May Sometimes Be Lengthy, Alternatives Should Be Brief. If the purpose of a test item is to measure student understanding of a concept, the definition should appear in the stem, and the alternatives should include the names, titles, or labels for the concept. Figure 7.10 provides a poor and a better example of stem development. In the first example, the alternative choices lack uniformity and/or have too much text.

Avoid using negatives, particularly double negatives, and other terms that qualify conditions or circumstances, including "always," "never," "none," and in particular "all of the above" or "none of the above."

Students tend to select these choices or avoid them by simply guessing about the likelihood that alternatives including these expressions are not likely to be the correct answer or are likely to be the correct answer. Additionally, they diminish the validity of the item for most assessment purposes because the student is asked to apply reasoning regarding

FIGURE 7.10   Good and Poor Examples of Stem and Choice Writing

Poor example:

During Western expansion, manifest destiny was used to justify

    a. the establishment of new states throughout North America.
    b. the trail of tears.
    c. slavery as an economic necessity in new states.
    d. the history of military conflict with Mexico.

Better:

The relentless movement of immigrants and the growing American population into the Western territories of the United States, despite their occupation by Native Americans, was justified by which principle?

    a. The pursuit of happiness
    b. Personal property rights
    c. Manifest destiny
    d. Self-determination

language usage, rather than simply expressing knowledge related to the stem of the question (Thorndike, 2005).

Distractors Should Be Similar in Length and Structure to the Correct Alternative.
Students will often guess that the shortest or longest alternative is the correct answer (Thorndike, 2005). As a general rule, have students select the correct answer from four alternatives. Three alternatives reduce item reliability by introducing chance as a substantial factor, and five alternatives introduce reading proficiency and extraneous test-taking skills as factors (Haladyna, 1999). Including "all of the above" or "none of the above" in questions with four alternatives is almost equivalent to writing a three-alternative question.

Distribute Correct Answer Placement across All the Possible Positions in the List of Alternatives. The old adage, "If you don't know, choose B," suggests that students believe teachers are more likely to place the correct answer in the second position among a set of alternatives. The placement of correct answers should approximate a random distribution across the four possible placements in a listing of alternatives.

Keep in mind that the power of multiple-choice items is in the quality of the stem and the distractors (Haladyna, 1999). The stem should be a clear, coherent statement that makes a complete assertion through the addition of the correct answer. The reader should not have to figure out the meaning or the intent of the stem through an analysis of the alternatives.

Distractors should be appealing as possible answers. Readers of the question who have only casual familiarity with the content or skills of the stem should judge distractors to be reasonable and logical explanations. Knowledgeable and prepared students should be able to recognize the fine distinctions between alternatives that make the correct answer unimpeachable.

Examine publicly released test items for major tests that students will encounter in your discipline or grade level. Replicate these items in form and content, but with appropriate variations in content, to help your students prepare for high-stakes assessments. It is possible to avoid "teaching to the test" while providing students with experiences in assessment that prepare them for testing important to their futures. Given the inclination of our society to measure student advancement to next steps in life through the use of tests that use multiple-choice items, it is appropriate to provide students with the experience of expressing their knowledge and skills with this item type, especially if they will encounter multiple-choice items on high-stakes tests.

CONSTRUCTED RESPONSE ITEMS

Constructed response items require respondents to enter information, not choose from among alternatives presented on the assessment. The information may be as brief as a number or word or as developed as a portfolio or lengthy essay. Constructed responses are more frequently used by teachers than professional test writers. They take time to evaluate and grade, which can introduce low reliability and be prohibitively expensive for large-scale assessment. We will begin our review of constructed response items with a review of sentence completion exercises.

Completion Items

Completion items are commonly used because they are relatively easy to write and easy to grade (Thorndike, 2005). Typically, a completion item is a sentence that is completed by the addition of a word, a number, or a short phrase.

EXAMPLE

The city at the southern end of Lake Michigan that became the railroad hub of America during the early 20th century is:

Completion exercises are similar to true-false and matching items in the nature of the cognitive task they demand of the student. The prompt specifies a particular word or perhaps a short phrase that will make an incomplete sentence a complete idea. The student needs only to recall the word or phrase from memory that makes the sentence a meaningful statement, which is a task at the knowledge recall or comprehension level of Bloom's taxonomy. In comparison to matching and true-false, the task placed before students in completion exercises is more challenging. The correct answer is not visible among alternative choices, as is typically seen in selected response items. Further, the student must recall the correct answer from memory, rather than simply identify it from among other words printed on the exam form.

Completion items are frequently used by teachers because they are easy to write and easy to score in relation to other kinds of constructed response items (Airasian, 2000). They are not as easily scored as selected response items because student writing must be interpreted. Further, students can quickly read several completion items and respond to them almost as quickly as they respond to true-false or matching items. They are almost as amenable to the survey of broad areas of student knowledge in a short period of time as true-false and matching items.

When teachers are not careful in constructing completion items, they learn from their students during test administration that more than one word or phrase will make a completion item true (Linn & Miller, 2005). Problems can quickly develop when several items in a category can complete a statement. Although qualifying adjectives can serve to identify only one answer, the stem can become convoluted and difficult to read or interpret as provided in the following example. The example illustrates a problem that surfaces quite often.

The battlefield in northern Virginia where Union forces suffered their first defeat is _____.

The sentence can be correctly answered by two different names, "Bull Run" or "Manassas," despite the effort to delimit all possible battlefields by referring to location and specific event. If constructed carefully, completion items can measure student foundational knowledge efficiently while minimizing the need for complex reading skills.

Improving Completion Items. Suggestions for improving sentence completion items focus on maximizing the advantages of this item type: speed and efficiency in assessing student knowledge (Thorndike, 2005).

Keep the Prompt, or Sentence to Be Completed, Simple in Structure. Sentences with several clauses and conjunctions include expectations that students can interpret complex sentence structure, which can reduce the validity of this item type. It is best to avoid compound sentences in constructing this item type.

The Missing Term That Completes the Statement Should Come at the End of the Sentence, Not at the Beginning or Midpoint. If the term to be provided completes the sentence at its end, the student will be able to recall the term on one quick reading of the prompt.

In the Event Units of Measure or Two or More Words Are Needed to Provide a Correct Answer, These Should Be Included or Properly Prompted. In the following examples, "The maximum speed limit is _____ m.p.h.," "When added together, the total length of the porch would be _____ inches," and "One of the states that has a two-word name is _____ _____," we can see this consideration is evident in the item structures. When used in conjunction with item types that assess higher-order learning skills, completion items can provide a well-balanced and low-anxiety-producing assessment experience for students (Young, 1991).

Short Answer

Short-answer items are similar in structure to completion items. They consist of a written prompt that calls for students to provide a written response. By contrast, the prompt is a complete statement of thought with no blanks to be filled in. Typically, the prompt is a question or declarative statement that requires students to write an answer, perhaps as a word, a phrase, or a sentence or two. "Name a part of speech used in forming a predicate" is an example of a declarative short-answer prompt. "In what state can you find a large monument to four presidents carved from the side of a mountain?" is an example of an interrogative prompt. Short-answer items may expect students to provide some interpretation or analysis that gives them more power in evaluating higher-order reasoning skills than completion items. Additionally, they are similar in nature to classroom recitation experiences. In many classrooms, teachers follow a presentation or direct instruction experience with questions asked of individual students. As students are asked questions, they are expected to respond with brief statements that may be either factual or interpretive. Short-answer questions often resemble the questions teachers use in the recitation experience. Students are typically comfortable with this kind of exercise because the test experience resembles daily classroom routine.

Short-answer questions can provide challenges to the item writer that are similar to the challenges for writing completion items. The prompt should elicit one particular correct response. Some interpretation or latitude in expression is necessary, however, because students will express a correct idea through different phrases or sentences. This makes short-answer items somewhat subjective to evaluate and open to student challenges regarding acceptable correct responses.

Improving Short-Answer Items. Considerations for improving short-answer prompts are similar to those for improving completion items (Linn & Miller, 2005).

Prompts Should Be Written Simply, Without Extensive Use of Clauses and Conjunctions That Form Compound or Complex Sentences. Readability of the prompt should not be a factor in student assessment of content knowledge. Obscure words, jargon, and language unfamiliar to people outside the region should be avoided.

Specify the Nature of the Desired Response in the Prompt to Reduce Subjectivity in Assessing Responses. In the prior examples of short-answer prompts, the phrases "Name a state..." and "What part of speech..." specify attributes of correct answers that limit subjectivity in evaluating responses as either correct or incorrect.

Model Prompts from Recitation Questions Used in Class. When students read prompts that are similar in vocabulary and structure to questions they hear in class, they will be less anxious about the item type and able to respond based on their abilities and knowledge (O'Shea, 2005).

When Asking for More Than One Term or Idea as a Possible Correct Answer, Specify an Exact or Minimal Number of Responses That Will Constitute a Correct Answer. "State three causes of the Civil War" is preferable to "State the causes of the Civil War."

Short-answer questions can require higher-order reasoning or mere knowledge recall. Students can be asked to evaluate or analyze an expression and then provide an acceptable interpretation or response. Students must consider a concept and its defining attributes when answering the question, "Consider the life cycles of frogs, butterflies, and humans—what stage is common to all three organisms?"

Short-answer questions can be strategically placed between selected response items with low cognitive challenge and constructed response items that call for higher-order reasoning skills. When placed between these kinds of items, short-answer exercises provide a smooth transition from easier to more challenging item types without raising student anxieties.

Essay Items

Essay items consist of extended responses to a written question. They typically require the student to prepare an expository statement of one paragraph or longer. Essay items can be perilous traps for procrastinating teachers (Thorndike, 2005). When tests are planned at the last minute, it is possible to come up with a few questions for students to answer in essay form. If care is not given to properly writing the essay prompt, no clear and consistent means for evaluating student responses becomes apparent, resulting in low reliability in assessing this item type (Harris & Bell, 1994). Essay questions can require students to write lengthy responses that are time consuming, but their power in evaluating student creative expression and higher-order reasoning skills can justify the allocation of a large percentage of test time to this item type.

Some teachers will write essay questions that call for relatively brief responses. An example might include, "Describe food groups that are likely to provide problems in weight control." Given the difficulty and subjectivity in evaluating essay responses, a more appropriate item type for this nutrition prompt is a multiple-choice question. In a typical classroom test, students might have 40 minutes to an hour to respond to a variety of item types. Only two or three essays will be appropriate in tests of this duration that use multiple item types. Given this limitation to the number of essay items that can be asked in any one test administration, it is better to use the power of essays to tap into higher-order reasoning skills, which usually calls for an extended response by the student.

Improving Essay Items. Essay items are best improved by considering the nature of a high-quality student response. The following suggestions will help you write better essay items (Nitko & Brookhart, 2008).

Describe the Attributes of a Desired Student Response and Prompt the Production of Those Attributes in the Question Statement. The essay question, "Why was Napoleon so successful during his early career as a general?" fails to clarify for the student the critical attributes of a good response or the criteria that will be used to evaluate the student's answer. "Describe Napoleon's tactical and strategic military skills that were evident in his victory at Austerlitz." Students are expected to display specific knowledge about tactics and strategy in this second example. The teacher can evaluate the responses of students based on this clearer expectation.

Probe Deeper Understanding Guided by Phrasing Found in Many Explications of Bloom's Taxonomy Related to Analysis, Synthesis, and Evaluation. An example of an essay question that demands higher cognitive reasoning might be, "Evaluate the Jackson presidential administration from the perspective of a Native American and a New York industrialist. Be sure to identify the particular events of his administration that each individual would reference in their judgment of his presidency."

Clarify for the Student the Expected Length or Duration of Time to Be Used in Answering the Essay Question. This information should be provided at the beginning of the test if students are going to encounter essays at the end of the test and to allow them sufficient time to respond to the questions properly.

Decide on the Elements You Expect to See in a Complete and High-Quality Response and Look for These Elements in Each of the Essays That You Evaluate. When grading a large number of student essay responses, it is easy to change one's expectations during the grading, which would reduce reliability significantly (Taylor & Nolen, 2008). This tendency will be substantially reduced if the attributes of a model response are identified before the first essay is scored.

Avoid Having Students Write Their Names on the Paper Used for Writing Essay Responses. Essay readers have a strong tendency to attribute to the essay response characteristics that they see in the author of the essay (Linn & Miller, 2005). If the student's name is not on the response sheet, anonymous scoring becomes possible.

The two item types that are most likely to raise student anxieties are multiple-choice items and essay questions (Ory & Ryan, 1993). Some teachers attempt to reduce student anxiety by allowing students to choose essays they wish to respond to. This is not a good practice for purposes of a reliable and valid assessment experience. When students respond to different essays on a test, the teacher is using two or more distinct instruments to assess the same domain of learning. This reduces the validity of the assessment experience. Further, the lack of uniformity in the measurement instrument used from one student to the next reduces the reliability of the test for measuring equivalent student knowledge.

Standards-Based Constructed Response Considerations

Previously, we noted that a blueprint of evaluative criteria derived from standards and frameworks, along with performance ratings that reflect expectations of the state standards tests, will ensure that the content domains tested in the classroom and by the state are the same. Further, the evaluative criteria of a standards-based rubric, derived from process skills and expected levels of reasoning described in state standards and frameworks, ensure that items developed for the classroom-based test will have the same level of challenge and similar cognitive tasks as those that appear on school district benchmark exams and state standards tests. The following recommendation may help teachers prepare structure response items that elicit student performances in keeping with the expectations of state standards and their assessment (O'Shea, 2005).

Include the Academic Language of the Standards in Prompts. The vocabulary used in state standards is likely to be the vocabulary of items in state standards tests. Therefore, students should learn to respond to the vocabulary of the standards in unit tests and other classroom-based assessments to prepare them for items with similar vocabulary on state exams. Furthermore, students should be expected to use the academic vocabulary of the standards in their assessment responses. Assessment items should be structured to reflect this expectation, and students should be evaluated on their accurate use of standards-based terms, concepts, and principles.

English language learners and other students with special needs are more likely to experience challenges with constructed response test items, particularly essay exams (Hamayan & Damico, 1991). If students are expected to respond to essay prompts with the rich vocabulary of state standards and frameworks, they need prior acquaintance with concept terms and common usage vocabulary that may stump learners still mastering English. For example, if a state standard expects students to write about the life cycle of butterflies and to know the life cycle stages in proper sequence, the term *sequence* may be a major obstacle to English language learners. It a teacher anticipates that students will need to understand the meaning and usage of the term *sequence* on benchmark tests and state standards exams, then the term should be introduced and explained well in class, and it should be accessed during classroom-based assessments.

Some authors have suggested that state standards should be interpreted to students in "student-friendly" language (Reeves, 1998). Unfortunately, this recommendation will not help students when they are assessed by the school district and by the state. The language of the standards is used in unmodified form to write the test items on state standards exams. Therefore, teachers need to prepare students for these exams by developing the vocabulary of the standards through instruction and classroom-based assessment activities.

Ask Students to Apply Process Skills That Appear in State Standards. State standards convey high expectations for student learning. They include knowledge, skills, and dispositions. The skills included in state standards may require students to interpret a passage, recognize themes, analyze graphs and charts, or apply formulas or procedures to data. These higher-order reasoning tasks are well suited to constructed response items. State standards and frameworks may integrate process skills with content expectations, or they may describe process skills in a separate section of the state documents. The process skills should be identified and included in expectations for student performance on classroom-based tests.

Released state test items may be a useful guide in writing constructed response items that require students to apply process skills. In some states, students are expected to show their reasoning on parts of state standards tests that include constructed response items. Other sections of some state tests require students to produce a calculation and grid the response for electronic scoring. Both of these item types may be used for the state to assess student applications of process skills, and they should be reviewed for ideas that can lead to process skill assessment in classroom-based exams.

Refer to Suggestions for Teaching the Standards That Appear in Frameworks. In many states, frameworks and curriculum resources for teaching to the standards have been produced by the state department of education, and these documents can be rich repositories of pedagogical suggestions. Some of these pedagogical approaches may include process skill development within them. For example, the History-Social Science Framework for California Public Schools includes the suggestion that teachers have students prepare time lines that illustrate historical events and social changes. Time line development and interpretation is a process skill as well as a pedagogical device (California Department of Education, 2005). Teachers in California may choose to have students interpret time lines or similar graphic devices in constructed response questions prepared for classroom use.

Summary

Planning tests, writing item types, and arranging items into a coherent assessment experience for students is a time-honored and challenging task. Teachers can call on some useful resources to help design more valid and reliable tests. Test blueprints, state curriculum standards, and state curriculum frameworks are examples of resources that can guide test development. Thoughtful use of these resources can result in assessments that accurately and fairly measure content that was taught in the classroom.

Blueprints can serve as effective tools to incorporate state curriculum standards into the local curriculum. When content and process skills of the standards are included in rubric design, alignment with state standards can be brought into the curriculum as the rubric is used to plan instruction and assessments.

Item writing is both a skill and an art. Guiding principles of validity, reliability and fairness in testing can be expressed as principles of quality item writing. Selected responses and constructed response items have different properties and can be used for different kinds of assessment purposes. When thoughtfully integrated into one assessment instrument, they can provide balance, breadth, and depth of assessment.

Exercises

1. Examine the blueprint in Figure 7.1. Note the content domains at the top of the columns and the entries in the related cells to the right of the process skill, "Recognizes essential terms and definitions." Describe a selected response item type that would be appropriate for assessing knowledge of these domains at the given process skill level. Defend your choice of item type based on the expected skill to be demonstrated as described in the cells to the right of the process skills statement. What kinds of answers would be good in this case?

2. Examine Figure 7.1 and identify the cell with the blueprint entry, "Site selection of a colony based on identified concerns." Identify the process skill and content domain headings that give rise to the content in this cell. Describe a constructed response item type that would be well suited for assessing the skill and knowledge description in this cell, and state the criteria for evaluating student responses to the item type you identify. What should students display in their answer?

3. Figure 7.3 is a blueprint with process skills that have been extracted from state standards. After examining these process skills, review the process skills of the standards or frameworks in the area of your teaching assignment. Write a list of process skills

from your discipline in ascending order of cognitive challenge that could be entries in your own blueprint.

4. Examine the blueprint in Figure 7.2 that provides percentage weightings to the process skills and content domains. The products of these numbers would appear in the cells, and they would be adjusted for the fact that many cells are empty. For this blueprint, assume that half of the cells are empty, so the product of multiplication you arrive at for any one cell would be doubled to give the percentage of a test attributed to measuring the content of a given cell. With this reasoning, 6% of the test should measure the content in the cell titled "Jamestown, John Smith, and James River." Identify the percentage of a test that should be attributed to the cells that include "Site selection of a colony," "Essential ideas of the Mayflower compact," and "Williamsburg."

5. Examine a copy of a teacher-made test and look at the section of multiple-choice items. Critique these items regarding principles for writing good multiple-choice items described in Chapter 7. Do the same critique for all selected response items in the test. Then make a written statement appraising all the selected response categories in the test.

6. Examine a copy of a commercial or teacher-made test that includes essay items. Read the essay prompt to identify the presence of good essay features. Does the question guide the student with evaluative criteria? Are conditions and qualifications of a good response provided? Redraft the essay question using the principles of essay questions provided in Chapter 7

Resources and Suggested Readings

The advent of state curriculum standards has resolved much of the debate about the content and skills to be tested in core subjects at each grade level of our public schools. Since the 1990s, school districts have expended great energy in aligning their curricula with state standards. In most settings, these efforts focused on the adoption of textbooks and curriculum programs that aligned with the scope and sequence of the state standards. Following the alignment of curriculum, additional effort was put into the alignment of teaching practices. Across the country, administrators asked teachers to post the state curriculum standards in prominent locations in the classroom. Teachers were also asked to prominently display the standard currently under development. Lesson plans, when asked for, are typically expected to include the topic of the lesson and the standard that the lesson will address.

Now that attention is turning to the alignment of classroom-based assessment with state standards, educators are seeking advice from leading researchers and thinkers about the use of classroom assessments, district centralized assessment activities, and state standards tests. Two researchers from the University of Colorado at Boulder have observed the emergence of new assessment practices intended to support the achievement of state curriculum standards. Dr. Lorrie Shepherd and Dr. Robert Linn, nationally recognized authorities on assessment practices, have informed educators about the "do's and don'ts" of quality assessment within the current reform context. Dr. Shepherd's work is often cited in the writing of major contributors on standards-based teaching and learning. Douglas Reeves has cited her contributions in a number of his books. Dr. Robert Linn has written widely on assessment policy and practice, and he has authored a number of books, including *Measurement and Assessment in Teaching* (2005).

References

Airasian, P. W. (2000). *Assessment in the classroom: A concise approach* (2nd ed.). New York: McGraw-Hill.

Arvey, R. D., Strickland, W., Drauden, G., & Clessen, M. (1990). Motivational components of test taking. *Personnel Psychology, 43*(4), 695–716.

Ausubel, D. P. (1963). *The psychology of meaningful verbal learning.* New York: Grune and Stratton.

Barootchi, N., & Keshavarz, M. H. (2002). Assessment of achievement through portfolios and teacher-made tests. *Educational Research, 44*(3), 279–288.

Berliner, D. C., & Biddle, B. J. (1995). *The manufactured crisis: Myths, fraud, and the attack on America's public schools.* Reading, MA: Addison-Wesley.

Birenbaum, M., & Feldman, R. A. (1998). Relationships between learning patterns and attitudes towards two assessment formats. *Educational Research, 40*(1), 90–97.

Burton, R. F. (2001). Quantifying the effect of chance in multiple choice and true/false tests: Question selection and guessing of answers. *Assessment and Evaluation in Higher Education, 26*(1), 41–50.

California Department of Education. (2005). *History-Social Science Framework for California Public Schools.* Sacramento, CA: Author.

Carrasquillo, A. L., & Rodriguez, V. (2002). *Language minority students in the mainstream classroom* (2nd ed.). London: Multilingual Matters.

Clark, L. A., & Watson, D. (1995). Constructing validity: Basic issues in objective scale development. *Psychological Assessment, 7*(3), 309.

Darling-Hammond, L., Ancess, J., & Falk, B. (1995). *Authentic assessment in action: Studies of schools and students at work.* New York: Teachers College Press.

Doolittle, A. E. (2002). Classroom assessment: What teachers need to know. *Journal of Educational Measurement, 39*(1), 85–90.

Downing, S. M., & Haladyna, T. M. (1997). Test item development: Validity evidence from quality assurance procedures. *Applied Measurement in Education, 10*(1), 61–82.

Gaberson, K. B. (1996). Test design: Putting all the pieces together. *Nurse Educator, 21*(4), 28–33.

Gronlund, N. E. (1998). *Assessment of student achievement.* Boston: Allyn and Bacon.

Haladyna, T. M. (1999). *Developing and validating multiple-choice test items.* Mahwah, NJ: Erlbaum.

Haladyna, T. M., Downing, S. M., & Rodriguez, M. C. (2002). A review of multiple-choice item writing guidelines for classroom assessment. *Applied Measurement in Education,* 309–334.

Hamayan, E. V., & Damico, J. S. (1991). *Limiting bias in the assessment of bilingual students.* Austin, TX: Pro-Ed.

Hancock, D. R. (2001). Effects of test anxiety and evaluative threat on students' achievement and motivation. *Journal of Educational Research, 94*(5), 284–291.

Harris, N. D. C., & Bell, C. (1994). *Evaluating and assessing for learning.* London: Kogan Page.

Hattaway, H., & Jones, A. (1983) *How the North won: A military history of the Civil War.* Urbana: University of Illinois Press.

Hawk, P. P. (1986). Using graphic organizers to increase achievement in middle school life science. *Science Education, 70,* 81–87.

Hedge, T. (2000). *Teaching and learning in the language classroom.* Oxford, UK: Oxford University Press.

Horton, S. V., Lovitt, T. C., & Bergerud, D. (1990). The effectiveness of graphic organizers for three classifications of secondary students in content area classes. *Journal of Learning Disabilities, 23*(1), 12–22, 29.

Kubiszyn, T., & Borich, G. D. (2000). *Educational testing and measurement: Classroom application and practice.* New York: Wiley.

Lacelle-Peterson, M. W., & Rivera, C. (1994). Is it real for all kids? A framework for equitable assessment policies for English language learners. *Harvard Educational Review, 64*(1), 55.

Levine, M. V., & Rubin, D. B. (1979). Measuring the appropriateness of multiple-choice test scores. *Journal of Educational Statistics, 4*(4), 269–290.

Linn, R. L., & Miller, M. D. (2005). *Measurement and assessment in teaching* (9th ed.). Upper Saddle River, NJ: Merrill/Prentice Hall.

Marzano, R. J. (2001). *A handbook for classroom instruction that works.* Alexandria, VA: Association for Supervision and Curriculum Development.

McDonald, M. (2002). *Systematic assessment of learning outcomes: Developing multiple-choice exams.* Boston: Jones and Bartlett.

McDonald, R. P. (1999). *Test theory: A unified treatment.* Mahwah, NJ: Erlbaum.

McMillan, J. H. (2004). *Classroom assessment principles and practice for effective instruction* (3rd ed.). Boston: Allyn and Bacon.

Mislevy, R. J., Steinberg, L. S., & Almond, R. G. (1999). *On the role of task model variables in assessment design.* Los Angeles: National Center for Research on Evaluation, Standards, and Student Testing, University of California.

Nitko, A. J., & Brookhart, S. M. (2008). *Assessment and grading in classrooms.* Upper Saddle River, NJ: Merrill/Prentice Hall.

Notar, C. E., Zuelke, D. C., Wilson, J. D., & Yunker, B. D. (2004). The table of specifications: Insuring accountability in teacher made tests. *Journal of Instructional Psychology, 31*(2), 115.

O'Shea, M. (2005). *From standards to success: A guide for school leaders.* Arlington, VA: Association for Supervision and Curriculum Development.

Ory, J. C., & Ryan, K. E. (1993). *Tips for improving testing and grading.* Newbury Park, CA: Sage.

Popham, J. W. (1995). *Classroom assessment: What teachers need to know.* Boston: Allyn and Bacon.

Porter, A. C. (2002). Measuring the content of instruction: Uses in research and practice. *Educational Researchers, 31*(7), 3–14.

Reeves, D. B. (1998). *Making standards work: How to implement standards-based assessments in the classroom, school, and district.* Denver, CO: Center for Performance Assessment.

Ross, C. S., & Nilsen, K. (2000). Has the Internet changed anything in reference? The library visit study, phase 2. *Reference and User Services Quarterly, 40*(2), 147–155.

Rothman, R. (2002). *Benchmarking and alignment of standards and testing.* Los Angeles: National Center for Research on Evaluation, Standards, and Student Testing, University of California.

Story, C. (1998). What instructional designers need to know about advance organizers. *International Journal of Instructional Media, 25*(3), 253.

Taylor, C. S., & Nolan, S. B. (2008). *Classroom assessment: Supporting teaching and learning in real classrooms.* Upper Saddle River, NJ: Merrill/Prentice Hall.

Thorndike, R. M. (2005). *Measurement and evaluation in psychology and education* (7th ed.). Upper Saddle River, NJ: Merrill/Prentice Hall.

Usova, G. M. (1997). Effective test item discrimination using Bloom's taxonomy. *Education, 118*(1), 100–110.

Wiggins, G. P. (1999). *Assessing student performance: Exploring the purpose and limits of testing.* San Francisco: Jossey-Bass.

Wilson, M., & Sloane, K. (2000). From principles to practice: An embedded assessment system. *Applied Measurement in Education, 13*(2), 181–208.

Young, D. J. (1991). Creating a low-anxiety classroom environment: What does language anxiety re-search suggest? *The Modern Language Journal, 75*(4), 426–439.

Endnote

1. Information about the National Assessment for Education Progress, often referred to as the nation's report card, can be found at http://nces.ed.gov/nationsreportcard/.

Chapter 8

Using Assessment Results to Improve Learning

LEARNER OBJECTIVES

At the conclusion of this chapter, the reader will be able to

▶ Apply test construction methods that improve reliability and validity.

▶ Design tests that reflect important test construction principles.

▶ Identify item types used in construction of tests and quizzes.

▶ Recognize strengths and weaknesses in test item types.

GRAPHIC ORGANIZER

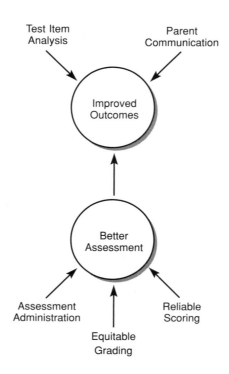

ASSESSMENT VOCABULARY

Mean: The average, or a value that would be found by adding up the total values of all scores and dividing by the number of scores.

Median: The score that can be found in the middle of a range of scores, such that one half of the scores fall below and one half fall above. The median is found by counting the number of scores and finding the score that has an equal number of scores below it and above it in ranked listing of scores.

Mode: The most frequently occurring score. There may be two or more modes, representing the second and third most frequently occurring scores. If scores tend to cluster near two values in the range, then the distribution is described as "bimodal."

Terms that describe the distribution of scores:

Range: The difference in measured units from the highest to the lowest score. If the highest performing student attains a grade of 98 on a test and the lowest performing student attains a grade of 42 on the same test, then the difference between the two values, 56, represents the range for all the ranked scores.

Normal curve (or bell curve): A distribution of scores where the mode is also the mean and the median. The number of scores diminishes the further the score value is from the mean.

INTRODUCTION

Planning and conducting fair and equitable assessments is only part of the process of using assessments to inform students of their progress with learning and to improve instruction. Administering assessments, evaluating student responses to test items, assigning grades to student work, using assessment results to improve instruction, and reporting student progress constitute the body of work to be done after an assessment activity has been planned and conducted. Several of these activities have been affected by standards-based reforms in public education. Most notably, conventional methods of assigning student grades and reporting student progress is undergoing change in many settings because traditional practices of norm-referenced grading are inconsistent with criterion-referenced student performance evaluation in standards-based settings (Wolfe, Viger, Jarvinen, & Linksman, 2007).

Many educators can recall high school and college classes where students were assigned either high or low grades relative to the performance of other students. Students who turned in better work got the As and Bs, and students who performed relatively poorly got the Ds and Fs in norm-referenced grading practices. The shortcomings of norm-referenced grading can be seen in low grades assigned to students in the most selective professional schools in the country. Some of the best and brightest students in the land, upon entering prestigious medical schools, find themselves achieving lower grades because they did not perform in the top 20% or 30% of the students in their class. In norm-referenced grading, some students must rank lower than others, even if all the students in the population demonstrate thorough understanding of the subject matter. This assumption is now being challenged by the criterion-referenced testing systems that are used to measure state standards achievement (Airasian, 2000).

The standards movement is grounded in criterion-referenced assessment practices, where student performances are measured against descriptions of proficient practice and understanding. This new perspective allows all students to be seen as performing well, not just those found to be above average (Meskauskas, 1976). In this final chapter, we will introduce new educators to the promise of fair and equitable grading in the evolving criterion-referenced and standards-based educational system currently in development across the country. These new practices will help teachers align their system of grading with the system used by states as they assess student understanding of state content standards.

We will begin this chapter with a presentation of the vocabulary and essential concepts of descriptive statistics used in the application of norm-referenced grading systems. This presentation will be followed by discussions of assessment activities that typically unfold for the classroom teacher in chronological order, beginning with assessment administration and ending with reporting of student progress. Along the way, we will examine distinctions between both conventional and standards-based assessment practices.

ESSENTIAL CONCEPTS FOR THIS CHAPTER

In norm-referenced grading systems, a core indicator of academic performance is the ranking that students demonstrate in relation to the class average. This convention is so pervasive that it has become a source of humor when used by entertainer Garrison Keillor during his *Prairie Home Companion* radio shows, when he declares that all the children in fictional Lake Woebegon are "above average." Statisticians might suggest to the Lake Woebegon community that their students might perform well in relation to a national sample of test takers, but someone needs to be below average within the local community. Measures of central tendency and score dispersion from the central measure are important concepts for describing the distribution of a set of scores obtained from a test, quiz, or other assessment experience. Several of these essential terms may be found in the section on assessment vocabulary at the beginning of this chapter.

For our purposes, the measure of central tendency most frequently used in assessment activities is the **mean**, or average. If the sum of all test scores is divided by the number of scores used to achieve that sum, the average is determined. Perhaps most laypeople believe that the average will be found in the middle of the scores. That is not always the case. A better measure of the middle point of a set of score is the **median**. This is the score that is found at the halfway point when all scores have been sorted from lowest or highest. The score that has half the values below and half the values above is the median value.

The pattern of dispersal of scores is of interest to educators. Sometime scores cluster around one or two values. The score that appears most frequently is the **mode**. Occasionally, two scores appear frequently with scores clustered around them. This is referred to as a bimodal distribution (Thorndike, 2005).

We are also interested in the **range** of scores, or the difference between the highest and the lowest score. All other scores should have a value within the range.

As we proceed with our discussion of classroom-based assessment, we will be using the terms *mean, mode,* and *range* with frequency.

ADMINISTERING ASSESSMENTS

Classroom administration of assessments is typically handled informally, because teachers rightly assume that students are familiar with testing as a common routine in daily life in schools. Nevertheless, there are a number of considerations to keep in mind while preparing an assessment.

Consider the Student Perspective

Students express considerable anxiety about tests and quizzes, and much of this may arise from the uncertainty they face before the test or quiz (Zeidner, 1998). Students will want to know how to prepare for an exam, how long the exam will last, and if they will have sufficient time to complete it. They may want to know the nature of the items they will encounter. Most important, they will want to know the content and skills that will be assessed. We want to reduce anxiety as much as possible and eliminate it as a contributing factor to poor student performance on tests (Hembree, 1988). We should disclose as much information about the test as possible without compromising its purposes. When students understand the nature of an experience that is before them, uncertainty will be reduced, and the reliability of the assessment experience will be enhanced.

WHAT RESEARCH CAN TELL US ...

• About Test Anxiety

Will humor help students perform better on major exams? If the humor appears in the writing of test directions and test prompts, will it set minds at ease or add to student anxiety? Two researchers affiliated with Johns Hopkins University reported a research study of the effects of humorous directions and prompts placed within a statistics exam on student anxiety levels (Berk & Nanda, 2006). The results suggested that student achievement was positively affected on constructed response items, but negatively affected on multiple-choice items. Conclusions were not reached regarding the actual anxiety levels of the subjects.

Describe the Testing Conditions and Circumstances before the Test Is Administered

Begin preparing your students for a major test 1 week prior to its administration. As the test date approaches, inform students of the time that the test will begin and when it will end. Indicate that the duration of the test must be the same for all students for a test to be fair. Provide information about the test structure in terms of its length, estimated duration, the number and type of items, and the amount of time that should be allocated to each section. Clearly describe the resources students may bring to class and/or use during the assessment. Describe any changes in the normal classroom routine that will apply on test day. If you are making special seating arrangements for an exam, tell students this information no later than the day before the exam.

Students should understand test response formats and procedures before test day arrives. We want to measure student knowledge and skills of the curriculum, not test-taking ability. To that end, have students examine electronic or commercial response sheets and give them the opportunity to practice test reading and response skills under the more relaxed circumstances that occur before test day. Students can become confused and upset if allocated test time is used to explain test-taking procedures beyond a few reminders about procedures already conveyed.

Suggested Routines for Test Day

Have the classroom arranged for the assessment prior to admitting students. If supplemental resources are needed (e.g., calculators and rulers), then distribute these items first and be sure all students have the required materials before the test is distributed. It is best to provide students with assessment questions and response sheets facedown. Then, on the teacher's direction, the students will all be told to begin at the same time by turning over their test materials. Inform students of the remaining time for the exam in a manner that least interrupts their concentration. Let them know the expected behavior when time is up (i.e., all question and response sheets must be turned facedown again). Adherence to the same routine by all students contributes to the reliability of the assessment experience.

Accommodating Students with Special Needs

Prior to test administration identify accommodations to be provided to students with special needs (Thurlow, Elliott, & Ysseldyke, 1998).

These should be made clear in the student Individualized Education Program, or IEP. Students may need accommodations in the format of the test. For instance, some students may need a large-print copy of the exam. Further, some students with special needs will need additional time or special resources to respond to test items. Measures should be taken to provide these resources, and the affected students should be informed of the efforts made before test time. Ideally, the teacher will have a brief conversation with each student with special needs to describe the accommodations that have been planned and to check with the student to see if any other accommodations were to be provided.

Every effort should be made to provide the accommodated student with all other conditions and circumstances of the assessment experience that are provided to all other students. Avoid having students feel that they have been singled out for advantages other students would resent. It is appropriate to inform the general student population of the class about the Individuals with Disabilities Education Act and how the school meets the needs of all students in a fair and equitable way that may include adjustments to conditions not experienced by all students (Hyatt, 2007).

Arrangements That Reduce Temptations to Cheat

The issue of cheating as a moral question needs to be developed as an important understanding among young children. Students in the primary grades may not have a clear understanding of appropriate boundaries when it comes to acceptable and unacceptable behavior in an assessment situation. In these circumstances, it is best to look at violations of appropriate behavior as important teaching opportunities. Structures that prevent inappropriate sharing of information should be established and their purposes made clear to students.

As children enter the upper grades, their understanding of the moral dimensions of life and their ability to equate cheating on tests with dishonesty deepens (Damon, 1999). Nevertheless, violations in these grades should be seen as opportunities to clarify appropriate behavior and to teach proper conduct. Consequences should take the form of doing it correctly on the next occasion. As students enter the middle grades and beyond, grades become important measures of achievement, and consequences for improper action become an important issue. As students enter high school, measures should be taken to limit temptations to cheat.

Cheating during exam administration can be reduced by limiting opportunities for students to see the work being done by students nearby (Kerkvliet & Sigmund, 1999). Tables and chairs can be placed in rows and columns that are farther apart than usual. Declare to students before the test that your intention is to ensure equitable and fair assessment to all by removing unfair advantages one student might have over others. Describe specific behaviors that, when seen, will constitute evidence of cheating. These include glancing at other students' work. Describe how students can avoid suspicious behavior in terms of where they should look or how they might behave to relieve stress during the test experience. Tell students that as a teacher, you cannot see intentions but you can see behaviors that are indicative of dishonesty, and papers of students who exhibit prohibited behaviors will be picked up at the time of the offense. Consequences for cheating should not include course failure or reduction of grade, for these sanctions are not consistent with academic achievement evaluation (Stiggins, 2001).

Inform students that they should not approach you for assistance during test time unless they have identified an error or confusing direction in the test. In the event that a student approaches you seeking clarification about a test item or direction, you need to provide all students with the clarifying explanation, not just the student that approaches you.

SCORING STUDENT RESPONSES TO TEST ITEMS

When students complete an exam or test, the teacher's first task is to gather the testing materials from the students to be sure that each student who took the exam submitted response forms, exam forms, and other paperwork used or produced during the exam. This will ensure the confidentiality and integrity of the test. After all exams have been administered, it is time to score the responses. This is often done by scoring item types of the same kind for all students. If a test began with a matching exercise, then all students' matching responses are scored and graded before moving on to the next item type. This approach will lead to consistent use of methods for scoring each type, which can contribute to the reliability of the assessment activity (Thissen & Wainer, 2001).

Scoring Selected Response Items

Selected response items are typically easy to score because answers are unequivocally correct or incorrect. There may be some need to interpret student responses if a modified true-false section is provided. Otherwise, the use of a scoring template placed sequentially over each student's response sheet that allows the teacher to see correct and incorrect answers will make the scoring process of selected response items move along quickly. True-false and multiple-choice items can also be scored quickly by having students respond to commercially available response sheets that can be run through a scoring machine to identify correct and incorrect responses very quickly (Ward, Frederiksen, & Carlson, 1980). At the end of a few minutes, selected response items can be scored, and the number of correct items in each item type category can be multiplied by the point value attributed to each item. For instance, if 30 multiple-choice items appear on the test, and they collectively account for 60 points of a 100-point exam, then each multiple-choice item marked correctly has a 2-point value. If one student gets 28 items correct in the multiple-choice test described, then the student will receive 56 points from a possible 60 points for the section.

Objective scoring of selected response items has undergone little change with the emergence of the standards-based reform movement, but there does seem to be a lot more of it to do. Technology has contributed to a reduction in the amount of time needed to score selected response items, which may benefit teachers who also use constructed response items and wish to allocate more time to the evaluation of these item types. Moreover, scoring considerations of constructed response items have been affected by the introduction of standards and frameworks, and these additional considerations will be described in the next section (Porter, 2002).

Scoring Constructed Response Items

It is no wonder that many teachers prefer selected response items because of the speed with which these items can be scored. As we discussed previously, however, essay and short-answer items are part of a comprehensive assessment process, but these item types take more time and the exercise of careful judgment to score. The evaluation of the essay part of an exam is inherently subjective. This subjectivity contributes to low reliability and attendant concern for fairness and equity in the grading process (Hughes, Keeling, & Tuck, 1983). Although it is possible to identify and even quantify anticipated elements in a constructed response item, there are qualitative factors sought in student responses that are typically scored by comparing each student's response to an ideal response worthy of a best obtainable score.

Recall from Chapter 7 that the values placed on individual test items should reflect the blueprint used to develop the test. If high-order process skills of the blueprint are to be given a weight of 40% on the assessment, then test sections that assess those process skills should all add to 40 points on a 100-point test. If half of the higher-order process skill assessment items consist of essay items, and the test will contain two such items, then each item should have a maximum score of 10 points. The rubric or checklist used to score a constructed response item should reflect these point attributions.

Effective scoring of student written work ultimately calls for a compromise between ideal methods that raise the reliability of the process and the limitations in time that teachers have to allocate to grading student work. If a high school English teacher assigns a theme to all students in five sections of 10th-grade English composition, it will take more than 18 hours to grade all the themes if the average class size is 28 and approximately 8 minutes are attributed to reading and scoring of each them. The following recommendations are intended to maximize reliability and efficiency in scoring constructed response items while recognizing constraints found in typical teaching situations.

Identify the Critical Attributes Used in Scoring. An essay question, if properly written, will clarify for students the nature of a good response. These attributes should have been conveyed to students during instruction, and expectations for their production should be evident in the prompt. Only these critical attributes should be identified as criteria for scoring student constructed responses, or content validity will be minimized. Students should know what they must provide to get the best possible outcome on the test item.

Choose between Holistic and Analytical Scoring. When teachers use holistic scoring, they form a general impression of each student's response based on the critical attributes of a good response that were communicated to students before and during the assessment (Bacha, 2001). A single score is provided for each item reflecting the extent to which all desired attributes were evident in the response. For instance, a teacher may assign a score of 8 to a student response on a 10-point essay item that is part of a 100-point test because the teacher believes that four of five critical attributes were evident in the response. When teachers use a checklist to evaluate each student response in this manner, rather than merely forming a general impression that an essay is worth about 8 of 10 points, the likelihood that each essay will be evaluated in the same manner will be substantially increased.

Given the time to do so, a teacher might opt for analytic scoring of essays, projects, and other student products. In analytic scoring, each of the desirable attributes in a student response becomes an evaluative criterion that is scored separately. Checklists or rubrics are commonly used to score each student response. If a checklist is used, a statement of the critical attribute with the maximum number of points possible is provided for as many as four or five evaluative criteria. One checklist is completed for each essay item. The total number of points are added together to calculate the essay score, and the scoring sheet is returned to the student. Through this process, analytic scoring provides students with informative feedback about the constructed response they prepared. Figure 8.1 illustrates a sample essay question and the checklist a teacher would use for analytic scoring of student responses (Oermann, 1999).

Rubrics were introduced as a constructed response scoring tool in Chapter 7. They are growing in popularity as a method of scoring constructed responses. They consist of a series of performance descriptions that characterize expected student responses at various levels of proficiency (Butler & McMunn, 2006). Better rubrics consist of descriptions of features in anticipated student products that are readily observable. Figure 8.2 includes an essay prompt and a rubric used to evaluate responses to the prompt in relation to three or four evaluative criteria.

Note that the evaluative criteria appear at the start of each row, and the columns are headed by point values to be attributed to responses. In this rubric, a maximum of nine points could be assigned to the items related to this rubric. The following guidelines are helpful in constructing rubrics that are reliable, fair, and equitable (Arter & McTighe, 2001).

1. **Limit the number of evaluative criteria.** Three to five evaluative criteria, leading to three to five rows in the rubric, are optimal for evaluating essays used in classroom

FIGURE 8.1   Sample Essay Questions

Essay question. 10 pts. Compare and contrast the defensive preparations of the Athenians before Salamis and the Spartans before Thermopylae, and state how the differences reflect differences in the governmental and social organization of the respective societies.	
Both succeeded in protecting city states against devastation.	(2 pts.)_____
Spartans relied on the king, Athenians on collective preparation	(3 pts.)_____
Spartan individual heroic character, Athenian social complexity.	(3 pts.)_____
King and his royal guard in contrast with army of a democracy.	(2 pts.)_____

FIGURE  8.2   **Describe the Chronology of Events and Support the Argument That the Missouri Compromise Was a Cause of the Civil War.**

	One Point	Two Points	Three Points
Recalls proper historical events	The Civil War	Bleeding Kansas Civil War	Bleeding Kansas Dredd Scott Civil War
Proper chronological order	Places compromise in 1820s before the Civil War	Includes description of one event between the compromise and the war	Two or more events between the compromise and the war
States negative consequences of the decision	Identifies subsequent violent acts only	Identifies violent acts and political changes	Identifies violent actives, political changes, and court decision outcomes

tests. More than five evaluative criteria are unlikely to be fully addressable by students responding to a prompt in a limited time period.

2.   **Be sure evaluative criteria map back to the prompt.**   The prompt must provide sufficient direction to elicit all responses needed to achieve a maximum score in each of the evaluative criteria. Students should have the opportunity to provide the optimal response expected.

3.   **Rubric cells should clearly discriminate between various levels of proficiency.**   Two or more teachers, given the same set of student responses, should arrive at the same score when each of the evaluative criteria of a rubric is used to evaluate any given student's response. Assessment experts refer to this agreement in scoring between two different evaluators as interrater reliability. Although it may not be possible to have a colleague examine your rubric cell descriptions, it is a helpful exercise to review the criteria for their usefulness in discerning one level of proficiency from another. As a suggestion, evaluative criteria that describe expected quantities or clearly observable physical characteristics are easier to score consistently.

4.   **Score all essay questions at one time and in a randomized order that does not disclose the name of the student.**   If essay questions, or student products of any other form (labeled and explicated diagrams, charts, and time lines), are a part of the test, the subjectivity needed to score these items leaves a door open for bias to intrude on the scoring process. When all constructed response items are graded as a group, in contrast to simply grading the entire test of each student, one test after the other, the reliability of the assessment process will be increased.

GRADING THE TEST

After all sections have been scored, their contributions to the total points earned on any one test should reflect the extent to which each section contributes to the assessment described in the test blueprint. If the blueprint suggests that 30% of the test should measure student knowledge recall and comprehension of essential facts and concepts, and a true-false and a matching section were used to measure these abilities, then the total score maximum for these two sections should add up to 30 points on a 100-point test.

Grading Conventions of the Past and Present

Many readers of this text will be familiar with two conventional grading options. The first of these is student performance in relation to a criterion, which can be 100% of items correct or predetermined proficiency levels that lead to letter grades (Airasian, 1991). The following scenario describes a grading experience based on the percent of items scored correctly. It takes place in a conventional classroom in 2002.

A scenario of assessment based on percentage of items correct:

> Susan Walker just finished scoring her 7th-grade test on New York state history in her small high school just outside New Paltz, New York. She had allocated 30 points to a 15-item true-false section, 20 points to a 10-item matching section, 40 points to 10 multiple-choice items, and 20 points to the essay section consisting of two essay items. She was pleased with this point allocation because each true-false item was worth two points, each matching item was two points, each multiple-choice item was worth four points, and the essays were worth ten points. She sees the higher values for multiple-choice and essay items as appropriate to the value she places on applications and analysis of problems. She scored all the tests to determine the total each student obtained of 110 possible points, which she converted to a percentage score by dividing total points earned for each student by 110 and multiplying the resulting quotient by 100. From the set of percentile scores obtained from this simple arithmetic procedure, she simply gave students with 90% or above an A, students with 80% to 90% at B, and so on, with students scoring below 60% receiving a failing grade.

Susan Walker's experience is not uncommon. Other teachers might have adjusted the number of test items to reach an exam total of 100 points, thereby eliminating the need to determine a percentage score through an arithmetic operation. Susan placed a priority on having the point value allocations reflect the nature of the item types and the number of items in each category reflect the value she placed on various kinds of reasoning she wanted students to display.

We have all gone through school accustomed to the idea that a certain range of scores, perhaps 80% to 90% correct work, is deemed "good," or a B effort. Further, we have accepted without question the determination of values placed on student work through these conventional assignments. In conventional grading systems based on the expectation that each student's target for learning is a perfect score on each graded activity, there is an underlying assumption that a quality performance is inherent to work that falls within 90% of an ideal performance. This assumption may not be valid, however, because the actual challenge in performing at the 100% level will vary significantly based on the expectations set by the teacher. We have all participated in conversations about teachers who were thought to be "tough" graders and others seen as "easy" graders (Stiggins & Bridgeford, 1985).

A different criterion-based grading system focuses on the expected skills and knowledge students are to display through the teacher's selection of test item types and the number of items in each category. For instance, a teacher might analyze a blueprint and determine that an A performance means 35 of 40 points of the lower cognitive skill items were answered correctly, and 50 of 60 total points of the higher-order sections of the test were answered correctly. Hence, 85 points or higher would be declared an advanced performance. The following scenario displays a teacher in Ocala, Florida, using this system in 2004.

Criterion-reference grading in Ocala Florida:

Jordan Brown had finished his unit on plate tectonics in his sixth-grade earth science class. He prepared a unit test consisting of 30 multiple-choice items and two performance questions worth 10 points each. The first performance question called for students to label and explain a diagram about the formation of the Hawaiian Islands, and the second item was an essay on the history of the plate tectonic theory. Mr. Brown told the students before the test that he was going to place particular value on the performance items because he wanted students to express their knowledge through visuals and through writing. He had explained that students will need these skills later in life.

He distributed the scoring guidelines to each of his students based on these expectations. The guidelines may be seen in Figure 8.3.

Mr. Brown used an electronic scoring machine to score the multiple-choice items, which students had recorded on a sheet of paper. He scored the two performance items using a checklist of specific attributes he wanted to see in each item. Student grades of A through F were then assigned in keeping with totals observed on the scoring sheet in Figure 8.3.

Mr. Brown's grading system uses points to achieve a total score to which he assigns a letter grade value. His setting is typical, A means excellent, B means good, C is fair, D is poor, and F is failing. He is not concerned about a percentage of items correct, not does he assign a value to such a percentage.

The other conventional grading system is the norm-referenced approach, where grading is done by comparing each student's performance with the performances of the rest of the class. As students, we have also become accustomed to comparative performance ratings when we have enrolled in classes where teachers prefer to grade on the **normal curve**, (or

FIGURE 8.3   Mr. Jordan Brown's test scoring criteria

Multiple-Choice Items Correct			Performance Items Score		
27–30	=	A	18–20	=	A
24–26	=	B	16–17	=	B
22–23	=	C	14–15	=	C
20–21	=	D	12–13	=	D
19 or less	=	F	11 or less	=	F

Grades in the two sections will be treated equally and averaged to determine the final grade. If two contiguous grades were average, the score would be the lower grade with a "+" added (e.g., B and A = B+).

bell curve). In this system, the instructor arranges scores into a range, from highest to lowest. In a popular approach to comparative grading, a teacher assumes that student performances should tend to cluster around an average score, with a lower number of scores that are substantially above or below the average. A teacher might decide to assign the top 10% of achieved scores a grade of A. Those students in the next 15% might receive a B. Unfortunate students who fall in the bottom 10% of the grade distribution would fail the exam, solely on the basis of how they performed in relation to other students.

Of course, one teacher can assign a value of C for an average grade in a normal or bell curve distribution, whereas another teacher can reason that the average performance is a C+ or B− grade. It is not uncommon for teachers in a high school department to rationalize the average grade is equal to a C performance in general ability classes, while allocating a B to the average grade in an honors or high-ability class (Sizer, 1992).

Other assumptions besides the bell curve model have been used by teachers to assign grades to a range of scores on a comparative basis. One popular approach is to look for a modal distribution, where scores tend to cluster around certain values in the range of scores. For instance, a teacher might note that several scores are found from 78 to 85 out of a possible 100 points, and another cluster of scores is found from 67 to 75, with no scores for 76 or 77. In this instance, a teacher might assign B grades to the cluster ranging from 78 to 85 and C grades for students scoring from 67 to 75. Here, the teacher might rationalize that the exam is a valid measure of achievement that "sorted" students into acceptable and good performers. However, this assumption rests on the premise that scoring between 78 and 85 points constitutes a good understanding of the subject matter, when in fact it may simply indicate a common level of understanding for a group of commonly performing students (Resnick, 1995).

For years now, high school and college students have gone from one class to another, finding one teacher who grades by comparing student performances with the ideal performance in percentage terms, and another teacher down the hall who grades on the bell curve by simply comparing one student's performance with the performances of all other students in the class taken as a group. And then there are all the possible compromises in between, where teachers will look for modes of score distributions and assign grades to clusters of student scores or simply use the percentage of the optimum score method to be followed by "curving" the grade distribution to attain a desirable distribution of high and low grades.

GRADING STUDENT WORK IN A STANDARDS-BASED SYSTEM

Now that criterion-referenced assessment has come to dominate large-scale testing in response to the standards movement, principles of criterion-referenced student performance evaluation are beginning to reach some classrooms. School district–operated benchmark testing programs, which generally emulate the criterion-referenced performance measures of state standards tests, are imposing a dichotomy of competing grading philosophies in schools across the country.

Many teachers are continuing to conduct norm-referenced or conventional percentage-based grading systems using their teacher-made tests and quizzes, whereas the district administers criterion-referenced benchmark tests in classrooms on a periodic basis. In some settings, this dichotomy of systems and philosophies of performance evaluation is leading teachers to the development of compatible criterion-referenced grading schemes that are coherent with state and district assessment processes (Brindley, 2001).

A scenario of assessment planning in a contemporary middle school:

> Janet Musgrave and Carolyn Nichols teach introductory physical science in Mortimer Bradshaw Memorial Middle School in Feldspar, Colorado. For several years the Feldspar schools have been evaluated in terms of the performance of their students on Colorado's Student Assessment Program, or CSAP. For years, student scores have been reported, and underperforming schools have been identified, based on student performances falling into one of four categories: unsatisfactory, partially proficient, proficient, and advanced. Lately, Janet and Carolyn have been planning common assessments that they administer to all physical science students eight times as year. These major unit exams are standards based, and they are intended to conform to student achievement of science as measured in Grade 10 in the CSAP and the National Assessment of Educational Progress, or NAEP. Janet and Carolyn would like to have their common assessments conform to the state program, and they recognize that the proficiency levels of the CSAP could be readily translated to letter grade equivalents. However, the two teachers do not agree on how to proceed.
>
> "Carolyn, I have trouble relating a system with two gradations below proficient to the conventional system of letter grades that has two grades above proficient, meaning A and B are above proficient, and we have one grade at proficient, namely, C. If we were to declare that partially proficient is a D, then what would be the letter equivalent grades for the other state proficiency levels?" asked Janet, with some frustration after 2 years of going around in circles on grading decisions.
>
> "I'm pretty convinced that the top proficiency levels of our two systems need to be equated with our top letter grade," said Carolyn with some conviction. "I see advanced as the same as an A, proficient as the same as a B, and partially proficient as the same as a C. For me, the issue comes down to equating unsatisfactory with either a D or an F," she concluded.

Janet Musgrave and Carolyn Nichols are confronting a dilemma arising in school districts across the country. How will teachers find common ground between the state's method of reporting student academic proficiency in our standards-based system and the expectations of parents and higher education institutions that want to see student achievement expressed in the competitive arena of letter grades and class rank?

Mr. Jordan Brown and his grading system in Jacksonville, Florida, approximates the criterion grading system seen in large-scale state standards assessments. The important difference in his grading system is the interpretation of student outcomes in conventional symbols of A through F grades.

Implementing Your Grading System

The following guidelines may be helpful in reaching decisions about grading student work in schools and districts that are changing the way grades are assigned due to the influence of state standards and state criterion-referenced exams (McTighe & O'Connor, 2005).

1. **Obtain local guidance regarding grading norms.** Schools are responding to changing expectations for grading in many ways. If the local norms focus on percentage-based

grades and conventional reporting, then the individual teacher should conform to these expectations.

2. **Determine your grading system before the school year begins.**   Students have a right to know the grading system by which their work will be evaluated, and they have a right to consistent application of grading procedures throughout the year. If students know in general terms the kinds of work that will be graded, frequency and total numbers of tests they will encounter in a marking period, and the criteria used to assign different grades, they will be less anxious or confused and able to perform to their best ability.

3. **Make changes in grading policy with your colleagues.**   If the school as a community decides to change from a percentage-based evaluation system to a proficiency-based system, you can time your changes with that decision, which will lead parents and students to accept your grading practices with less confusion.

IMPROVING INSTRUCTION THROUGH ANALYSIS OF TEST OUTCOMES

In conventional teaching settings and before the onset of the standards movement, assessment practices would begin with assessment planning and close with the assignment of grades to student work. Grades would be recorded, the grade book would be closed, the textbook opened, and plans to move on to the next unit of instruction would begin. In some settings, a few teachers would insert a critical step into the assessment cycle between the recording of grades and starting the next unit. This critical step is the analysis of assessment results to improve instruction.

Scored and graded tests and quizzes contain valuable information about the knowledge and skills that students have mastered. They can also reveal patterns of misconceptions, areas of confusion, skills that are insufficiently developed, and concepts that are poorly understood. Item analysis is a method that can be applied to selected response test items to identify patterns of student misconception or misinterpretation (Ebel & Frisbie, 1991).

Item Analysis for Selected Response Test Sections

Consider for the moment that a teacher reviews the results of a true-false section on a test. The teacher might be pleased to note that the majority of students in class obtained 8 or more items correct on a 10-item exercise. Typically, the observation that students did well on the true-false section would bring to an end any further consideration of student performance on this item type. Further analysis might disclose, however, that one of the items was incorrectly marked "true" by almost half of the class when the statement was false. Clearly, the students as a group found this particular item challenging. Once discovered by the teacher, an error of fact or misconception can be clarified. If the teacher scored the true-false section with a template or scoring machine, then wrong choices would be appropriately marked and the frequency with which each item was missed could be evaluated.

Item analysis of selected response items can be a powerful tool for teaching improvement when it is thoughtfully combined with careful item writing during test construction.

The effective use of item analysis reaches its maximum, however, when it is applied to well-crafted multiple-choice items.

If multiple-choice item distractors are written as appealing choices that can capture the attention of students who misunderstand content, then item analysis will reveal the misunderstandings for teacher intervention (Haladyna, 1999). For instance, a mathematics teacher can use values in distractors that result from common procedural errors. If students select the carefully provided wrong answers with high frequency, then the teacher can infer that many students were performing the incorrect procedure. When the test results are provided to the students, the error in procedure can be corrected. Most electronic scoring machines can provide a frequency distribution of distractor selection on multiple-choice tests. Armed with this information, the teacher can identify the most frequently selected distractors and correct misunderstandings.

Many of us may recall when some of our teachers of the past reviewed test results before moving on to a new unit. We may further recall that some of these teachers pointed out common mistakes made by many students, and they clarified the class understanding of the material where confusion or misunderstanding was evident. These teachers were doing their job well when they spent time in class reviewing assessment results to clarify student misunderstanding.

Analysis of Constructed Response Items

The analysis of student essay, short-answer, and sentence-completion items may not be conducted as efficiently as item analysis for selected response items, but the value of the exercise can still be found in improvements in teaching and learning. When students write a single word to complete a sentence, it is likely that students with shared misunderstanding will write the same incorrect word at the end of a completion item. As a teacher grades a completion section of a test, a record can be made of repeated errors. If the same wrong answer keeps appearing for a given completion item, the teacher can address the apparent misunderstanding during subsequent instruction.

Response analysis for short-answer and essay exam questions is problematic because patterns of misunderstanding are difficult to detect in a class set of extensive narratives. Patterns of misunderstanding can be detected, however, by using a scoring checklist. If each essay or short answer is graded with a corresponding checklist or rubric, then the checklists and rubrics can be examined as a group after grades are recorded. If a pattern of low scores appears for one or two of the evaluative criteria used in the scoring guide, it will reveal an area of misunderstanding or poor skill development. Corrective measures can then be taken during subsequent instruction.

EVALUATING STUDENT PERFORMANCES AND PRODUCTS

Student performances are typically evaluated in specialized courses, including physical education, performing arts, and skilled trades. Occasionally, teachers in general education classes will expect students to provide a performance that will be evaluated. This is most likely to happen in courses where language arts skills are taught and evaluated. For instance, students may have their speeches evaluated in a public speaking class. In science classes, students may be asked to move from one setting to another in a constructed assessment exercise, often referred to as a practicum (Ladewski, Krajcik, & Harvey, 1994).

When students exhibit performances, one of two possible circumstances specify the manner by which the performance can be evaluated. A description of the event can be obtained during the performance, and derivative products resulting from the performance can be examined at a later time.

An example of a performance in the first category includes a student oral report combined with a presentation of lasting products that will be evaluated at a later time. On such occasions, teachers can take notes during the event and evaluate the activity after its completion or they can use a scoring guide and evaluate elements of the performance as they are performed. Alternatively, ratings and notes can be taken as a recording is also produced. Regardless of the particulars involving these methods, the general approach is to produce written data that can be considered after the performance is concluded (Haertel, 1999).

On occasion, a judgment or opinion must be rendered at the conclusion of a performance. Ice skating, dance, and gymnastic competitions are familiar examples of situations where performances are exhibited and rated shortly after their conclusion. In some instances, a videotape record of the event can be considered, but this is typically not the case at a school-sponsored competition. It is not within the scope of this text to consider these specialized circumstances, because they are rarely exhibited in the classroom. We shall see, however, that many suggestions that enhance the validity and reliability of classroom-based performances that have the benefit of residual data will also apply to settings where an immediate rating following a performance is called for.

Student performance evaluations are not commonly used by teachers, which is unfortunate. Speaking is one of the four language arts and possibly the least developed as a skill during elementary and secondary education. Student research and preparation for a presentation that leads to a speech, a written report, and a visual display is an example of a fine authentic learning and assessment experience that emulates performances expected in the world of work. The following vignette reflects a conventional performance evaluation that could have been observed in a typical fourth-grade classroom in the recent past.

A scenario of a public speaking exercise in 1997:

> It was customary for Mrs. Ferguson to assign a public speaking exercise as a part of her fourth-grade social studies curriculum focusing on the history of the Commonwealth of Virginia. For this year she decided to have students select a topic within the Colonial era of Virginia, and one topic available for students was the homes of Virginia's founding fathers. Eddy Childs selected Thomas Jefferson's Monticello as his topic. Other students selected the homes of other Virginia statesmen, including George Washington's Mount Vernon, but other topics included the lives of the founding fathers and the history of Williamsburg, Virginia. The diversity of topics placed an expectation on Mrs. Ferguson to evaluate student preparation for the speech and its presentation in relation to characteristics that all the student speeches could hold in common.
>
> In planning this comprehensive activity, Mrs. Ferguson chose to allocate 100 points to this entire exercise, giving it the same value as a unit test in the calculation of quarterly marks. Figure 8.4 shows Mrs. Ferguson's grading criteria and possible scores for this activity.

An examination of Figure 8.4 reveals that 25 of the 100 points for this comprehensive activity will be attributed to the speech each youngster will make. All the other points will be awarded based on an examination of student written products. For each of these written items, checklists or rubrics can be developed to evaluate each in succession. But what of the evaluation of the speech?

Mrs. Ferguson decided to conduct four separate activities so that each student would have the best opportunity to perform well in their public speaking exercise. These activities included

► Instruction in public speaking for all students, with modeling;

► Presentation of the evaluative criteria to be used in the form of a checklist;

► Opportunity for students to practice their speech with peers; and

► Individual consultation with each child to review the final draft of the speech and the visual to be used.

One week before speeches were to begin, Mrs. Ferguson discussed skills of public speaking, including posture, elocution, eye contact, use of notes, and projection. She demonstrated each of these features in a brief speech she made to the class. After students asked questions to clarify the nature of their public speaking assignment, Mrs. Ferguson gave them a homework task: devise a brief, 5-minute speech to present in a small group to be practiced by the children before their speech would be delivered.

The next day, Mrs. Ferguson discussed the evaluative criteria for the public speaking sessions and shared the rating checklist she would use during each speech. The rating sheet appears in Figure 8.5

Mrs. Ferguson dedicated 3 days to the public speaking activity, and she determined the order of presentations by student random selection of a number from 1 to 28, representing each member of the class. Students were informed that they would be called to the front of the classroom. They would be given about 2 minutes to organize their materials, and they would be allocated 10 minutes to conduct their speech. As each child came forward to speak, she completed two copies of the rating sheet. Points were allocated in each category of performance, and comments were written about specific areas of

FIGURE **8.4   Mrs. Ferguson's Virginia History Rating Sheet**

Student notes from library research	10 pts	due Nov. 3
1st draft of speech outline	10 pts	due Nov. 9
1st draft of three-page written report	15 pts	due Nov. 12
Visual prepared for speech	10 pts	due Nov. 15
Final draft of speech outline	10 pts	due Nov. 21
Speech	25 pts	Nov. 22–25
Final report due	20 pts	Dec 2

FIGURE 8.5 **Mrs. Ferguson's Public Speaking Rating Sheet**

Clear introduction of topic and purpose of speech	_____ 2 pts.
Student eye contact with the audience	_____ 3 pts.
Elocution and clarity of speech	_____ 5 pts.
Organization and development of topic	_____ 5 pts.
Effective use of notes	_____ 3 pts.
Display and explication of visual	_____ 5 pts.
Conclusion, interaction with audience	_____ 2 pts.
Total	_____ (25 pts.)

Comments:

_____

_____

_____

accomplishment and areas for improvement. One checklist copy was given to each of the students when the speeches were completed, and the other was retained for her records.

Principles of Performance Evaluation Evident in Mrs. Ferguson's Teaching

Mrs. Ferguson attempted to provide each student with a fair and equitable opportunity to perform well in the public speaking exercise. Of course, the first student to speak would be unable to learn from the experience of others, but random chance was used to identify the order of student presentations so that students would not infer any bias on the teacher's part. These other aspects of her instruction formed the foundation of a fair performance evaluation (Newmann, Marks, & Gamoran, 1996).

1. **Prior instruction in expected behavior was provided.** Mrs. Ferguson discussed each aspect of public speaking that would be evaluated, she described the evaluative criteria that would be used in grading each speech, and she showed students copies of the checklist she would be using as students were speaking. It is evident that she wanted each child to perform at his or her best.

2. **Students learned how they would be evaluated.** Mrs. Ferguson showed the checklist to the children. The checklist displayed the evaluative criteria and the relative number of points that would be attributed to each criterion. Her disclosure of the assessment methods involved students in understanding the elements of the public speaking event that were essential to a good performance.

3. **Students were evaluated under uniform conditions.** Students conducted their student teaching performances under similar conditions, with the exception of the order in which students would be called to speak. They were each provided the same

amount of time to arrange their materials, and each child had 10 minutes to speak to the class.

4. **Students received feedback about their performance, with commentary.**   The rating checklist provided point values for seven performance criteria. For a 10-minute speech, seven skill areas could be easily demonstrated, and they would represent a significant set of public speaking skills for students to acquire. More than seven criteria would be difficult for children to demonstrate. The checklist provided space for teacher comments, allowing for specific feedback for students. Further, all students would receive their feedback at the same time, after all children presented, which would reduce anxiety and contribute to the reliability of the evaluation process.

One particular feature of the scenario involving Mrs. Ferguson and her lesson in public speaking is indicative of conventional assessments of performances. This feature is the grading system she used to evaluate aspects of student performances and the means by which she evaluated the public speaking exercise in relation to other grades that would ultimately be used to determine course marks. Mrs. Ferguson arbitrarily determined that the preparations, written work, and speech would collectively equal a unit test. Given that unit tests have a value of 100 points, she then used checklists and other rating tools to evaluate the quality of student written work, visuals, and the speech. The speech was worth 25 of the total 100 points for the preparation and delivery of a speech.

We do not have information about student grading beyond the accumulation of points that may reach, or fall short of, the maximum 100 points for the entire exercise. In conventional teaching, students with 80 to 90 of the 100 possible points might earn a B grade, which would then be evaluated with other letter grades to derive a letter grade as a course or semester report card mark.

Alternatively, Mrs. Ferguson might simply add the points earned in this exercise (e.g., 83 of 100 points) to all the other points earned in the marking period. Students would then receive letter marks of A for excellent, B for good, and so forth, depending on the percentage value they obtained by calculating points earned in relation to the total number of points in the marking period. Perhaps 800 points is the maximum a student could earn for perfect performances on all tests, quizzes, and other graded material, including the public speaking exercise, in the marking period. If one particular student earned a total of 685 points across the marking period, then 685 would be divided by the 800 points possible, leading to 86% of the total possible points earned. This final numerical average would then be evaluated as a B grade if 80% to 90% of possible points were identified as the required achievement for that grade. In grading systems based on student achievement of a percentage of an ideal performance, the criterion of excellence is a perfect score. Students receive lower grades to the extent that their performance deviates on a percentage basis from a perfect outcome.

Articulating Classroom Assessment with District and State Assessment Programs

The articulation of classroom-based assessment with district and state standards-based assessments is leading to a system of layered assessments (Stiggins, 1991). Collaboratively planned common assessments in a given elementary school grade or high school subject prepare students for success on district-administered benchmark assessments. The benchmark assessments, in turn, prepare students for success with state standards tests. In a system where lower-level assessments prepare students for success on higher-stakes tests administered by a higher level of authority, certain conventions can be established across the system for students to gain value from one experience to the next. The first of these conventions is standards alignment.

In a well-articulated and layered assessment system, all levels of authority are assessing students on the same domain of knowledge. In our evolving reform environment, the domain of knowledge is state curriculum content standards. If each level of the hierarchy of assessment is limiting related assessment content to skills and knowledge of a set of state standards, then students will see that the layered assessment activities are complementary. For the classroom teacher, collaboratively planned common assessments should assess the same domains of knowledge found on benchmark tests.

School districts that provide standards-based curriculum guides with pacing calendars and benchmark exams are focused on standards articulation. When teachers plan their common assessments to measure student achievement of state standards identified in their school district's pacing guide, they are assessing students on the same domain of content that will appear on the district's benchmark tests. In these circumstances, the common exams developed by classroom teachers prepare students for success on the benchmark tests through content alignment. If students experience classroom-based exams that have an appearance and distribution of item types similar to the district's benchmark tests, then students will be comfortable with the benchmark assessments and familiar with the tasks they encounter as they sit for these exams (Bhola, Impara, & Buckendahl, 2003).

Finally, each of these related exams will become a part of a coherent standards-based assessment system to the extent that each of them is criterion referenced and similarly scored. For the most part, state standards tests and many school district benchmark tests are already criterion referenced. Progressive school districts that have installed benchmark assessment systems will use the same criteria and ratings in their benchmark assessment system that they see on state standards tests. For instance, a school district in California should emulate California's state standards performance ratings by establishing a criterion of proficiency for its benchmark tests, then identifying related performance criteria for advanced, basic, and far below basic ratings. These are the ratings used on the state standards tests. If the benchmark assessment system of the school district is intended to display predictive validity in relation to the state standards tests, then the percentage of items needed to attain proficiency on the benchmark tests should be close to the percentage of items needed to attain that same rating on the state standards tests (Stern & Ahlgren, 2002).

Unfortunately, few classroom-based assessments are criterion referenced, and teachers rarely use performance criteria and performance ratings found on state standards tests when they construct classroom tests. Although many teachers are beginning to include released test items from state standards tests in classroom-based unit tests, few teachers have moved away from the conventional system of norm-referenced, letter-based grading of unit tests.

Their reluctance to move in this direction is understandable. Parents are familiar with conventional As, Bs, and Cs along with student performance rankings based on relative placement in relation to other students in the class. The public is reluctant to move from assessment conventions with which parents and students are familiar. In many settings, teachers are struggling to interpret the language of standards-based proficiency ratings (e.g., "advanced," and "proficient") as conventional grades that appear on traditional reporting systems.

Furthermore, receiving authorities, including employers, colleges, and universities, expect to see student transcripts and grade reports that identify class rank and grade point average based on the numbers of each kind of letter grade that students have received. A truly articulated and coherent criterion-referenced system of K–12 assessment will need acquiescence to this form of student grading by agencies, colleges, and universities that review and compare transcripts.

DETERMINING FINAL MARKS FOR REPORT CARDS

Grade reports take on increasing importance as students mature, but they are certainly important at the outset of schooling as parents learn of a small child's success in acquiring the essential literacy and numeracy skills the child will carry through life. The compilation of grades into a final mark that appears on a report card or a transcript results from adding total points and setting scores for each mark, establishing a grand total of possible points and assigning marks based on the percentage of the total points attained, or averaging a set of letter grades with consideration of the relative weights or work products for which grades were assigned. Whichever method is used, the following suggestions should be considered, based on research into the reliability and validity of teacher-made tests (Winger, 2005; McMillan, Myran, & Workman, 2002).

1. **Consider the limitations in the accuracy of your assessment instruments.**   Is a student with an 89% average over the semester worthy of a full grade less than another student with a 90% average? It is unlikely that tests, quizzes, and student work are so error free that the one-point distinction between an 89 average and a 90 average can, of itself, justify a full grade difference between the two students.

2. **Take a holistic view.**   Student marks for a course or term may reflect growth in knowledge, effort, what the student knew at the end of the course, or average performance over an extended period of time. Invariably, a teacher is making a value judgment about different kinds of evidence when assigning a final mark. The principle of triangulation should play a confirming role. When a final mark is determined, try to corroborate the judgment implied by the mark in terms of other evidence of achievement the student presented during the course of the term.

3. **Assign marks for student academic achievement.**   Do not let issues of concern, including deportment, punctuality, motivation, or attitude, intrude into the course or subject grading exercise. Others who will read the report card or transcript will infer that a course or subject grade conveys information about student knowledge and skills, not other extraneous factors. If you need to communicate to parents or other officials about other attributes of learners, use other means than course grades to do so.

Ultimately, grade others according to the principles and procedures on which you would like to be graded. Make a conscious effort to consider bias or unfairness that may be present in your methods. Attempt to be flexible in considering all legitimate sources of evidence in assigning final marks, and give the evidence its appropriate weight in determining the final grade, while not compromising standards.

REPORTING STUDENT ACADEMIC ACHIEVEMENT

New teachers often experience discomfort with the process of reporting student marks to parents in report cards. After years of being a student, the change in role from student to teacher becomes apparent when grades are to be assigned. Further, parents will often express anger and frustration to a teacher and the teacher's principal in response to their child's low marks. The following guidelines will be helpful to teachers who are getting started in their careers (Brookhart, 1993).

Make Grading Policies Known to Parents

College professors make their grading policies known to students when they distribute the course syllabus on the first day of classes. Schoolteachers should communicate their grading policies as well, but to a wider audience and through different means. It is appropriate to send a packet of information home at the start of the school year that includes grading policies and procedures. The communication should invite questions from parents seeking clarification of grading practices. Last, have parents sign and return a copy of a memo that states they have reviewed the grading procedures and other important information pertaining to rules and policies. Keep these signed memos for future reference.

Inform Superiors of Your Practices

As a new elementary school teacher, you should take the time to talk to your principal about grading policies and procedures. Ask the principal for guidance in this area and include, as appropriate, suggestions made by the principal in your own grading policies. Provide the principal with copies of the information about grading that you provide to parents.

Maintain Communication with Parents

Parents want to know how their students are performing in school. Back-to-school night and a letter of introduction at the start of the year are necessary but minimal forms of communication. Messages and phone calls to homes should be made throughout the year, particularly at the first signs of academic difficulty. Be sure to contact parents with good news as well. Effective communication with parents about grades begins with telling them that you as the teacher want to be their partner in achieving the academic success of their child. Secondary school teachers should avail themselves of the academic warning notification system. They should also call parents when trouble is first detected.

Make a Record of All Grades and Make a Note of Efforts to Communicate with Parents

In the event a dispute arises about a student's grades, a record of efforts to reach parents, including dates when calls were placed or notes were sent home, will be invaluable resources if the principal receives a call from an angry parent about grading policies.

Summary

Much remains to be done after a test is written and prepared for administration. Students need to be informed about testing procedures and the particular expectations of various kinds of assessments. As students mature, assessment takes on more significance in their lives. Anxiety that arises from confusion about tests and quizzes and uncertainty about the assessment experience should be avoided. We want students to perform at their very best when they sit for an exam.

Scoring and grading test items are largely dependent on item type. Selected response items can be quickly scored, leaving time for thorough evaluation of constructed response items. Scoring student written work and projects requires preliminary preparation and the use of a scoring guide, perhaps a checklist or a rubric. When scoring guides include explicit evaluative criteria, fairness and validity in assessment result.

The evaluation of test outcomes to improve instruction is a frequently overlooked role in teaching. Selected response items lend themselves to item analysis, which can reveal to the teacher areas of student misunderstanding or poor skill development. Multiple-choice items can be written to anticipate item analysis. This item type is particularly useful in the item analysis process.

If checklists and rubrics are used to score constructed response items, patterns of student underperformance can be revealed by examining student responses in relation to the evaluative criteria used to rate student work.

The assignment of grades for tests, quizzes, and other student work is undergoing reevaluation due to the influence of the standards movement. Criterion-referenced testing is finding its way to the classroom, and teachers in progressive schools are developing grading schemes that are consistent with state standards assessment.

When grades are reported to parents and other stakeholders, two guiding principles will serve the teacher well. The first is to establish a partnership role with the parent with the goal of fostering student success. The second is more practical: If concerns about student performance arise, call home early and often.

Exercises

1. Following a review of the suggestions for administering classroom tests and quizzes, write a policy statement to students that describes your responsibility as the test administrator and your students' responsibilities as test takers before and during the administration of an exam. Describe the information you will provide to them before exam day and during the exam period. Be sure to include your policy about cheating, describing the kind of behavior that constitutes cheating. Include a statement of consequences if you teach at the middle or high school level. Exchange your policy

statement with another educator, and identify improvements leading to a final draft you would use in the classroom.

2. If you are working at a school site, become acquainted with the test scoring technology that is available. If you do not visit a school regularly, use the Internet to identify a product for scoring student response sheets. The technology may consist of a machine through which forms are fed or a peripheral device that reads completed scoring sheets and sends data to a computer for analysis. What kinds of selected response test items can be scored? Does the machine perform an item analysis? What kinds of assessment reports will the machine prepare? Describe the device and its features in a brief descriptive essay.

3. Select or write an essay question that follows the recommendations provided in Chapter 7. Be sure that the evaluative criteria used to score the essay are communicated to the students in the essay question. Examine your essay and prepare a rubric to score student responses. The rubric should include the evaluative criteria as row headings and performance ratings as column headings. When completed, compare the rubric with the essay question to check its validity with the content domains of the question.

4. Find a colleague or small group of colleagues and hold a discussion about grading practices. Engage in a discussion of your personal experiences as a student and the kinds of grading practices you encountered. Present your philosophy of grading and describe grading practices that align with that philosophy. Listen to, and evaluate, the philosophies, principles, and practices of others. Then prepare a written statement describing your grading practices and the grading principles and philosophy that support your practices.

5. Become acquainted with the assessment program of your school district. The district's website may be helpful as a starting place, but a visit with the assessment coordinator should be included in this exercise. Identify the assessment practices at the district level, the school level, and the classroom level. Evaluate the practices with respect to coherence and common purposes. Is the district program a layered system focused on state standards achievement? Describe the program's strengths and shortcomings, and provide recommendations for its improvement.

6. Working as a teacher or with a teacher, conduct an item analysis of selected response and constructed response items after a test is scored. For the constructed items, you will need a record of student performances as provided by a scoring sheet (e.g., a checklist or rubric). Identify patterns of inadequate performance. Suggest next steps to shore up student skills and knowledge in areas of concern identified through the item analysis exercise.

7. Prepare a memo about your grading policies to be distributed to parents at the beginning of the year. Include information about the nature of the assessments you will use, your grading policies, and the role of parents in supporting their student's success. Inform the parents of your availability to respond to their concerns. Describe how you will report each child's progress during the course of the year.

Resources and Suggested Readings

The use of assessments to improve instruction has gained new impetus with No Child Left Behind. School districts are expected to use the results of state standards testing programs to provide remediation or supplemental instruction as needed when test scores reveal that student performance among language, ability, and ethnic groups may vary. Formative assessment has long been used to improve instruction soon after it happens. When teachers assess learning as it develops in the classroom, formative assessment can be used to avoid learning incorrect procedures or concepts.

In recent years, a movement has grown calling for the analysis of student work to improve instruction. Protocols for conducting this process have been described on the Internet. When teachers develop common assignments and assessments for their grade level or subject area, they can examine the results collaboratively to improve their instruction. The examination of student work as a collaborative exercise among teachers with common assignment is a part of this growing trend. Readers may choose to look at the work of certain online communities involved with this work, including the educators at http://www. lasw.org/ and members of the Philadelphia Education Fund at http://www.philaedfund. org/slcweb/guideli.htm. The protocols suggested by these groups can guide teachers in their work as they improve their instruction by collaborating with colleagues.

References

Airasian, P. W. (1991). *Classroom assessment.* New York: McGraw-Hill.

Airasian, P. W. (2000). *Assessment in the classroom: A concise approach* (2nd ed.). New York: McGraw-Hill.

Arter, J. A., & McTighe, J. (2001). *Scoring rubrics in the classroom: Using performance criteria for assessing and improving student performance.* Thousand Oaks, CA: Corwin.

Bacha, N. (2001). Writing evaluation: What analytic versus holistic essay scoring tells us? *System, 29* (3), 371–383.

Berk, R. A., & Nanda, J. (2006). A randomized trial of humor effects on test anxiety and test performance. *International Journal of Humor Research, 19*(4), 425.

Bhola, D. S., Impara, J. C., & Buckendahl, C. W. (2003). Aligning tests with states' content standards: Methods and issues. *Educational Measurement, 22*(3), 21–29.

Brindley, G. (2001). Outcomes-based assessment in practice: Some examples and emerging insights. *Language Testing, 18*(4), 393–408.

Brookhart, S. M. (1993). Teachers' grading practices: Meaning and values. *Journal of Educational Measurement, 30*(2), 123.

Butler, S. M., & McMunn, N. D. (2006). *A teacher's guide to classroom assessment.* San Francisco: Jossey-Bass.

Damon, W. (1999). The moral development of children. *Scientific American, 281*(2), 72–78.

Ebel, R. L., & Frisbie, D. A. (1991). *Essentials of educational measurement.* Englewood Cliffs, NJ: Prentice Hall.

Haertel, E. H. (1999). Performance assessment and education reform. *Phi Delta Kappan, 80*(9), 662–667.

Haladyna, T. M. (1999). *Developing and validating multiple-choice test items.* Mahwah, NJ: Erlbaum.

Hembree, R. (1988). Correlates, causes, effects, and treatment of test anxiety. *Review of Educational Research, 58*(1), 47–77.

Hughes, D. C., Keeling, B., & Tuck, B. F. (1983). Effects of achievement expectations and handwriting quality on scoring essays. *Journal of Educational Measurement, 20*(1), 65–70.

Hyatt, K. J. (2007). The new IDEA: Changes, concerns, and questions. *Intervention in School and Clinic, 42*(3), 131.

Kerkvliet, J., & Sigmund, C. L. (1999). Can we control cheating in classrooms? *Journal of Economic Education, 30*(4), 331–343.

Ladewski, B. G., Krajcik, J. S., & Harvey, C. L. (1994). A middle grade science teacher's emerging understanding of project-based instruction. *Elementary School Journal, 94*(5), 499.

McMillan, J. H., Myran, S., & Workman, D. (2002). Elementary teachers' classroom assessment and grading practices. *Journal of Educational Research, 95*(4), 203.

McTighe, J., & O'Connor, K. (2005). Seven practices of effective learning. *Educational Leadership, 63*(3), 10–17.

Meskauskas, J. A. (1976). Evaluation models for criterion-referenced testing: Views regarding mastery and standard-setting. *Review of Educational Research, 46*(1), 133–158

Newmann, F. M., Marks, H. M., & Gamoran, A. (1996). Authentic pedagogy and student performance. *American Journal of Education, 104*(4), 280–312.

Oermann, M. (1999). Developing and scoring essay tests. *Nurse Educator, 24*(2), 29–32.

Porter, A. C. (2002). Measuring the content of instruction: Uses in research and practice. *Educational Researcher, 31*(7), 3–14.

Resnick, L. B. (1995). *From aptitude to effort: A new foundation for our schools.* Boston: Daedalus.

Sizer, T. R. (1992). *Horace's school: Redesigning the American high school.* Boston: Houghton Mifflin.

Stern, L., & Ahlgren, A. (2002). Analysis of students' assessments in middle school curriculum materials: Aiming precisely at benchmarks and standards. *Journal of Research in Science Teaching, 39*(9), 889–910.

Stiggins, R. J. (1991). Facing challenges of a new era of educational assessment. *Applied Measurement in Education, 4*(4), 263–273.

Stiggins, R. J. (2001). *Student-involved classroom assessment* (3rd ed.). Upper Saddle River, NJ: Merrill/Prentice Hall.

Stiggins, R. J., & Bridgeford, N. J. (1985). The ecology of classroom assessment. *Journal of Educational Measurement, 22*(4), 271–286

Thissen, D., & Wainer, H. (2001). *Test scoring.* Mahwah, NJ: Erlbaum.

Thorndike, R. M. (2005). *Measurement and evaluation in psychology and education* (7th ed.). Upper Saddle River, NJ: Merrill/Prentice Hall.

Thurlow, M. L., Elliott, J. L., & Ysseldyke, J. E. (1998). *Testing students with disabilities: Practical strategies for complying with district and state requirements.* Thousand Oaks, CA: Corwin.

Ward, W. C., Frederiksen, N., & Carlson, S. B. (1980). Construct validity of free-response and machine-scorable forms of a test. *Journal of Educational Measurement, 17*(1), 11–29.

Winger, T. (2005). Grading to communicate. *Educational Leadership, 63*(3), 61.

Wolfe, E. W., Viger, S. G., Jarvinen, D. W., & Linksman, J. (2007). Validation of scores from a measures of teacher's efficacy toward standards-aligned classroom assessment. *Educational and Psychological Measurement, 67*(3), 460–474.

Zeidner, M. (1998). *Test anxiety: The state of the art.* New York: Kluwer.

BIBLIOGRAPHY

Airasian, P. W. (2000). *Assessment in the classroom: A concise approach* (2nd ed.). New York: McGraw-Hill.

Black, P., & William, D. (1998). Inside the black box: Raising standards through classroom assessment. *Phi Delta Kappan, 80*(2), 139–148.

Bloom, B. (1956). *Taxonomy of educational objectives: The classification of educational goals. Handbook I: Cognitive domain.* New York: Longmans.

Boaler, J. (2003). When learning no longer matters: Standardized testing and the creation of inequality. *Phi Delta Kappan, 84*(7), 502–507.

Briars, D. J., & Resnick, L. B. (2000). *Standards, assessments—and what else? The essential elements of standards-based school improvement* (CSE Technical Report). Los Angeles, CA: Center for the Study of Evaluation.

Buckendahl, C. W., Plake, B. S., Impara, J. C., & Irwin, P. M. (2000, April). *Alignment of standardized achievement tests to state content standards: A comparison of publishers' and teachers' perspectives.* Paper presented at the Annual Meeting of the national Council on Measurement in Education, New Orleans, LA.

Butler, S. M., & McMunn, N. D. (2006). *A teacher's guide to classroom assessment.* San Francisco: Jossey-Bass.

Busick, K., & Mann, M. (2001). Weaving standards into learning. *Pacific Resources for Education and Learning.* Honolulu, HI.

Darling-Hammond, L., & Ball, D. L. (1998). *Teaching for high standards: What policy makers need to know and be able to do* (CPRE Joint Report Series, JRE-04). Philadelphia: Consortium for Policy Research in Education and the National Commission on Teaching and America's Future.

DuFour, R., Eaker, R., & DuFour, R. (2005). On common ground: The power of professional learning communities. Bloomington, IN: National Education Service.

Elmore, R. F. (2002). *Bridging the gap between standards and achievement: The imperative for professional development in education.* Washington, DC: Albert Shanker Institute.

Falk, B. (2000). *The heart of the matter: Using standards and assessment to learn.* Portsmouth, NH: Heinemann.

Gall, M. (1984). Synthesis of research on teachers' questioning. *Educational Leadership, 42*(3), 40–47.

Gardner, H. (1983). *Frames of mind: The theory of multiple intelligences.* New York: Basic Books.

Gullickson, A. R. (1993). *The student evaluation standards: How to improve evaluation of students.* Thousand Oaks, CA: Corwin.

Hawk, P. P. (1986). Using graphic organizers to increase achievement in middle school life science. *Science Education, 70,* 81–87.

Herman, J. L., & Baker, E. L. (2005). Making benchmark testing work. *Educational Leadership, 63*(3), 48–54.

Horton, S. V., Lovitt, T. C., & Bergerud, D. (1990). The effectiveness of graphic organizers for three classifications of secondary students in content area classes. *Journal of Learning Disabilities, 23*(1), 12–22, 29.

Hyatt, K. J. (2007). The new IDEA: Changes, concerns, and questions. *Intervention in School and Clinic, 42*(3), 131.

Kubiszyn, T., & Borich, G. (2007). *Educational testing and measurement: Classroom application and practice.* Hoboken, NJ: Wiley.

La Marca, P. M., Redfield, D. W., & Winter, P. C. (2000). *State standards and state assessment systems: A guide to alignment.* Washington, DC: Council of Chief School State Officers.

Leahy, S., Lyon, C., Thompson M., & William D. (2005). Classroom assessment: Minute by minute, day by day. *Educational Leadership, 63*(3), 18–24

Lerner, J. W. (2000). *Learning disabilities: Theories, diagnosis, and teaching strategies* (8th ed.). Boston: Houghton Mifflin.

Linn, R. L., & Herman, J. L. (1997). *A policymaker's guide to standards-led assessment.* Denver, CO: Education Commission of the States and National Center for Research on Evaluation, Standards, and Student Testing.

Marzano, R. (1998). *Implementing standards-based education.* Washington, DC: National Educational Association.

Marzano, R., & Kendall, J. (1996). *A comprehensive guide to designing standards-based districts, schools and classrooms.* Alexandria, VA: Association for Supervision and Curriculum Development.

McMillan, J. H. (2004). *Classroom assessment: Principles and practice for effective instruction.* Boston: Allyn and Bacon.

McMillan, J. H., Myran, S., & Workman, D. (2002). Elementary teachers' classroom assessment and grading practices. *Journal of Educational Research, 95*(4), 203.

National Commission on Excellence in Education. (1983). *A nation at risk: The imperative for educational reform.* Washington, DC: U.S. Government Printing Office.

Notar, C. E., Zuelke, D. C., Wilson, J. D., & Yunker, B. D. (2004). The table of specifications: Insuring accountability in teacher made tests. *Journal of Instructional Psychology, 31*(2), 115.

Ogawa, R. T., Sandholtz, J. H., Martinez-Flores, M., & Scribner, S. P. (2003). The substantive and symbolic consequences of a district's standards-based curriculum. *American Educational Research Journal, 40*(1), 147–176.

O'Shea, M., & Kimmel, H. (2003, January). *Preparing teachers for content standards: A field study of implementation problems.* Paper presented at the American Association for Colleges of Teacher Education, New Orleans, LA.

O'Shea, M. (2005). From standards to success: A guide for school leaders. Arlington, VA: Association for Supervision and Curriculum Development.

Overton, T. (2003). *Assessing learners with special needs: An applied approach.* Upper Saddle River, NJ: Merrill/Prentice Hall.

Rosenthal, R., & Jacobson, L. (1968). *Pygmalion in the classroom: Teacher expectations and pupils' intellectual development.* New York: Holt, Rinehart and Winston.

Salvia, J., & Ysseldyke, J. E. (2001). *Assessment* (8th ed.). Boston: Houghton Mifflin.

Spillane, J. (2003). *Standards deviation: How schools misunderstand educational policy.* Cambridge, MA: Harvard University Press.

Stiggins, R. J., (2001). *Student-involved classroom assessment* (3rd ed.). Upper Saddle River, NJ:Merrill/Prentice Hall.

Tell, C., Bodone, F., & Addie, K. (2000, April). *A framework of teacher knowledge and skills necessary in a standards-based system: Lessons from high school and university faculty.* Paper presented at the American Educational Research Association. New Orleans, LA.

Thorndike, R. L., & Hagen, E. (1969). *Measurement and evaluation in psychology and education.* New York: Wiley.

Tomlinson, C. A. (1999). *The differentiated classroom: Responding to the needs of all learners.* Alexandria, VA: Association for Supervision and Curriculum Development.

U.S. Department of Justice, Civil Rights Division, Disability Rights Section. (2005, September). *A guide to disability rights laws.* Washington, DC: Author.

Winger, T. (2005). Grading to communicate. *Educational Leadership, 63*(3), 61.

Zmuda, A., & Tomaino, M. (2001). *The competent classroom: Aligning high school curriculum, standards, and assessment: A creative teaching guide.* New York: Teachers College Press.

Fact Sheet for Mathematics CSAP–Grades 3–10

Construction Information:

   60 items–45 multiple choice, 15 constructed response
      Of the constructed response items:
            3 are extended constructed response worth 4 score points
            6 are medium constructed response worth 3 score points
            6 are short constructed response worth 2 score points

   Total test score points–87
   - Multiple choice score points –45 or 52% of total
   - Constructed response score points–42 or 48% of total
            {Grades 4 & 5–69 items, Total test score points–96
            - Multiple choice score points–54 or 56% of total
            - Constructed response score points–42 or 44% of total}

   Test is designed to be given in three 65-minute sessions (Grade 3 has only two sessions)
   - Each session has a similar composition of item types
   - Sessions 1 and 2 the use of calculators is **not** allowed
   - Session 3 the use of calculators is allowed **only** at Grades 9 and 10

Weighting of Standards by Grade Level for Mathematics CSAP

Standard	Grade 3 %ScrPts	Grade 4 %ScrPts	Grade 5 %ScrPts	Grade 6 %ScrPts	Grade 7 %ScrPts	Grade 8 %ScrPts	Grade 9 %ScrPts	Grade 10 %ScrPts
1	20	20	20	20				
6	20	20	20	15	30	25	20	20
2		15	20	20	20	25	30	30
3	25	15	20	20	20	20	25	25
4 5	35	30	20	25	30	30	25	25

   Example of contextual reference of items (From the 2003 grade 10 test, similar for other tests)
   - 60% problem solving–involves both conceptual and procedural   {Grade 5=> 55%}
   - 20% mostly conceptual in nature   {Grade 5=> 25%}
   - 20% mostly procedural in nature   {Grade 5=> 20%}

Test Scoring
   - Multiple choice are machine scored
   - Constructed response are scored by readers hired and trained by the test contractor under specific guidelines from CDE personnel and Colorado teachers
   - Performance category cut-lines are set using the Bookmarking Process (description on CDE website) and a Modified Bookmarking Process

Associated materials available on the CDE webside (www.cde.state.co.us)
   - Assessment Frameworks
   - CSAP Item Maps
   - Released Items
   - CSAP Performance Level Characterization
   - Student work from selected Release Constructed Response Items (Anchor Papers)
   - Technical Reports and other information

Fact Sheet for Mathematics CSAP–Grades 3–10

Sub-Content Area Descriptions:

4th Grade:
Number and Operation Sense: The Student demonstrates meanings for whole numbers, commonly-used fractions, decimals as money and the four basic arithmetic operations including the use of manipulatives, drawings, and decomposing and composing numbers.

Patterns: The student reproduces, extends, creates and describes geometric and numeric patterns as problem-solving tools. Note:

Measurement: The student demonstrates knowledge of time, and understands the structure and use of US customary and metric measurement tools and units.

5th Grade:
Number and Operation Sense: The student demonstrates the meaning of whole numbers, commonly used fractions, decimals and the four basic arithmetic operations through the use of drawings, decomposing and composing numbers, and identify factors, multiples and prime/composite numbers.

Patterns: The student represents, describes, and analyzes geometric and numeric patterns using tables, graphs, and verbal rules as problem solving tools. Note:

Data Displays: The student organizes constructs, and interprets displays of data including tables, charts, pictographs, line plots, bar graphs, and chooses the correct graph from possible graph representations of a give scenario.

6th Grade:
Number and Operation Sense: The student demonstrates and understanding of relationships among benchmark fractions, decimals, and percents and justifies the reasoning used. The student adds and subtracts fractions and decimals in problem solving situations.

Patterns: The student represents, describes and analyzes geometric and numeric patterns using tables, words, concrete objects and pictures in problem solving situations.

Geometry: The student will reason informally about the properties of two-dimensional figures and solve problems involving area and perimeter.

7th Grade:
Number Sense: The Student will demonstrate understanding of the concept of equivalency as related to fractions, decimals, and percents.

Area and Perimeter Relationships: The student demonstrates understanding of perimeter, circumference, and area, and recognizes the relationships between them.

8th Grade:
Linear Pattern Representation: The Student represents, describes, and analyzes linear patterns using tables, graphs, verbal rules, and standard algebraic notation and solves simple linear equations in problem-solving situations using a variety of methods.

Proportional Thinking: The student applies the concepts of ratio, proportion, scale factor, and similarity including using the relationships among fractions, decimals, and percents in problem solving situations.

Geometry: The student describes, analyzes and reasons informally about properties of two and three-dimensional figures to solve problems.

Fact Sheet for Mathematics CSAP–Grades 3–10

Sub-Content Area Descriptions Continued:

9th Grade:
Multiple Representations of Linear and Non-Linear Function: The student represents functional relationships which model real world phenomena using written explanations, tables, equations, and graphs, describes the connections among these representations and converts from one representation to another.

Proportional Thinking ng: The student applies the concepts of ration, proportion, scale factor, and similarity including using the relationships among fractions, decimals, and percents in problem-solving situations.

10th Grade:
Multiple Representation of Function: The student represents functional relationships which model real world phenomena using written explanations, tables, equations, and graphs, describes line connections among these representations and converts from one representation to another.

Probability and Counting Techniques: The student applies organized counting techniques to determine a sample space and theoretical probability of an identified event which includes differentiating between independent and dependent events and using area models to determine probability.

	Grade 3	Grade 4	Grade 5	Grade 6	Grade 7	Grade 8	Grade 9	Grade 10
Sub-Content Area#				Sub-Content Area				
1	Not applicable	Number & Operation Sense	Number & Operation Sense	Number & Operation Sense	Number Sense	Linear Pattern Representation	Multiple Representations of Linear/Nonlinear Functions	Multiple Representation of Function
2	Not applicable	Patterns	Patterns	Patterns	Area & Perimeter Relation-ships	Proportional Thinking	Proportional Thinking	Probability & Counting Techniques
3	Not applicable	Measure-ment	Data Displays	Geometry		Geometry		
4	Not applicable							
5	Not applicable							

INDEX